A REVOLUTION
OF COMMON
SENSE

A REVOLUTION OF COMMON SENSE

How Donald Trump Stormed Washington
and Fought for Western Civilization

Scott Jennings

WM

WILLIAM MORROW
An Imprint of HarperCollins*Publishers*

HarperCollins books may be purchased for educational, business, or sales promotional use. For information, please email the Special Markets Department at SPsales@harpercollins.com.

hc.com

FIRST EDITION

Designed by Michele Cameron

Library of Congress Cataloging-in-Publication Data has been applied for.

ISBN 978-0-06-347217-4

25 26 27 28 29 LBC 5 4 3 2 1

To Everett, Winston, Thatcher & Harlan:
I'm so proud to be your dad. I love you.

CONTENTS

A REVOLUTION OF
COMMON SENSE

I first met Donald Trump on February 10, 2025, three weeks after he had taken the oath of office a second time.

It was strange to finally meet the man who had dominated most of my on-air (and quite a few of my off-air) conversations since he launched his presidential campaign back in 2015. And to meet him in the Oval Office, where he was surrounded by senior members of his cabinet and team, was even more surreal.

But there I was on a cold, bright Monday afternoon in Washington, DC. "He's expecting you," said the bubbly aide. We opened the door, and the hushed confines of the outer office gave way to the vibrant bustle of the Oval, where Trump was presiding over a gathering of several top advisors.

"Look at this guy," the president said as I entered the room, doing a double take as he looked up from the Resolute Desk. "You look terrific in person. Wow!"

Ever the casting director, I thought as I stepped onto the newly re-installed cream-colored rug from the Reagan presidency, the last time a true celebrity made the leap from entertainment to the presidency. "Thank you, Mr. President. So do you!"

Making my way to the golden couches that face each other in front of the presidential fireplace, it was flattering to be favorably sized up by the commander in chief. The "in person" part reminded me that Trump only knows me from CNN, where I occupy the role of senior political commentator, and as the conservative often battling several liberals at a time over his policies. He has seen me fight ferociously for him and, on some occasions, take issue with something he's said or done. He's seen it all—I never hold back when I have an opinion or a hot take.

"Have a seat," the president said.

On the couch closest to the door, I sat next to Scott Bessent, the new secretary of the treasury. Of all the people in the room, he was probably the person I knew the least about and had never met. But I was impressed by him during his confirmation hearing and his subsequent media engagements.

He leaned over and said, "Thank you for flagging my comments to *Bloomberg* on your X account. Very helpful."

The previous Friday night, as I prepared for an eleven p.m. tussle on CNN, my close friend and frequent collaborator Joe Arnold sat just outside of camera range and showed me a clip of Bessent's calm smackdown of a *Bloomberg* reporter who was assailing him on DOGE's efforts inside the Treasury Department. I was impressed by Bessent's riposte and posted it for my followers on X, the platform where my following exploded during and since the 2024 campaign. Bessent obviously took notice and his comment reminded me that even a late-night post from Louisville, Kentucky, can find its way to the most important decision-makers in the world.

The influence of X on our public discourse is vast, more than people realize, I thought. Yet another feature of the Trump era: diluting the influence of mainstream media outlets and ramping up the importance of other new media and information-sharing platforms like X (formerly Twitter).

As I began to take in the room—which I hadn't been in since the summer of 2008—Trump asked the assembled: "Does everyone here know Scott? He's terrific on CNN. Just terrific."

The people in the room all nodded. And I did know most of them in one capacity or another. Secretary of State Marco Rubio (earlier that morning I had interviewed him for nearly thirty minutes while guest hosting on SiriusXM radio). CIA Director John Ratcliffe.

Deputy Chief of Staff Stephen Miller. Mike Waltz, who was then the president's national security advisor. Commerce Secretary–designate Howard Lutnick (who would be confirmed a few days later). Deputy Chief of Staff Taylor Budowich.

Then Trump added: "To be honest, he used to be, frankly, a little bit average. But now, he's terrific!"

A light chuckle rippled over the room, and I allowed myself a laugh. I always wondered whether Trump had noticed the times in which we had not been aligned; obviously the answer is yes.

I've been one of Trump's most ardent defenders on cable TV, especially since the 2024 campaign and subsequent transition to Trump 2.0. I tore apart his political opposition daily (they deserved it for being unhinged and blatantly dishonest in many of their attacks on him). And I gave half the country a voice during a campaign and ensuing transition that countered the gaslighting and insane takes from Trump's most hysterical opponents.

I was hired by CNN as a pundit in 2017, just a few months after they signed up JD Vance, a fellow politico with ties to rural Kentucky who also emerged from humble beginnings. He was to be the "Never Trump" Republican voice and I was to serve as an emblem of the average Republican voter that largely supported the president but could call balls and strikes, too.

I wasn't hired to read talking points. Rather, I was hired to authentically translate from Red America to fellow panelists and CNN's audience about how average Republicans were absorbing the news during the new Trump era. Plus, I had years of high-level campaign and government experience under my belt at that point. Not every "strategist" you see on TV does, I am sorry to report. It amuses me when I see someone proudly carrying the banner of "strategist" as their title when they possess little to no experience to back it up.

But I digress. Eight years later, JD Vance is Trump's vice president (after earning the president's GOP primary endorsement during a successful run for US Senate in 2022) and I am still putting on makeup for a living (among other endeavors, such as my public affairs firm

RunSwitch back in Kentucky and my nationally syndicated radio show on the Salem Network). And as of this writing, Vice President Vance, after a stellar performance in the 2024 campaign, is the front runner for the 2028 GOP presidential nomination.

But like Vance, I, too, had expressed some misgivings about a few things Trump had done or said over the years. And like Vance, over time, I had come to find a new respect for Trump, in no small part because I began to see him as a necessary and strong bulwark against a political opposition that had lost its damn mind.

I wrote in a 2019 op-ed for the *Los Angeles Times*:

Unencumbered by the pablum that traps most politicians, Trump is a perfect mirror when he takes the rally stage. The attendees see themselves in him; they don't talk or think like politicians, either. And though their lives don't permit them to attack those they find aggravating, they can live vicariously through a president who does it for them. This is especially true for rural folks, looked down upon as hicks and rubes by the coastal elites for a very long time. Bless your hearts, we do cling to our guns and religion because they are a deeply meaningful part of our heritage.

Is Trump a perfect representative of the disrespected rural Republican, who goes to church on Sunday and worries about what cavalier, liberal attitudes toward life and marriage mean for the future of their country? No, of course not.

But . . . We didn't hire a barbarian to sing soprano in the choir; we hired him to beat back the savages.

It was true then and it is very true today. Trump is the Republican Party's fighter, and indeed a fighter for Western Civilization against enemies that have only gotten crazier and more dangerous. The future of the West hangs in the balance, and Trump is leading the fight to save it, as far as I am concerned.

Throughout 2024 and certainly by February of 2025, I felt politically closer to Donald Trump than ever. Like many Republicans, I had ridden the Trump roller coaster for years—mostly thrilled but a little green around the gills during certain loops. And the ride demanded some reconciliation on issues like trade and various aspects of foreign policy, where he veered from the old tracks laid down by the likes of Ronald Reagan and George W. Bush.

If there's one thing Trump gave the American people, it was a presidency unbound by previous political orthodoxy. Across the board, Trump refused to be encumbered by opinions set by the entrenched Washington political establishment.

There's no politician I agree with 100 percent of the time, but Trump's "revolution of common sense" line from his inaugural address resonated deeply with me and crystallized how I had come to view the Republican Party in its battle with the radical, progressive left.

Beyond that, Trump's "f–around and find out" attitude in the early days of his second term seemed like the perfect way to handle Washington, DC. After what establishment Washington did to cripple his presidency the first time around, I certainly didn't have a problem with him fighting back, because it felt to most Republicans like he was fighting back *for us*.

"Have you been in here before?" the president asked me as I settled into the Oval.

"It's been a few years, sir. Two thousand eight," I said.

"Well, I've done some redecorating. Look at these paintings. George Washington over the fireplace. And Reagan here over the desk. The conservatives love that. Place of honor over the fireplace—who would you put there, Reagan or Washington?" Trump asked.

I paused to consider a decorating question that only presidents usually ponder. And I've marveled at his constant redecorating of the most important office in the world. The paintings. His own mugshot. The Declaration of Independence. He's restyling the Oval visually as fast as he's reshaping all of American politics.

Trump's redecorating is a metaphor for the way he has governed in his second term—adding new elements at such a rapid pace that hardly anyone can keep up. It's clear that he has a vision for what he wants, and it is up to the rest of us to figure it out and embrace it.

"Sir, you're asking a Kentuckian, so I am biased. But I would've chosen Lincoln," I said.

"Well, we have Honest Abe over here," Trump retorted, pointing to the wall opposite Reagan where a picture of Lincoln indeed hangs.

Another that caught Trump's attention was a portrait of Franklin D. Roosevelt, perhaps the most powerful president of the twentieth century. Not since FDR has anyone busted Washington's norms, challenged the judiciary, expanded executive power, reshaped the government, and acted on the will of the people like Trump. The historical parallel is unmistakable.

"Some of the Republicans don't like that," Trump said, briefly nodding toward the thirty-second president.

"I'm thinking of putting a chandelier in here," Trump then said, still seated behind his desk. "Right through the shield there on the ceiling. If there's any room that needs a chandelier, it's this one. What do you think, Scott?"

"I think it will come in handy at night, Mr. President," I said. The Oval was awash in sunlight that day, brighter than I remembered it from frequent visits during the Bush 43 years, where I served as special assistant to the president. I wasn't quite sure that it needed any more lighting fixtures, but I thought to myself *if anyone knows where to put a chandelier, it is this man.* (I learned several weeks later that the White House staff investigated the possibility but concluded the ceiling couldn't hold the weight.)

These days, there is another portrait hanging in the Oval—James Monroe, he of Monroe Doctrine fame. It was a gift from Secretary of State Marco Rubio, who shipped it over from the Washington, DC, neighborhood of Foggy Bottom. As Secretary Rubio told me during an interview, he presented President Trump with a book of art from the State Department's collection—art that, in Rubio's words, was "hanging somewhere that no one sees." The president flipped through the book and immediately chose Monroe. "Obviously a lot of people point to its link to the Monroe Doctrine," Rubio said, "but for the president, and for me, it's a reminder that foreign policy works best when it's anchored in the national interest."

Now down to business. But not mine, *his*. I was about to be knitted into "the weave," Trump's description for his communication style, for the first time in my life.

"What do you think of the Panama Canal?" he asked me.

"They are violating their treaty obligations, sir. Well within your rights to push back on Chinese influence," I said.

"Greenland?"

"Don't forget about this one. Strategically located, rare earth minerals, and I think an inspired idea."

"Canada, fifty-first state?"

"Intriguing, but I am worried about two additional Democratic senators stalling out your agenda."

A laugh from the president, but then another note from him: "The conservatives are doing well, they will win the next election. The people of Canada are unhappy." *Ever the optimist*, I thought.

In the weeks that followed, Trump's running commentary roiled Canadian politics. Conservative leader Pierre Poilievre distanced himself from Trump at one point, which caused Trump to immediately attack back. On April 28, the Canadians elected liberal leader Mark Carney, who'd run against Poilievre (and against Donald Trump). Although the conservatives, it should be noted, had their best showing since 2011 and the liberals fell a few seats short of an outright majority.

I realized in his line of questioning that I had stumbled into what was essentially the president conducting two meetings at the same time—one on foreign policy, and the other on steel and aluminum tariffs, which he planned to sign later that day.

But both meetings were really about the same thing—what is in the best interest of the United States of America? What choices can we make that put America First?

After a few final instructions for his advisors, they began to collect their binders and notes. Trump then beckoned for me to approach the Resolute Desk.

Also in the room was Special Envoy Steve Witkoff, who, unbeknownst to me, was about to leave for Russia to secure the release of American hostage Marc Fogel, one of the most triumphant moments of Trump's first months in office. Witkoff would later take on several other huge responsibilities, including dealing with the Russians over Ukraine.

Today's business, though, was reacting to Hamas, which had just announced it was going to pause releasing hostages after agreeing to do so around the time of Trump's inauguration.

"I think we give them forty-eight hours to release them all," Trump said to Witkoff and me. "What do you think?" he said, looking for my opinion.

"I think they are savages, and you cannot trust them one bit. Forty-eight hours sounds generous to me, sir. Look what they've done to these hostages. The videos of these people are terrible, and they make them participate in public relations stunts to humiliate them."

Trump agreed, but Witkoff was circumspect and offered that waiting until the following Saturday was the best option, as that was the typical day for hostage release. Trump sided with Witkoff and that was that. He and National Security Advisor Waltz took down the president's words for a statement on the matter.

Trump said to Waltz, "Go write that up and bring it back to me. I want to see it." And then to Witkoff, "You will brief Bibi on this?"

Both agreed to their assignments and left the room. It was obvious how much Trump respected Witkoff. Witkoff left our meeting, flew to Russia, and secured Fogel's release. Just thirty hours after that encounter in the Oval, the two friends would be standing next to Fogel, an American teacher held hostage in Russia, in the White House, with Trump inviting him to the Lincoln Bedroom.

In the opening months of the administration, Trump dispatched Witkoff to several hot spots. His engagement with Hamas soon took a sour turn; in fact, I had been right. You can't trust these guys. The terrorist organization reneged on agreements they made with Witkoff, prompting Israel to relaunch attacks. Hamas released their final American hostage—Edan Alexander—on May 12, although as of this writing the terrorist organization is still holding nearly sixty Israelis even as hostage negotiations continue. There's no doubt that Israel has severely degraded Hamas and worked with Trump to defang its sponsor, Iran. In fact, because of Trump's leadership, the summer of 2025 saw the Middle East moving toward peace, with expansion of the Abraham Accords on the horizon following a serious degradation of Iran's nuclear and terrorist capabilities in the 12-Day War.

Watching Trump command the issues and his people was remarkable. I thought *I have no idea who was in charge of the country the last four years, but I sure as hell know who is in charge now: Donald J. Trump.*

Incidentally, the more we learn about Biden's capacity—or lack thereof—the more it is clear that we just lived through one of the biggest scandals in modern American politics. Reporter Alex Thompson of *Axios*, one of the few journalists who had the courage to report on Biden's decline while the former president was still in office, called it a "cover-up" in late April of 2025 as he spoke of his profession's damaged credibility at the White House Correspondents' Dinner in Washington, DC.

"We bear some responsibility for faith in the media being at such lows. I say this because acknowledging errors builds trust, and being defensive about them further erodes it. We should have done better," Thompson said. *Amen,* I said to myself sitting in the crowd. I couldn't help but notice that his obviously true statement received, at best, scattered applause.

Thompson, along with my CNN colleague Jake Tapper, released a book in May 2025 called *Original Sin*. It detailed the enormous conspiracy that took place to hide Biden's mental decline and diminished physical condition from the American public. Every story in the book is worse than the last one. If I had a nickel for every time I heard an anchor or Democratic pundit use the phrase "the big lie" after the 2020 election, I'd be a rich man.

But as it turned out, the real "big lie" was what Biden's White House and family did to hide his diminished state from the American people. The Biden cover-up, in my opinion, is the biggest scandal in modern American political history. It required the cooperation and capitulation of virtually every member of Biden's inner circle, his family, every senior Democratic elected official, and untold others who all undoubtedly knew that Biden should not have been serving as president, at a minimum in 2023 and 2024 (and perhaps even before).

At the end of Biden's presidency, there was credible reporting that Hunter Biden, the son to whom he granted a blanket pardon, was effectively running the White House along with First Lady Jill Biden, among the most power hungry and duplicitous people in this scandalous episode. And a senior Department of Justice official from the Biden years told me that the DOJ, which Democrats claim to hold as sacred, was not given a heads-up on any of the last-minute pardons Biden issued to his family, Hunter's included.

Since Biden left office, he has barely been seen or heard from at all outside of a widely mocked speech he gave in Chicago on April 15, 2025, and a disastrous appearance on *The View* on May 8. The fact that Biden and his closest aides are still arguing with a straight face that he should have been the Democratic nominee in 2024—that he was anywhere near capable of holding the office for another four years—is brazen gaslighting that ought to see them all drummed out of the political business forever.

But with Trump commanding the room from behind the Resolute Desk, giving orders, questioning staff and offering quick decisions on matters large and small, I thought *there's really no question who is running the country now.* As I said on CNN the night of Trump's inauguration, as our political panel watched live as the new president signed order after order all the while narrating the details of each one: "I'm just struck by the fact that we have a president again."

Back in the Oval, with his business out of the way, the president looked me square in the eye and said, "Scott, I'm glad you are here. Can we have kind of a quick meeting because, as you can see, I'm dealing with a lot of shit today."

I suppressed a chuckle. Trump has a way of speaking that gets right to the point.

"Yes sir, Mr. President. I don't need much of your time. I simply came by to congratulate you on your victory, and to ask you for your cooperation on a book I want to write. I think you revolutionized presidential campaigning last fall, and now you're revolutionizing governing in the modern era. You've smashed your enemies and they don't know what to do. You are the 80–20 president, and I think your first hundred days are going to be remembered as one of the most remarkable periods in presidential history."

The president leaned back in the chair.

"Well, how do you know the first hundred days are going to be a success?" he asked me. I was a little surprised, to be honest. Trump isn't known for navel-gazing or second-guessing himself.

At this point Trump had been in office less than three weeks. But among the flurry of executive orders, foreign affairs wins, brash statements, and the DOGE effort uncovering waste, fraud, and abuse across the federal bureaucracy, I felt confident that we were living through a historic period and that Trump deserved a review from someone who was willing to look at the facts instead of creating just another narrative.

"Sir, I think you're already a success, and I have no reason to believe you're going to stop. The momentum is remarkable," I said. "But I want to write this book as soon as possible, and to do that I need to start now."

As I complete the book in the summer of 2025, it's safe to say that the first few months of Trump 2.0 have been wildly successful. He has fulfilled campaign promises, handily won the culture wars, and restored strong American leadership in the world.

Internationally, Trump has the Middle East in a better place than it has been in years. He has supported our ally, Israel, in its fight to defeat Iran and its terror proxies. He has opened up solid lines of partnership with Arab states in the region and is on the brink of expanding the Abraham Accords, one of the best accomplishments of his first term.

In Africa, Trump and Secretary of State Marco Rubio announced a peace agreement between the Democratic Republic of Congo and Rwanda, helping end a conflict that had been raging for decades. And in the dealmaking, they gained access for the United States to critical minerals in the region.

In Europe, Trump reaffirmed the US commitment to NATO and convinced all allies in the organization to spend 5 percent of GDP on national defense, the first time that's ever happened.

Domestically, the stock market had reached all-time highs after months of predictions of a market crash. Inflation had cooled significantly. Blockbuster private investments and reshoring of manufacturing jobs are announced with regularity by some of the biggest companies in the world. Gas prices are at a four-year low. Egg prices, often derisively cited by Democrats in February and March as evidence of Trump's failure, are down 69 percent.

On the southern border, nothing short of a miracle has occurred. Border crossings are nearly nonexistent after millions of illegal aliens flowed in during the Biden years. ICE has arrested over one hundred thousand illegal aliens, including 2,700 members of the violent Tren de Aragua gang.

Politically, Trump led the narrow Republican majority in Congress to pass his "big beautiful bill" by July 4, just as he asked. It made his 2017 tax cuts permanent, implemented work requirements for Medicaid, invested heavily in border security, and re-focused American energy policy on fossil fuels instead of wind and solar. This was, in effect, the fulfillment of Trump's campaign agenda.

In the courts, Trump's pushing of the envelope has paid off. The Supreme Court has ruled in his favor on several major cases, affirming the powers of the presidency and curbing the ability of individual district court judges to grind a presidency to a halt with nationwide injunctions.

Culturally, Trump strongly confronted the radical left on boys playing in girls' sports, antisemitism, and DEI, making it safe for businesses to abandon the nonsense of the last few years. He kept up his longtime passion of holding the media accountable, forcing several multimillion-dollar settlements in the process.

Indeed, by summer, Trump was winning and his supporters were more than thrilled with the results, despite wishcasting from Democrats and pundits that he was losing altitude with his own people.

Back in the Oval Office, Trump was quizzing me about the book.

"But you aren't a writer, are you?"

I realized that Trump only knew me from TV. During the campaign and in the early days of the presidency, a few of his advisors told me he enjoyed watching clips of my nightly sparring with four or five Democrats at a time.

"I've written a lot of newspaper columns, sir. And this would be my first book. But I imagine that the usual Washington suspects are already lining up to write books shitting on these first hundred days. I think more than half the country is thrilled with what you are doing and deserves a book that tells the real story about how you smashed the Washington bureaucracy before your enemies even got out of bed."

A nod from the commander in chief.

"Oh, we smashed them last fall, too. They still don't know what to do," Trump said, musing as he thought about my proposition. He gazed away for a moment, allowing himself a quick second to relive the satisfaction of having won such a decisive victory last November.

Talking to Trump in private is remarkable. He is fully engaged in the conversation. He is quick, funny, and authentic. Part of Trump's secret sauce for political success is exuding authenticity. For Kamala Harris, his vanquished opponent, it was her weakest attribute. She gave off the appearance of simply being an actor reading someone else's script, while Trump's vibe is that he's very much the producer, director, writer, and leading man in his own play.

"Okay, call me next week!" the president said. And he shook my hand as he turned his attention to Howard Lutnick and Scott Bessent to prepare for the steel and aluminum tariff signing, which would take place later that afternoon.

* * *

To say I was impressed by Trump that day is an understatement. This was a man in control of the news, his views, and the moment. He's charming, and it was easy to see why he was beating his enemies to a pulp. He moves fast; they don't. He's funny; they aren't. And he is far more in tune with the daily zeitgeist than they could ever hope to be.

"Did you see the crowd last night? Oh, they booed Taylor Swift like crazy. But they cheered me!" he said at one point during our meeting, reliving the previous night's trip to New Orleans and his historic attendance at Super Bowl LIX. It was true, too. When Donald Trump walks into a football stadium—college or pro—the ovation is deafening.

When I worked for President George W. Bush, I visited the Oval for personnel meetings where the president and sometimes Vice President Dick Cheney would listen to a small group of advisors make recommendations on presidential appointments.

Those meetings were somewhat formal and relatively scripted. President Bush was handed a binder of recommendation memos and the staff would talk through them all. He occasionally asked questions (my job was to chime in with political information that proved the recommended appointee truly supported the president's agenda), and for the most part what came into the Oval in those memos was signed off on without much fuss.

The meeting I had just witnessed with Trump was the opposite. And that's not a pejorative comment. What you see of Donald Trump in public is what you get in private—freewheeling, witty, affable, and in command of more topics than the press wants to give him credit for. As Treasury Secretary Scott Bessent would later put it to me during an interview, "[President Trump] takes in information from everybody. He's happy to have you disagree with him. Sometimes he'll run you over, but he's listening. He remembers when you were right. He's always thinking about how to get leverage. What's the move, and what's the move *after* the move?" When Secretary Bessent prepares people for meetings with the president, he'll often ask, "How many points do you have to make?

You're probably not going to get past one and a half. If you get in two, that'll be a lot."

As I sat outside marveling at the last hour I'd spent with the president, I couldn't help but think of how much the Republican Party—of how much *everything*—had changed since my days in the Bush 43 White House. And it had changed because of one man—Donald J. Trump.

He transformed the Republican Party's attitude from passive to aggressive when dealing with the Democrats and the media. His style scared off some of my old Bush colleagues but also inspired millions of Americans to vote Republican for the first time in their lives. Old "blue dog" Democrats like my father came to see Trump as a voice for the working man. And millions of other people with no previous interest in the Republican Party have gravitated to the GOP because of Trump's imprint.

I'm often asked how someone can go from a Bush/McConnell/Romney aligned Republican to becoming Donald Trump's most visible defender on national television.

And while it is true that those men are basically on the outs with Trump and his allies, there is a through line that is clearer to me than ever—each of them, Trump included, were the most important defenders of Western Civilization during their moment.

They all strongly believed in free speech. And they all understood that it was outright dangerous to allow the progressive movement to drag the country drastically and radically to the left.

The difference, of course, is that the Republican Party's previous leaders chose to play within the lines drawn by the media and the opposition party. Trump tore up their lines and remade the entire playing field, and everyone in politics is still catching up to this day.

For whatever policy quibbles any old-guard establishment Republican might have with Trump, you cannot deny that he's fighting a much larger battle against forces that believe the American founding was somehow rotten at its core, that the speech of their political enemies should be suppressed and even censored, and that Western Civilization itself should be upended in favor of a world divided into two groups—the oppressed and the oppressors. And they fundamentally think America is an oppressor and therefore deserves to be punished.

Simply put, Trump is defending the free world and traditional American values. And if we lose our freedoms, especially the freedom of speech, we won't be around to argue about any of the rest of our policy disputes.

It took me awhile to understand the Trump phenomenon and why his brand of politics is such a potent force. I just didn't get it at first. I came up in politics through the establishment lanes that most operatives followed. Incidentally, my aforementioned father was the first person to tell me Donald Trump would be the next president. I, of course, laughed it off, like most other political insiders. But he was right and I was wrong.

But over time, I have come to admire and respect Trump's most impressive attributes. He doesn't succumb to the corrosive attitude of *we've always done it that way before*. He is on the attack all the time against his enemies in the Democratic Party and the press, institutions that have relentlessly dedicated themselves to tearing him down using any means necessary. And he rarely accepts *you just can't do that* as a final answer. He doesn't always get his way, but he has certainly defeated enemies and created pathways for conservative progress that had eluded Republicans for years.

And his aggressive style, I believe, is born of a desire to rein in the uncommon nonsense of the radical left and restore some sanity to American life. My interactions and observations of the president have convinced me that, despite what you hear his enemies say, he does, in fact, care about changing America for the better.

"He's obsessively in love with America," Secretary Marco Rubio told me during an interview. "Everything he does is about what's good for America."

He has a knack for finding overwhelmingly popular positions and making them his own. I once dubbed him on CNN "the 80–20" president because he finds issues that 80 percent of us agree on and somehow tricks his enemies into dying on every 20 percent hill. Deporting illegal immigrants? Paper straws? Keeping boys out of girls' sports? Check, check, and check—Trump takes an obviously politically popular position and Democrats lose their minds.

"I can't wait until American women can't get blueberries for their smoothies," Democratic strategist Jenna Arnold said in a debate with me on CNN, as I argued for Trump's plan to deport illegal immigrants from the country.

"This is just stupid . . . this move is pointless," said progressive social media personality Ed Krassenstein of Trump's executive order banning paper straws.

Representative Jasmine Crockett, one of the Democratic Party's leading voices in the new Trump era, offered this screed on X: "On National Girls & Women in Sports Day, Trump is: - banning trans kids from playing sports - trying to cut Title IX women's and girls' athletics grants - removing references to women, female and equality on government websites. LET ME BE CLEAR. This. Doesn't. Protect. Women."

And that preceded every Senate Democrat voting against the Protection of Women and Girls in Sports Act on March 3, blocking the bill from even being considered on the Senate floor.

If you are still wondering how Trump could have possibly come back from the political dead after January 6, look no further than the contrast of his commonsense instincts versus those of his deranged opponents. Time and again, his enemies choose to die on bizarre progressive hills while never stopping to wonder why most Americans are not up there with them.

"I don't know who the leader of the Democratic Party is, but I know who runs it—Donald Trump," I said to CNN's Kasie Hunt during a March 2025 appearance. The only real ideology of the Democratic Party is to reflexively oppose Trump's every move, even when it is clearly not in their political interest to do so.

The intervening period between Trump's two terms was illuminating to millions of people who were essentially misled about what a Joe Biden presidency would mean for the country. He promised a return to normalcy and moderation as the nation emerged from COVID's upheaval.

Instead, we were treated to a period of economic and cultural turmoil. Excessive, outright insane amounts of government spending led to the inflationary crisis that crippled working families. The borders were effectively opened, and millions of illegal aliens invaded America in record-breaking numbers. Many committed heinous crimes, like the murders of Laken Riley and Jocelyn Nungaray. Americans living in small towns and big cities suffered the consequences and were told to sit down, shut up, and stop being so racist.

Biden, despite presenting himself as a moderating influence on American life during the 2020 campaign, threw in with the most radical social progressives in his party, embracing the fever swamp ideas of the American Left like no other Democratic president before him. He jerked the wheel of American life so hard to the left that the ensuing G-forces pulled millions back into Trump's orbit. He campaigned as a moderate and then turned the government over to Bernie Sanders and Elizabeth Warren. It was a bait-and-switch that had enormous policy and political repercussions.

After four years of Biden and Harris, the American people came running back to Trump for one reason: America was off the rails under radical Democrats, and someone had to restore common sense and American optimism.

Americans were tired of being told to accept the random and extreme as the new normal. They don't want men changing in their daughters' locker rooms. They don't want their morning commute blocked by protestors gluing themselves to roadways. They don't want their favorite sport to become a vehicle for "social justice." And they don't want to be told they are the crazy ones for even raising an eyebrow to this!

Voters were desperate for any political leader who appeared to be *normal*. And that's how Trump has redefined the ideology of the GOP today: his is the party of common sense, and Democrats have become the party of uncommon nonsense.

In his inaugural address on January 20, 2025, Trump made a simple promise: to usher in a "revolution of common sense." From his Day One executive orders to his pragmatic approach to foreign affairs to his clear-eyed determination to get control of the southern border, the unifying thread to Trump's governing style is simply to ask whether a certain action presents as common sense.

As I stood on a press riser in the back of an arena in Macomb County, Michigan, on April 29, Trump's one hundredth day in office, he returned to the phrase that had launched his new term in office to a throng of cheering rally goers:

"What the world has witnessed in the past fourteen weeks is a revolution of common sense. That's all it is," Mr. Trump boomed. "You're conservative, you're liberal, whatever the hell you are—it's about common sense."

This book is about the opening salvos of Trump's second term, how he swept like a hurricane into Washington, DC, smashed his enemies before they knew what hit them, and pulled off the most consequential opening months of a presidency since Franklin D. Roosevelt. As Secretary of the Interior Doug Burgum put it to me in an interview, "President Trump was courageous in his first term. This time he's fearless."

For years, conservatives have been desperate for a leader audacious enough to fulfill the big promises—cutting government bloat, standing up to the radical cultural bullies, and putting a hateful, activist media in its place.

Through DOGE (the Department of Government Efficiency), executive orders, and a press team that understands the new media landscape better than anyone, Trump has delivered on those promises and more. A common theme of anti-Trump commentary was that Trump's voters would eventually recoil from his decisions, but nothing could be further from the truth. Trump's voters were thrilled with the first act of Trump 2.0 and were giving him all the latitude any politician could hope for.

"Everybody I know who voted for Trump is gleeful and supportive of everything he is doing!" lamented commentator Ana Navarro on

March 20. She, like so many of the elites who make their living by feeding the Trump Derangement Syndrome (TDS) industry, keep waiting for Trump's supporters to give up on him for one thing or another.

But they never will.

If Trump is anything, he is a "genius empath," a comment coined by former *Saturday Night Live* star Darrell Hammond (who, in my opinion, will always be the best Trump that *SNL* ever cast). Trump knew the American people were emotionally primed for an active president, someone willing to swing into action, to think big, and to risk a few mistakes if it meant getting America out of the left-wing, elite-dug ditch and back onto a better path.

If Trump was interested in beginning a revolution of common sense, he knew he couldn't simply rest on the laurels of an incredible comeback victory in November's election. He could not simply treat his second term as a valedictory exercise, content to enjoy the trappings and pomp of the presidency.

Trump knew that to assuage the distress of the American people after four disastrous years of the Biden administration, he had to act and act fast. He learned all too well in his first term what happens when official Washington fights back. It can wrap itself around the neck of a presidency like an anaconda, its only goal to choke, crush, and devour it whole.

Despite having some successes in his first term, Trump was buried with investigations, impeachment, and so much poppycock that he was never truly afforded the running room that most new presidents get. And he left unfinished business on the table as his enemies and the COVID pandemic effectively robbed him of a full term to execute some of his biggest ideas.

But this time would be different.

For this book, I interviewed the president of the United States, his senior staff, members of his cabinet, his political advisors, and countless others in Washington, DC, and around the country who are shaping the second Trump administration or have a front-row seat to it. I met with the president in the Oval Office and flew with him on Air Force

One. I sat down with Elon Musk in a quiet corner of the Eisenhower Executive Office Building (EEOB) on the White House complex, a conversation that took place just days before he would depart and break with the president. And, of course, I have been in the middle of analyzing the president through my perch at CNN, which has given me unique insights into how the debate over Trump's second-term actions are being absorbed by Democrats and Republicans alike.

As President Trump texted me on June 27: "*A great 6 months, and incredible 2 weeks, including the 12 Day War! Maybe the best period of time in history for a president.*"

The president is right—he did have an incredible open to his second term, fulfilling campaign promises and rampaging through opponents who had no idea how to fight back. For virtually every Trump voter I know, their reaction to Trump's retaking office was "This is exactly what I voted for."

This is the story of how a determined Trump—aided by a focused, no drama team—crushed and defeated the snake before it ever got out of bed.

CHAPTER ONE

No Holds Barred

"Every day, my administration is fighting to deliver the change America needs, to bring a future that America deserves, and we're doing it. This is a time for big dreams and bold action."

—PRESIDENT DONALD J. TRUMP, MARCH 6, 2025

I spent election night 2024 in what most Republicans would consider hostile territory. But not for me—a CNN television studio has been my natural habitat for over eight years, where I am more than comfortable speaking for half (and sometimes far more than half) of the country on lopsided panels full of punditry legends like Obama strategists David Axelrod and Van Jones, who have become good friends. Sometimes people ask me if I thought these panels were "fair." I stopped to think about it once and said, "No, not really. But if they added two or three more liberals it might be."

Over the years, I have argued about everything from tariffs to tax cuts to Brett Kavanaugh to men competing in women's sports to the legitimacy of the Russian collusion investigation. But nothing could prepare me for the ferociousness of the anti-Trump discourse during our coverage of the 2024 election, or the second Trump administration that would come after.

I came to see my job at CNN as a representative for Flyover Country, USA. Though the shows would typically draw just a few hundred thousand live viewers, clips of my appearances during the 2024 election began to generate millions of views on social media, particularly on the X platform, formerly Twitter. The flood of positive comments was certainly good for my self-esteem, but more importantly they revealed what turned out to be the truth of the 2024 election: the elites who control our political narratives were deeply out of touch with the mood of the country.

And Americans were hungry for someone to call BS on all of it.

While cable TV anchors were obsessed with Kamala Harris's "brat summer," regular people were seething over the state of affairs in Joe Biden's America. Middle Americans did *not* care about Governor Tim Walz's silly camouflaged hats. They didn't care that some shock-jock comedian had made a joke about Puerto Rico at a Trump rally. They weren't persuaded by obviously flawed, outlier polling in Iowa showing Harris with momentum. Regular people never took their eyes off the real issues, even as our political pooh-bah desperately tried to distract them from it.

Regular people cared that inflation and crime were rising. They cared that the border was being overrun. They cared that Joe Biden had been the worst president of their lifetime, and that Kamala Harris was promising more of the same. And they were tired of smug pundits and arrogant Democratic operatives telling them things were fine, and that Biden was "sharp as a tack."

More than anything, they cared that instead of fixing these problems, the Biden-Harris administration (and the Left in general) seemed to care more about policing language and catering to "woke" interest groups than they did about helping ordinary Americans. As I told Dana

Bash on CNN's *State of the Union* program one month before the election: "A lot of men think Democrats care more about dudes who want to become women than dudes who just want to be dudes." My sparring partners that morning were aghast, but in the end, I was proven dead right.

The election results that began rolling in on the evening of November 5, 2024, felt like vindication to millions of Republicans, including me.

Around ten o'clock I looked at the sunken faces of my fellow panelists, all dedicated Harris supporters, as they came to grips with the reality that Trump was going to prevail rather easily. For months, our CNN band had traveled together, walking the snowy streets of Des Moines, Iowa, witnessing the fateful June debate in Atlanta, Georgia, and taking in both party conventions. We had absorbed the undulations of the campaign as a team, and I had come to appreciate them as good-faith players with solid experience. Indeed, CNN deserves a lot of credit for platforming an outspoken conservative like me and creating situations where real debates can occur.

But on this night, my colleagues and I found ourselves on opposite ends of expectations and desired outcomes.

In the days leading up to the election, Democrats had talked themselves into a narrative of Harris momentum that just wasn't true. Their delusion was understandable. During our election coverage, these people had consistently made the case that Donald Trump was a fascist and a fundamental threat to democracy. More than one had not only compared him directly to Adolf Hitler, but claimed that his supporters were, therefore, Nazis!

They jumped the shark when Trump scheduled a massive rally at New York City's storied Madison Square Garden in late October. The storied venue, monikered "The World's Most Famous Arena," hosted historic events such as the 1971 "Fight of the Century" between Muhammad Ali and Joe Frazier, Marilyn Monroe's birthday serenade to President John F. Kennedy in 1962, a Mass celebrated by Pope Francis, legendary concerts by Bruce Springsteen and Billy Joel, and countless college and pro basketball thrillers. The radical left and the media instead drew a parallel between Trump and a February 1939 Nazi rally at the Garden, threatening anyone who dared to attend Trump's rally with being branded as a Nazi.

Many conservatives were surprised by these unhinged invectives, but I wasn't. Over the course of a twenty-five-year career in Republican politics, I've heard just about everyone called Hitler by the Left. I served as special assistant to President George W. Bush for three years during his second term and saw too many protests on Pennsylvania Avenue depicting the affable Republican president as Hitler, complete with mustache and uniform. The same was true for Ronald Reagan and Mitt Romney. To Democrats, every Republican is Hitler. And to Republicans, the epithet no longer has any meaning.

Another of my old mentors, Senator Mitch McConnell of Kentucky, a staunch defender of institutions, the Constitution, and human rights, was once called "the gravedigger of American democracy" by a left-wing historian of the Holocaust.[1] This seems to be the default claim of liberals who run out of respectable arguments. It would be funny if it wasn't so serious. Why does the Left call everyone they hate Hitler while curiously ignoring the antisemitic left-wing protestors and terrorists who have made life miserable for Jews around the world, including on the streets and college campuses of America?

Sadly, the offensive tirades usually worked. For years, conservative voters were disappointed by Republican candidates who tried to appease their left-wing detractors by backing down in the face of this outrageous criticism. If there's one lesson I've learned in my work at CNN, it is this: it's never enough. No amount of appeasement or self-flagellation ever satisfies the left-wing mob.

Donald Trump took a different approach, to put it mildly. The only way to stop a bully is to punch them in the nose. Rather than shrinking away from the Left's criticism, he gave it right back to them—usually twice as hard and ten times as loud.

To silence the Left's media echo chamber, Trump popularized the term "fake news" as a blanket epithet to respond to the narratives being spun against him. Never before had an American politician, let alone a *president*, cut through the clutter to speak so plainly, truthfully, and authentically to the people. And he'd done it without needing to go through the typical filters and conventional channels.

Instead, he simply broadcast his thoughts and feelings to millions of people at a time, usually in a straightforward, stream-of-consciousness style that was all his own. Some establishment Republicans blanched at this newfound GOP aggression, and the left-wing press and its affiliated pundits were powerless to stop him no matter how much they raged from their podcast studios and cocktail parties.

There were, of course, bumps in the road. At the end of his first term, following January 6, a group of censorious tech executives at Twitter banned President Trump from using the platform he had mastered. A similar thing happened at Facebook. In the aftermath, it seemed that President Trump's political career might be over. Even I thought so, and I said as much on the air and in my written commentary. Well, I was wrong. And I fully admit that it took me a long time to understand the power and potency of the Trump political phenomenon. I learned in 2024 that not only was Trump back, he had never really left, at least as far as Republicans were concerned. They wanted vindication for what was done to Trump in his first term. For the Russia hoax. For the weaponization of the criminal justice system against Trump. For the impeachments. For all of it.

And only Trump returning to the White House could deliver that satisfaction.

The political realignment that began with Donald Trump's first election in 2016 was far from over.

If anything, it was just beginning.

As Joe Biden's first term in the White House labored on, I realized just how dominant the Trump phenomenon had grown. In a sense, he had become the head of both parties. Republicans never really left him, even after a momentary drop of support following January 6, and he was all that Democrats could talk about.

Even Joe Biden, who'd run as a moderate dealmaker in the vein of

Bill Clinton's campaigns of the 1990s, couldn't shut up about Trump. On a surreal evening in September 2022, Jill Biden led her husband out the front door of Independence Hall in Philadelphia. Floodlights on each side of a walkway illuminated their path to a riser where plexiglass teleprompter screens waited. As President Biden stepped to the podium, the historic backdrop was bathed in an ominous red light and the US Marines posted at the door became silhouettes. The scene gave off serious super-villain vibes. Punctuated by phlegm-clearing coughs, an angry Biden warned us all that "ultra-MAGA Republicans" were one of the most dangerous threats we faced as a nation.[2]

At the time, our streets were being ravaged by crime. The price of gas, housing, and groceries—and virtually everything else that makes up your cost of living—had been skyrocketing for months. Illegal border crossings were surging. And all the president of the United States seemed able to focus on was the man who'd held the office before him . . . and who, Biden obviously thought, could well hold it again.

Throughout his four years in the White House, Joe Biden was wrong about a lot of things. But he *was* right about that, his laughable post–2024 election musings that he would have defeated Trump notwithstanding. Obviously, someone in the know had told him that the appeal of Donald Trump and the rest of the MAGA movement hadn't died when Trump left office the first time. If anything, it was only getting stronger. I sensed during the 2024 campaign a resolve among Republicans like none I'd experienced since 2004, when I worked on Bush 43's successful reelection effort. The MAGA movement—and indeed most Republicans—wanted vindication for what happened in 2020 and in the intervening period. During the 2024 GOP primary, only one man could create and then meet the moment of truth: Donald J. Trump.

And it makes sense, doesn't it? When you find yourself watching a disastrous withdrawal from Afghanistan coupled with economic upheaval at home followed by a brutal invasion of Israel by bloodthirsty Hamas terrorists, you tend to reminisce about times when things weren't so chaotic. Simply put, life had been better under Trump than it was under Biden. The world had been calmer. And the United States had a mentally competent president.

Perhaps it wasn't surprising, then, that in 2024 voters were still willing to wait hours to attend rallies for the man who could deliver the United States from the misery of the Biden years. By the time the Republican primaries really got underway, former President Trump was packing venues just like he had during his historic 2016 run. He proved once again that he was the center of the American political universe and that pundits who counted him out were wrong. As he continued his seemingly inevitable climb out of the political wilderness to become the first American president to win nonconsecutive terms since Grover Cleveland, the Left threw everything they had at him.

There were congressional investigations led by "Never Trump" Republicans who would soon cash in on their fame with book deals and media contracts. A complicit news media posted countless negative articles and tirelessly platformed every Trump hater in Washington. The Biden FBI raided Trump's home at Mar-a-Lago in search of classified documents (and reportedly rooted through Melania Trump's wardrobe), while Biden himself was stashing classified material in open boxes stacked in his own garage!

And the "lawfare" against Trump reached its ridiculous climax when New York District Attorney Alvin Bragg filed thirty-four felony counts over Trump's 2006 encounter and subsequent payment to Stormy Daniels, not a single one of which would have been brought against anyone whose last name wasn't "Trump." This kind of case had never been prosecuted anywhere in the United States until Bragg used what we call "lawfare" to try to stop Trump's return to the White House.

In a piece for *New York* magazine, my fellow CNN contributor Elie Honig, a former federal prosecutor, said the charges against President Trump "[weren't] just unusual. [They were] bespoke, seemingly crafted individually for the president and nobody else."[3] The prosecutors, he wrote, "got their man, for now at least—but they also contorted the law in an unprecedented manner in their quest to snare their prey." Later, on an episode of *Somebody's Gotta Win with Tara Palmeri*, he said, "If they were trying this case in a jurisdiction that would have gone 50–50 Trump-Biden, I would say there's no chance of a conviction."[4]

Amusingly, once Trump regained the presidency, he hung his New York City mugshot in the hallway outside the Oval Office—a reminder, perhaps, that when you aim for the "King," you best not miss.

Against the backdrop of metaphorical slings and legal arrows, two actual snipers *trained their sights* on Trump during the 2024 campaign. In Butler, Pennsylvania, one of them opened fire, grazing the ear of the once-and-future president, coming within a centimeter of taking his life.

The moment President Trump stood up, blood streaming down his face, his return to the White House was virtually sealed. An iconic—historic—photograph taken by Evan Vucci of the Associated Press became the defining image for the rest of the campaign: Trump standing defiantly, his fist raised as he charged the terrified crowd to *"FIGHT, FIGHT, FIGHT!"*

Every newscast, every newspaper, every outlet showed the defining and inspiring moment. On that July 13 night, I happened to be on the CNN set in Washington, DC, with legendary anchor Wolf Blitzer. As it became clear that Trump had narrowly survived an assassination attempt, anger welled up inside of me. *My God,* I thought. *Has it come to this? Has the American left fomented so much hatred for Trump that this man can no longer leave his home?* I unleashed a tirade that rocketed around social media—there was no "both sides" tonight. The Republican nominee for president was bleeding. And I was seething.

The Left, I noted, was "dedicated to telling half the country that if Donald Trump wins an election, the country will end. The Constitution will go away, and so on and so forth. What I wanted to hear from all elected officials is that this kind of hyperbolic extremism has consequences, and it must end." When Wolf tried to tell me that there were problems on both sides, and that President Trump's rhetoric had been equally bad, I shot back: "Who's in the hospital?"

I was hardly the only media person to be outraged by the attempts of some to blame Trump for his own assassination. Political journalist Mark Halperin summed it up a year later:

"The mentality in the immediate aftermath of the near-murder of the former president and leading presidential candidate—to turn to flyspecking his statements rather than the many, many statements of Democrats hostile to Donald Trump—is quite something," Halperin said.[5]

"I'm all for the press scrutinizing Donald Trump, but you see in the immediate aftermath of the near-death of Donald Trump people wanting to hold him accountable for his own near-murder. It's kind of incredible," he continued.

"To jump to the conclusion that what contributed to the shooting was Donald Trump's own words—a lot of Americans look at that and say this is why the press has lost so much credibility—why their credibility has plummeted so far."

Even as the press tried to "both sides" the political violence that was squarely aimed at one man, Trump endorsements began to pile up. Actors, comedians, and thought leaders who never would have publicly supported President Trump during his first campaign—or even his first *term*—came out of the woodwork to show their support. Trump's heroic stand was met on X by a full-throated endorsement from Elon Musk, the platform's new owner. Writing in the direct, plainspoken style that he'd soon use during his interviews about the Department of Government Efficiency, or DOGE, Musk said, "I fully endorse President Trump and hope for his rapid recovery." A few months later, Musk would cast a vote for President Trump.

And so would just over 77 million other Americans.

THE MANDATE

On Election Night, I paced between my laptop in the CNN war room and the broadcast studio where reporters and anchors were crunching the numbers. Like a Kentucky family navigating a route home from a Florida spring break through I-75 bottlenecks, our election experts exhausted every possible escape route for Kamala Harris. The initial returns from key counties were the canary in Harris's coal mine. Because Virginia polls close early, her weaker-than-expected performance in heavily Democratic Northern Virginia portended a disastrous night for the blue ticket.

Political journalists and pundits had promoted as fact that people of Puerto Rican descent would soundly reject Trump after a comedian made a joke about the island at Trump's October MSG rally. The propeller heads who crunch election data tagged Osceola County, Florida, a traditional Democratic stronghold, as a bellwether for the blowback. The county's 56 percent Hispanic population is mostly Puerto Rican.

So it was with disbelief and resignation that my colleagues watched Trump flip Osceola County to his favor. At every subsequent turn—in every swing state—Harris's path was blocked by the American people turning out for—and back to—Trump.

By the time Pennsylvania was called at 2:04 a.m., Kamala Harris's chances of victory had been dashed. President Trump was going to be the forty-seventh president of the United States. The election had not been close. When CNN finally unleashed me at 3:38 a.m. to analyze how and why Trump had won such a decisive victory, I didn't hold back.

"This is a big deal," I said. "This isn't backing into the office. This is a mandate to do what you said you were going to do." The numbers crawling across the screen told the story: Trump would win by 8.2 million votes, the largest electoral victory for a Republican since George H.W. Bush in 1984.

I framed it as a reckoning. Regular, working-class Americans—people the media had dismissed and mocked—had stood up and voted. "They're not garbage," I said. "They're not Nazis. They're just regular working people who get up and go to work every day and are trying to make a better life for their kids."

This, more than anything else, was the message that I felt people needed to hear, both in the building and in our audience. Later, in my short monologue, which reverberated loudly across X, Facebook, and countless websites that night, I said that the 2024 election was "an indictment of the political information complex." I wasn't singling out my own network; I meant the broad, unholy alliance that had formed over the past several decades between mainstream media and the Democratic Party to create false narratives that misled the American people. And the narratives were almost always designed to help Democrats and hurt Republicans.

The political information complex kicked into high gear during the 2024 election, when the mainstream press parroted increasingly unbelievable Democratic talking points. First came the narrative that Joe Biden, behind closed doors, was definitely not cognitively impaired. Then came "cheap fakes," the term coined by White House press secretary Karine Jean-Pierre to discredit clear video evidence that Biden was failing mentally and physically. For months, they told us that Donald Trump was a grave threat to democracy and that Joe Biden was sharp as a tack, that he juggles knives and rides unicycles while doing trigonometry (behind closed doors, of course).

After special counsel Robert Hur's report expressed concerns that a jury would regard Biden as an "elderly man with a poor memory," the president's sycophants lined up to insist that the emperor was wearing plenty of clothes. They ruthlessly smeared Hur, a dedicated public servant that told the American people the truth—Joe Biden is a confused old man who could never be convicted by a jury who would see him exactly that way.

"He is sharp, intensely probing and detail-oriented and focused," Homeland Security Secretary Alejandro Mayorkas told *Meet the Press*.[6]

"He was sharper than anyone I've spoken to," said Representative Dan Goldman of New York.[7]

"His mental acuity is great, it's fine . . . all this right-wing propaganda that his mental acuity has declined is wrong," according to Senate Majority Leader Chuck Schumer.[8]

And on and on it went. Democrat after Democrat lining up to attest to something they knew was total BS.

"We're looking forward," Schumer would dodge in 2025, when asked to explain his statements in the aftermath of reporting done by Jake Tapper and Alex Thompson in their book, *Original Sin*, which documented the clear cover-up by the Democratic Party and its top officials of Biden's cognitive issues.[9]

Then, when Biden dropped out of the race and Kamala Harris—who had never won a single vote for president, let alone an entire primary—was installed, the same people who lied about Biden pivoted to explaining that Harris was the best person to "save democracy." (Never mind the fact that just weeks before, many Democrats were openly musing in the press that Biden should dump the bumbling Harris from his ticket.) And on top of that, they repeated over and over the Nazi and fascist slurs, stiffening Republican resolve and desire for vindication that had been growing since 2021.

The overcooked rhetoric portended a desperation in the Democratic Party's message, which the election results proved was well-founded. Near the end of my election night analysis, I looked over at my friends and fellow commentators David Axelrod and Ashley Allison, who were both part of Barack Obama's campaigns. I reminded Ashley that on election night in 2012, she and I had both been in Ohio, but on opposite ends of the election. Axe, Ashley, and the Obama folks were popping champagne and listening to a victory speech, while I (the head of the Romney campaign in the Buckeye State) was licking my wounds.

I didn't bring this up to gloat. If anything, the opposite was true. I brought it up to remind everyone that the American political system is cyclical and that today's winners could be tomorrow's losers. In 2024, voters were simply fed up with being disrespected and ignored, with being told what they can and can't say, with being told their concerns aren't valid, and that they were racist and bigoted for disapproving of DEI and transgender policies. Voters felt they had been backed into a corner—economically and culturally—and they reacted accordingly.

When the dust and ballots had settled, President Trump had shocked the world once again by pulling off the greatest *comeback* in the history of American politics, just eight years after scoring the greatest *upset* in American political history.

But I wondered, how would he govern this time?

After he won in 2016, President Trump constructed a fairly

conventional Republican administration. His appointees, policies, and judicial appointments were center cut, normal Republican stuff. Not exactly expecting to win, and without a cadre of people with governing experience supporting him and waiting in the wings, Trump inherited the old-guard infrastructure of a political party that he had only recently commandeered. While Trump was served well by many fine Republicans in his first term, it could be argued that their collective experience and worldview were, on some issues, a mismatch for Trump's leadership style.

But on election night 2024, I had a suspicion that Trump 2.0 would be different. This time around, Trump knew what he wanted to do and would not be restrained by lack of experience. Nor did he feel compelled to accept personnel recommendations that didn't fit his personality.

Nine years after the ultimate political outsider descended the Trump Tower golden escalator, he was now the Republican Party's boss. He fully owned and operated the GOP, and he did not lack for ideas and personnel to implement his governing vision. This time, I suspected, we'd get the full Trump experience. And in the early days of his second term, I was proven right.

What signals would the president-elect send the country upon winning a popular and electoral vote mandate? That very evening, we got the beginnings of an answer.

When Trump bounded onto the stage to address his victory rally at the Palm Beach Convention Center, he set the tone for a commonsense second term:

"We're going to help our country heal," Trump flexed. "We have a country that needs help, and it needs help very badly. We're going to fix our borders, we're going to fix everything about our country, and we've made history for a reason tonight, and the reason is going to be just that."[10]

There was something profound and terrifically insightful about Trump's call for healing the nation. The Democratic Party under Biden had divided the country by taking nonsensical, fringe positions on many issues and forcing everyone to accept them as mainstream. They chose to force-feed the American people insane positions on race and gender ideology while driving up inflation. They let millions upon millions of illegal immigrants into the country while pooh-poohing concerns about crime and community impacts.

Biden had promised to heal the "soul of the nation" but had done the exact opposite by allowing freak progressive ideologies to dominate his term. Now, Trump was back to restore common sense.

Over the next few weeks, rumors swirled. The cabinet came together. Policy propositions leaked. Elon Musk and Vivek Ramaswamy announced a joint venture known as DOGE, promising to cut government waste and save Americans billions of dollars. Others worried that President Trump, with no more campaigns to run, might not have as much juice as people said he did. After all, he was a lame duck, wasn't he?

Exactly seventy-six days after election night, the world got an answer to that question. This duck was anything but lame.

His inauguration moved indoors due to dangerously cold temperatures in Washington, but Trump's speech would bring heat to the Capitol Rotunda. There was nothing laid back or limited about Trump's message to the nation. This was a liberated Trump, fully embracing his mandate to make sweeping changes for the American people.

At 11:47 a.m., with Donald Trump and JD Vance in their rotunda seats and Senator Amy Klobuchar of Minnesota, in her capacity as chairman of the Joint Congressional Committee on Inaugural Ceremonies, delivering opening remarks, TV anchors broke in with shocking news. On his way out the door, Biden had issued preemptive pardons for his siblings and their spouses, who had been clearly exposed as corrupt during an investigation by Representative James Comer of Kentucky, head of the House Oversight Committee. Back in December, Biden had already pardoned his son, Hunter, for any crime committed dating back to January 1, 2014.

"The committee found that nearly $30 million in payments from foreign sources was paid to the Biden family and their associates with no known products or services being provided in exchange . . . aside from vague claims of networking and advising, all while Joe Biden served as vice president," Representative Comer wrote in his bestselling exposé *All the President's Money*.[11]

The audacious and unprecedented pardons left Trump little choice but to excoriate Biden as part of his inaugural address. From the rotunda—a regal, intimate setting that only amplified the drama— Trump delivered a stunning indictment of his predecessor and the political class that had protected him. Biden, seated just feet away with his family, had no choice but to sit and take it.

"My recent election is a mandate to completely and totally reverse a horrible betrayal, and all of these many betrayals that have taken place," Trump blasted the defeated president. "And to give the people back their faith, their wealth, their democracy, and indeed, their freedom."[12]

Moments later on CNN, I called it one of the most remarkable inaugural addresses I'd ever seen. Trump had just stood in the Capitol rotunda and, without flinching, delivered a blunt message to the political class seated right in front of him. The imagery was unforgettable: Biden and his family watching quietly as Trump laid out a clear agenda that amounted to a sweeping rejection of their legacy.

I told the audience that the tone was serious and workmanlike. Trump didn't lean on lofty language or applause lines—he focused on action. The rotunda backdrop gave it a regal feel, but the speech itself was grounded in realism, which is a recurring theme of Trump's leadership style. In my conversations with Trump and observing him behind closed doors, you begin to understand how reality and the desire for outcomes shape his worldview more than any contours drawn and left for him by previous presidents.

Trump deals with the world as it is, warts and all. And in the rotunda, he spoke like a man who knew exactly what he planned to do and wasn't interested in wasting time.

"Today, I will sign a series of historic executive orders. With these actions, we will begin the complete restoration of America and the revolution of common sense. It's all about common sense," Trump said to loud applause. That line resonated with me deeply and became the inspiration for this book.

"The mandate is simple. It's economic relief. It's fix the immigration crisis, steer the country away from the cultural left, and restore American prestige . . . Republicans feel vindicated and Trump is back to fix the country," I reacted on CNN.

As Marine One prepared to lift the Bidens off the Capitol grounds, Trump used the moment to project strength. He talked about economic relief, restoring order at the border, countering the cultural chaos, and rebuilding American strength abroad. Republicans watching that day felt affirmed. The conservative movement had returned to power—and this time, it wasn't going to hesitate.

Of course, few predicted or even imagined how immediate, effective, and bold those changes would be. They would only have to wait a few hours to find out.

THE 80–20 PRESIDENCY

A little over twenty-five years ago, when I was still advising campaigns for Republicans like George W. Bush and Senator Mitch McConnell, the phrase "compassionate conservatism" became popular. "I felt compelled to phrase it in this way," President Bush once said, "because people hear 'conservative' and they think heartless. And my belief then and now is that the right conservative philosophies are compassionate and help people. Compassionate means you care about people and the policies you enunciate help people."[13]

This was a strong message. So strong, in fact, that it went a long way to delivering George W. Bush the White House. Twice. And Bush 43 was the last Republican before Trump in 2024 to win the national popular vote, which is no small thing.

A quarter of a century later, President Donald Trump won the White House for the second time in a very different world, and with his own unique branding.

In January 2025, people didn't hear "conservative" and think "heart-less." Many of them—especially the ones who tuned into mainstream news networks—heard conservative and thought "evil," "racist," "fas-cist," and "Nazi." Trotting out a bunch of policies that tried to appeal to "compassion" wasn't going to fix that. Democrats had long stopped debating Republicans in good faith and instead had embarked on a campaign of slander and over-the-top invective.

Trump instinctively knew that the old liberal vs. conservative con-struct was dead. There was no use trying to fight old battles when a new branding strategy was needed. So he came up with an interesting and politically ingenious idea by harkening back to another phrase that begins with a C, made popular 250 years ago by the political pamphle-teer Thomas Paine: *Common Sense*. In that pamphlet, Paine warned: "A long habit of not thinking a thing wrong gives it a superficial appearance of being right."

Paine's sentiment could have been written for the Washington swamp, where dysfunction, failure, and bureaucratic bloat are treated as business as usual. But as Paine also wrote, "We have it in our power to begin the world over again." That's exactly what President Trump set out to do—and what the American people demanded when they sent him back to the White House.

Trump's opening act came in front of twenty thousand cheering supporters during the inaugural parade at Capitol One Arena, also moved indoors due to the cold weather.

Whipping out his trademark presidential Sharpies for the first time in four years, Trump began to execute on his campaign promises, one huge signature at a time.

With White House staff secretary Will Scharf, who manages the presidential paper flow, standing and announcing the orders, Trump signed and held each order aloft in a display of presidential showmanship.

"Could you imagine Biden doing this?" Trump grabbed the micro-phone, chuckling. "I don't think so."[14]

In less than seven minutes, Trump did the following:

- Rescinded seventy-eight executive orders of the Biden administration
- Ordered a hiring freeze to shrink government
- Froze federal regulations
- Required federal workers to return to work full-time and in-person
- Ordered the government to address the cost-of-living crisis
- Withdrew the US from the Paris Climate Treaty (again)
- Directed an end to lawfare
- Protected free speech after the previous administration had pressured news media and social platforms to censor certain people and information

Trump could have signed those eight orders, headed to an inaugural ball, and called it a successful day, but he wasn't finished. Not by a long shot. Instead, by the end of the first day, the president signed an astonishing 196 executive orders and other presidential actions, thrusting open the floodgates of common sense in a torrent that still hasn't stopped. The deluge of governing and swift decisions hit especially hard because Biden had essentially disappeared after he was defenestrated by his own party in favor of Harris. The country was rudderless no longer. As one journalist told me on Inauguration Day: "Trump is doing so much we don't know what to cover."

The president held court in the Oval Office that night, narrating even more executive orders as he signed them. I watched and commented from CNN's studio, blocks from Capitol Hill:

Trump's pace was relentless. In a single day, he delivered multiple speeches, issued a staggering number of executive actions, held a lengthy press conference, and still had the energy to attend inaugural balls that night. The contrast with Biden was unmistakable—Trump was moving fast, operating with clarity and force.

The nation once again had a president who could speak in full sentences, taking his audience through the nuances of policy while entertaining them at the same time. Trump had chosen to come out of the gate with issues that appealed to just about every rational person in the country, including:

+ Unleashing American energy
+ Securing the southern border and ending the illegal immigration invasion of our country
+ Designating drug cartels as foreign terrorist organizations
+ Protecting female athletes from biological males entering their competitions
+ Ending DEI in the federal government
+ Establishing the Department of Government Efficiency (DOGE)

And for good measure, he literally rewrote the map—renaming the Gulf of Mexico as the Gulf of America and changing Denali back to Mount McKinley.

Despite predictions from the pundits, Trump chose to open his presidency with policy instead of vengeance.

And he did it on what I call "80–20 issues," where a large majority of Americans agree on what the commonsense position should be. For years, the political information distribution complex has been gaslighting Americans, amplifying fringe positions to make people believe they were mainstream, when in fact they weren't.

THE POPULARIST

During the campaign, President Trump had made more than a few liberal heads explode by joking he would "act like a dictator" in office, "but only on day one." This was used dishonestly by the left-wing press and the Harris campaign as further evidence that President Trump was going to trample the Constitution. They did the same dishonest thing when he said there would be a "bloodbath" for the auto industry if Biden won by repeatedly claiming that Trump would incite violence and kill people in the streets. When this man took office in January 2025, the Left assured us, we were going to get unimaginable pain and suffering and an end to democracy as we knew it.

What we got instead was an end to paper straws.

Now, I'm aware that the official executive order that ended the procurement and forced use of paper straws didn't actually come out until February 10, 2025 (the same day I visited President Trump in the White House, in fact). But I mention it here because it is about as good an example of the "80–20 rule" as we're likely to see. Everyone I know, and probably everyone *you* know, hates paper straws. We hate the way they dissolve in your mouth halfway through a Coke or an iced coffee. When you get one, you immediately realize your drink has been ruined. They contain chemicals that are extremely hazardous to our health, including "'forever chemical' PFAS (per- and polyfluoroalkyl substances) . . . which are known to be highly water soluble and can bleed from the straw into the drink," according to a government fact sheet.

They are more expensive and often wrapped in thick plastic, pretty much defeating the purpose of mandating them. And you might have forgotten how the paper straw phenomenon started in the first place—when a nine-year-old Vermont boy erroneously claimed in 2011 that Americans were using 500 million plastic straws per day.

Years ago, when I first got into politics, both parties would have jumped hard on this issue. Who wouldn't want to be the party that fixed something so stupid? Democrats and Republicans would have included bans on the forced use of paper straws in their platforms, competing to see who could use the strongest anti-straw language and whose plan would get rid of them the fastest. But in 2024, only one party was interested in listening to popular opinion. The other one, which had turned "trust the science" into a kind of religious mantra during the COVID-19 lockdown, was content to listen to a fringe mob that treats their causes like a religion despite overwhelming popular opinion (and evidence) to the contrary. In other words, the Left, ruled by fringe climate zealots, believed it knew better than most Americans and was willing to promote bogus stats to get its way. The Right, now led completely by President Trump, simply listened to most Americans, analyzed the facts, and did the commonsense thing.

Trump's strategy for gathering data was nothing like I had ever seen before. Every time he gave one of his freewheeling rally speeches, he would launch into "the weave," switching from his main topic and introducing new ones, always landing the proverbial plane at the end, by coming back to his main point. In terms of political communications, the Trump era is defined by the complete and utter defeat of rote, rehearsed political pablum. Voters crave authentic voices and language, not mediocre actors reading scripts handed to them by some faceless consultant. The era of the scripted politician is over, and the ones who succeed in the future will authentically speak their own minds, instead of someone else's. It requires a serious amount of talent to succeed in this environment; Trump blazed a trail and it will be fascinating to see if anyone, in either party, can ever approach replicating the connection he has with his people.

When I was working in the White House under President Bush, we often had a hard time finding out what the American public wanted, or even what they thought. The best way to figure it out was through polling, a complex art form that can often introduce more confusion into the process than certainty. We'd commission a group to test public opinion on a certain issue—say, school choice or tax cuts, for example—and then that group would start calling people on the phone. During a good poll, a large percentage of people would hang up. An even larger percentage would refuse to answer the questions. That left a tiny number of people (at least compared to the population of the United States, which was just over 300 million at the time) to give you the answers you were looking for.

There are tricks, of course. Most involve complex statistical math. These tricks can get you a reasonable approximation of what people in the United States thought about things. All you needed was a good sample size, say a few hundred people, and you could extrapolate based on available data to figure out what everyone else probably *would* have said. In the modern era, these techniques have gotten even more sophisticated. But all you have to do is look at the results of the three most recent presidential elections to see that opinion polling is less than perfect, and that there are certain populations and geographies that are simply hard to measure. There have been many times during my career in politics and public relations when I've found myself wishing I could just get a few thousand people in a room, ask them questions, and determine their stances on issues based on the crowd reaction.

Which, as it turned out, is exactly what President Trump had begun doing the first time he ran for president. If you study his speeches from that era, you'll notice how they evolved—day by day, city by city. Applause lines became policy. Muted responses led to rapid adjustments. He was, in effect, treating every rally like a live focus group. If the crowd roared for something, he expanded his pitch. If they didn't react to something else, the issue faded. To some, that might seem crude. But if you're going to be a president for the people, there may be no purer way than to simply listen to your people and act accordingly.

That approach had its critics. During a March 2025 CNN panel with David Axelrod—Barack Obama's former chief strategist—I drew a distinction between populists and what Axe had called "popularists." Trump, he argued, just wanted to be liked (don't most politicians?). And he warned that the public might soon grow uneasy with how quickly and aggressively the new administration was operating.

If Trump liked being popular, I said, then he was likely enjoying himself—because his popularity was surging. The public wasn't unnerved; people were energized by an activist president after four years of wondering who was actually running the country. What Axelrod derided as "the Musk effect"—that sense of disruption, speed, and unorthodoxy—was exactly the point. Trump was nimble and responsive in a way most politicians, who moved like battleships, simply couldn't match.

As I told Trump in the Oval Office, he had revolutionized political campaigning in many ways, in no small part because of his bias to action and his nimbleness. And now, from inside the White House, he was proving that he could do the same with governing.

Consider the administration's ban on biological men competing in women's sports, one of the most talked about and easily understood issues. Trump had been workshopping it at rallies for years and knew full well how powerful it was.

"So ridiculous," Trump said at a 2022 rally in Texas. "Young girls and women are incensed that they are now being forced to compete against those who are biological males. . . . It's not good for women. It's not good for women's sports, which worked for so long and so hard to get to where they are."[15]

More on transgender issues later in the book, but suffice to say, this is one of the purest 80–20 issues. Heck, 80–20 may not even do it justice. Even hardcore liberals I know don't want biological males in their daughters' locker rooms or spiking volleyballs in their faces. Call it 90–10 or 95–5, even.

"If this does not change," Trump said to his crowd, "women's sports as we know it will die."[16]

At a rally in Salem, Virginia, just a few weeks before election day in 2024, he added the trans issue to his list of campaign promises. After saying he'd get MS-13 off the streets using Immigration and Customs Enforcement, he said, "We'll stop the indoctrination of your children, and we will not let them try to change your kids' gender. They will not be doing that. They won't be changing your children's gender with their transgender craziness."[17]

The applause was louder than it had been for any issue he'd raised so far—so loud, in fact, that he needed to pause mid-speech and step back slightly from the microphone. The surest way to engender loyalty from someone is to do something for their kid, or to protect their child from danger.

Trump rang that bell. Hard.

Then he said, "Last year, the radical left's gender ideology arrived right here in Salem when a man was allowed to transfer onto the

Roanoke College women's swim team." (Boos erupted from the crowd.) "The brave members of the swim team stood up to the transgender fanatics—something new. And those strong—and I would say beautiful but I'm not allowed to use that term anymore with women because if you say beautiful it means the end of your career in politics. You're not allowed to say beautiful, so I will not tell you how beautiful they are, but they are beautiful. But those strong, beautiful, intelligent women? They won. They won."[18]

I must admit that I hadn't followed the story of the Roanoke College swim team too closely before President Trump brought it up at his rally, although, as a Kentuckian, I was quite familiar with a brave female swimmer from the University of Kentucky named Riley Gaines. She had stood up against the NCAA when forced to compete against biological male Lia Thomas and continues to this day to be one of the strongest voices in the nation for protecting women's sports from the radical left (incidentally, thanks to Trump's pressure, the University of Pennsylvania, which allowed Thomas to swim on the women's team, agreed to "restore to female athletes all individual Penn Division I swimming records, titles, or similar recognitions which were misappropriated by male athletes allowed to compete in female categories").

Rather than caving to the far left out of fear, these women stood up and fought for their rights to compete in separate, women-only spaces, a right they were given with the passage of Title IX so many years ago. I bring it up here only to illustrate just how in step President Trump is with the American public on this issue. He didn't need to see polling that said more than 80 percent of people do not believe biological men should be able to compete in women's sports. He didn't need to know that even *that* number was probably a little low, given that many respondents later reported being confused about what "trans woman" actually means. (Many believed, not unreasonably, that it referred to a woman transitioning to a man, not the other way around.) He only needed to know that when he raised this issue in front of crowds, the passion was there. And he, of course, knew that his opponents were stupidly on the wrong side of it, once again captured by a fringe mob that couldn't be further from the heart of American public opinion.

A few months after that rally in Virginia, President Trump sat in the East Room of the White House for one of the most iconic moments of his second term. On February 5, surrounded by dozens of female athletes, Trump made it official, signing the "Keeping Men Out of Women's Sports" executive order. Any president *could*, theoretically, have done this. The numbers would have supported it. But Democrats were not interested in popular support. They were interested in catering to a tiny minority of fringe, radical activists who insisted (successfully, at least for a while) that people could change their genders at will, including through the use of surgical and chemical castration on children who hadn't even reached puberty.

The first days of the Trump administration sent a clear message to the world that this kind of caving to left-wing activist groups was over. It also let the American people know that they were going to get what they voted for—a commonsense president unafraid to stand up to political and media mobs.

Applying the president's considerable pressure, the Department of Education's Office for Civil Rights scored what Secretary Linda McMahon called a "common sense" victory for women and girls when the University of Pennsylvania not only banned biological men from competing in female sports, they also restored the swimming records and titles of female athletes who had been robbed of their rightful place by a man posing as a woman. UPenn even sent a personalized letter of apology to each victim.

It is difficult to imagine any other presidential administration having the balls to stand up for civil rights the way Trump did in this case.

Unlike previous presidents who've talked a big game on the campaign and then complained about the slow-moving bureaucracy once in office, President Trump and his team were going to fulfill their promises at breakneck speed, allowing common sense to be their guide. If a program didn't make sense to the American people, that program would soon be gone. If there was an idea the American people had been enthusiastic about on the campaign, the team was going to ram it through, no matter how much the bureaucracy resisted or the media howled. The American people had elected an administration with nothing to lose and a clear sense that time was of the essence to rescue the country from the progressive ditch.

As Trump's pollster John McLaughlin told me in a conversation for this book, "[Trump] knows he has a finite amount of time to save the country. That's why he's doing so many things at once."[19]

CHAPTER TWO

DOGE

The Deep State Chainsaw Massacre

*"[Elon's] an incredible . . . brilliant guy. He was a
tremendous help both in the campaign, and in what he's
done with DOGE . . . He's a great patriot."*

—PRESIDENT DONALD J. TRUMP, APRIL 2025

*"I am saddened to watch Elon Musk go completely 'off
the rails,' essentially becoming a TRAIN WRECK over
the past five weeks."*

—PRESIDENT DONALD J. TRUMP, JULY 2025

When I started writing this book in February of 2025, Elon Musk
was serving as a special advisor to President Trump and riding high
as the Godfather of the DOGE effort inside the White House, the

hottest thing in conservative politics in years. The two titans appeared to have a political, a professional, and even a warm, friendly, and personal relationship.

By the time I was finishing the book in the summer, though, Musk had not only left the White House but was publicly assailing Trump over the "big beautiful bill," Trump's signature legislation that made permanent his 2017 tax cuts, invested in border security, encouraged work instead of welfare, and included vital energy deregulation. The vitriol in Musk's comments was shocking and personal in nature. By the time I turned in the final manuscript, Musk had launched a new political party (he called it "The America Party") that many conservatives—including myself—worried would split the conservative movement at a time when unity is required to maintain political and policy momentum created by Trump's huge win the previous November.

I don't know how this relationship is going to turn out. Recently, Elon went "completely off the rails," according to Trump, and at times Musk seemed to regret some of his more vitriolic statements.

I am writing this chapter from the perspective of someone who has admired Elon Musk's private sector work and his political engagement in 2024, but also as someone who harbors disappointment that his relationship with Trump soured so quickly and so publicly. During the spring of 2025, as Musk served in the Trump White House, the political left lost its collective mind and tried to destroy Tesla and SpaceX, two of his highest profile companies. The attacks on Tesla were particularly nasty, with Democratic politicians hoping for the company's failure and insane liberals vandalizing cars and firebombing dealerships across the country.

I believe Musk sincerely, as he told me in April, wants to save America from bankruptcy and defend Western Civilization. I can only hope he realizes that the Republican Party is the correct vehicle for those desires instead of a misguided third-party effort that could wind up empowering a radical left that hates Musk for supporting Trump in 2024 and working to eliminate waste, fraud, and abuse from the federal government.

INSIDE THE NERVE CENTER

It was a bright, sunny Wednesday in Washington in late April, but the traffic was brutal—a typical day in DC, especially since President Trump had ordered all the bureaucrats to return to their offices after years of "work from home" policies that lingered after the COVID era. As I arrived at the White House, what struck me immediately was just how active the place felt. The building wasn't functioning as a historic showpiece or ceremonial backdrop. It was alive—cabinet secretaries, senior government aides, and others were zipping in and out of meetings with the kind of purpose that's rare in government buildings. This was a direct reflection of President Trump's management style: hands-on, inquisitive, and centered on personal accountability. This president doesn't want a faceless memo. He wants the answers—face-to-face— from the people he has appointed to execute his agenda.

I was there to meet Musk, whom I had communicated with before but never in person. We met in the West Wing visitor lobby and walked together through the basement, across West Executive Avenue, and up into the Eisenhower Executive Office Building.

I asked him: What's the story of your stint in government that history might miss?

Without hesitation, he said, "I'm trying to figure out how America doesn't go bankrupt."[1] He talked candidly—no press staff, no polish— about his concern that the United States is spending itself into "oblivion." He warned, "We are going to have a worthless currency. Inflation has devalued the dollar. We cannot keep doing this." It was a raw, passionate assessment of the country's fiscal trajectory. He clearly believed the stakes couldn't be higher.

Then he pivoted: "One other issue I obviously care about is . . . you know . . . humans. Humanity. I'm very concerned about the birth rate." He sees the demographic decline as an existential threat. In his view, if we don't address it, the United States simply won't be able to sustain itself: "We cannot import the world's worst people and not have babies and expect America to be okay." He said it twice—slowly, deliberately.

I don't think I'll forget that line anytime soon. This man cares about America and takes his patriotism seriously, a stark contrast to the narratives spun by his most unhinged detractors.

Elon wasn't naïve about the pushback he's received since joining the administration. He told me, "I thought there might be a boycott [of Tesla], but I wasn't expecting people to burn down so many cars and dealerships." He said, "It's not pleasant to think about, but yeah, I expect to be threatened for the rest of my life." He described his life as living in a "golden cage." But he's not fully stepping away from his interest in streamlining the federal government. Despite media rumors about DOGE's demise, he was emphatic: "We're going strong. We have great momentum right now."

In mid-May, the White House announced that Russ Vought would be taking over the core of the DOGE agenda from his perch atop of the Office of Management and Budget, picking up the ball that Musk had gotten rolling in January.

"Russ Vought, President Trump's top budget official, is looking to lock in many of Elon Musk's cost-cutting efforts once the billionaire CEO steps aside from government. A key part of his plan: steamrolling Congress," reported *The Wall Street Journal*.[2]

Elon also addressed the ongoing attacks about his citizenship. He was visibly frustrated: "I went through an incredibly difficult process. I came here on a student visa. I got a green card. It took seventeen years to become a citizen." He called accusations about foreign allegiance "totally ridiculous." And then he launched into a sharp critique of the Democratic Party's immigration strategy: "If they're losing criminal illegals, that means they're losing customers. It's an issue of customer retention." In his view, it's not a humanitarian mission—it's a cynical political strategy to "turn swing states into California."

He didn't mince words: "Not all Democrats are criminals, but all criminals are Democrats." And while some may recoil at that, Musk doesn't care. He sees his job as calling out what others are afraid to say. He warned that offering benefits to illegal immigrants while ignoring the needs of American citizens is "going to break America." I found

Musk in person to be what his X platform has become to the public—a haven for radical free speech in a world that sorely needs more of it.

Musk cares deeply about the future of Western Civilization, and he believes electoral outcomes today will have a profound impact on the world's future. He had mentioned it on the campaign trail in Wisconsin, where he spent heavily in time and treasure on a State Supreme Court special election in April 2025. His candidate was unsuccessful, but I admired deeply his willingness to engage. Ultimately, Musk has put himself—his reputation and his successful private career—on the line for the sake of America's future.

Elon Musk up close was stoic. Direct. No handlers, no pretense. Just an earnest guy, sitting in an office in the EEOB, eating a bag of chips and sipping a Diet Coke, offering his unfiltered view on the future of the country.

And I'll leave you with this: earlier that day, the full cabinet had gathered for a meeting marking the administration's hundredth day (though it occurred on the 101st day). Elon walked in wearing two hats—literally. The bottom one was black. The top one was bright red and read GULF OF AMERICA in bold white letters.

"Even my hat has a hat," Musk joked. Laughter broke out around the table.

President Trump addressed him directly: "You have really been a tremendous help, and you've opened a lot of eyes as to what can be done. You're invited to stay as long as you want. But he wants to get back home to his cars."[3]

By that point, DOGE had purportedly saved the American taxpayer just over $160 billion. And as President Trump noted during the meeting, that number might soon double. It might have fallen short of initial projections, but the effort is ongoing and administration officials believe more savings will be had in the future, especially with Vought keeping the DOGE flame alive.

But the unsung victory of DOGE went beyond financial savings. One of the biggest breakthroughs—ignored by the media, but just as important—was operational: information technology.

"They found things quickly that might not have ever been found," EPA administrator Lee Zeldin told me. "They really helped on the IT front, which helped reduce backlogs of issues. And we inherited a ton of backlogs from the previous administration."

Every cabinet secretary I spoke to had nothing but positive things to say about Musk, the DOGE effort, and the need to keep the reforms going.

"DOGE was a wonderful accelerant," Defense Secretary Pete Hegseth told me aboard Air Force One.[4]

That's what Elon Musk had done. He'd lit a fire under an entire federal bureaucracy. He had pushed government officials—some of them long accustomed to delay and dysfunction—to think faster, move smarter, and do more. And for an administration built on the idea of common sense, he became something close to a patron saint.

But even patron saints run into trouble sometimes.

In early June, the partnership between Musk and Trump hit a rough patch. Musk came out swinging against the president's marquee legislation—what Trump had branded the "one big beautiful bill"— calling it a "disgusting abomination" and warning it would drive the country off a fiscal cliff. Trump fired back, questioning Musk's loyalty and hinting at consequences for biting the hand that once praised him. For a few strange days, it felt like the most unlikely political marriage in modern memory might end in very public divorce.

During an appearance around that time with Jake Tapper, I grabbed a nearby trash can and stuck my head in it. "Let me just tell you what every Republican is doing," I said, mimicking someone who needed to vomit. "Heads are in the garbage can right now. That's the state of everybody I know at the moment." Then, in a more serious tone: "Not gonna lie. It's an ugly day, and you hate it when your friends are fighting. I continue to believe their partnership last year saved America, and I also continue to believe their goals are not mutually exclusive."

Later that night on CNN, appearing on Abby Phillip's *NewsNight* debating show, I poured myself a large cup of Pepto Bismol live on the air to cap a long day of commenting on the Musk-Trump public feuding.

What Elon did was extraordinary. He came into government, not as a politician or a bureaucrat, but as a citizen determined to prove the system could work better. And it did. He took risks, made enemies, and never once apologized for telling the truth as he saw it.

Did DOGE do everything perfectly? No, of course not. Perhaps Musk overpromised in a town that has a way of slowing even the fastest movers down. And perhaps he could have been better at public relations along the way.

But what Musk did was light a fire under Washington. He started a much-needed public conversation about waste, fraud, and abuse, and about America's fiscal future. And whether he returns to Trump or truly goes his own way, Musk's concerns about our future are valid and deserve public debate.

AIM ANYWHERE

"People ask how you can find waste in DC," said Musk, sitting on stage at the Gaylord National Resort in Maryland on February 20, just over two months before I sat down with him in the Oval. "It's like being in a room and the walls, the roof, and the floor are all targets. So you can close your eyes and shoot in any direction."[5]

The crowd at the Conservative Political Action Conference, or CPAC, roared. And with good reason. In 2019, the federal government spent about $5.47 trillion. In 2024, that number ballooned to 6.75 trillion. In 2019, the government had 2.1 million employees, excluding the military and the postal service. In 2024, it had just over 3 million employees.[6]

For years, Republicans have worried about the size and bloat of government. But I don't think anyone truly realizes just how much larger the government had grown since 2019, nor do they know that welfare programming such as Medicaid and SNAP massively ballooned during COVID but never returned to their pre-COVID levels despite the pandemic being long over (these topics would rise to the top of the public debate over Trump's "big beautiful bill").

During the Biden administration, the full-time government work-force grew by 6 percent. Every major agency saw an increase in staffing levels, according to *Government Executive*, a publication that covers the federal government. The State Department, for instance, expanded its workforce by 22 percent since 2021.[7]

Under Biden, the Food and Drug Administration (FDA) grew by 13 percent, the Centers for Disease Control and Prevention (CDC) swelled its workforce by 26 percent, and the National Institutes of Health (NIH) ballooned by 34 percent. The public health bureau-cracy that had badly failed the American people during COVID was, of course, expanded during Biden's four years.[8]

During Trump's first administration, the workforce grew a modest 2 percent, thanks mostly to personnel added in Homeland Security, Veterans Affairs, and Defense. Virtually every other department saw staffing reductions.[9]

The Department of Veterans Affairs added 100,000 workers over the last decade. A large part of the increase was due to the 2022 pas-sage of the PACT Act, or the "burn pits" legislation that expanded services to veterans who had been exposed to toxic chemicals during their service. President Biden often claimed that exposure to burn pits in Iraq killed his son, Beau, during his service there. The link between burn pits and Beau's brain cancer was never proven. Nevertheless, the story became another cog in the apocryphal wheel of Biden's personal narrative, much of which was true only in the former president's mind.

Official Washington was good at using big moments to expand government. As former Obama White House chief of staff Rahm Emanuel once said, "You never want a serious crisis to go to waste. What I mean by that—it's an opportunity to do things that you think you could not do before."[10]

For Biden, the crisis was COVID, which was still going on when he took office in January 2021. And the impossible dream was growing the size and scope of government beyond anyone's wildest imagination. "Biden oversaw a bigger growth in the federal workforce than any pres-idential term in the last 30 years," according to *Politifact.com*.[11]

The Department of Government Efficiency was born via one of President Trump's Day One executive orders. Trump had announced shortly after the election that Musk would be running the project, which entailed the world's richest man working impossibly long hours with a small, fiercely dedicated group of people who all shared a passion for making the government more efficient and less wasteful. A few hours before his CPAC remarks, Musk had been given a literal chainsaw by the president of Argentina, libertarian firebrand Javier Milei, and he'd waved it around with a big smile on his face for the cameras.

Musk's public appearances—during the campaign and in the period following Trump's win—were unlike anything we'd seen in American politics before. Not even the late-in-the-game campaign rallies for Kamala Harris and Tim Walz, whose team paid millions for celebrities to show up and act passionate about them, even came close. In appointing Musk as the head of an office that would slash government, Trump had once again recognized a deep sentiment in the American populace and harnessed it. That sentiment, in so many words, was: *Big Government Sucks.*

If you've been a Republican for longer than five minutes, you've probably heard at least one person say some variation of this in your life. Some of the most famous figures in the party have made cutting government a priority, at least in rhetoric. President Ronald Reagan still makes the rounds online for the immortal line: "The most terrifying nine words in the English language are, *I'm from the government and I'm here to help.*" Low-tax conservative activist Grover Norquist famously said he wanted a government so small "you could drown it in a bathtub." For years, examples of silly government programs would circulate online, usually with notes telling us how much they cost. Conservatives would read this and always ask the same thing: Why doesn't someone do something about this?

A few crusaders have been tilting at the waste windmill for decades. Five-term Wisconsin senator William Proxmire (a Democrat!) created the Golden Fleece Award in 1975 to "dramatize wasteful and extravagant spending to try to discourage it," as he explained it to *The Wall Street*

Journal.[12] The National Science Foundation was the first "honoree," after spending $84,000 on a study to determine why people fall in love.[13]

For many years, Senator Rand Paul of Kentucky has issued a yearly list of the most egregious ways the government wastes money, entitled the *Festivus Report.* It included gems like the $12 million the Department of the Interior spent on a Las Vegas pickleball complex, the $2 million grant to study kids looking at Facebook ads about food, and the $3 million sent to Brazil for a "Girl-Centered Climate Action" initiative. The Department of State squandered nearly $5 million on social media influencers to promote US foreign policy, and another $500,000 on a hashtag campaign in Ethiopia to publicize American investments. There was also $419,470 wasted on a study of whether lonely rats prefer cocaine more than happy rats, $365,000 to promote circuses in city parks, and $288,563 to ensure bird-watching groups have safe spaces known as "affinity groups." Year after year, reports like this confirmed what many already suspected—the federal government believed it had money to burn, and the bureaucrats who worked there were throwing it on the dumbest bonfires imaginable.

Incidentally, talking with Musk, I asked him if there was a particular member of Congress who stood out as someone who really gets it when it comes to cutting spending. He mentioned one: Rand Paul. (Paul, incidentally, voted against Trump's "big beautiful bill" in June, one of just a few Republicans to do so.)

"Most Republicans will tell you they want to cut spending, but just not in my state," Musk said, obviously disdainful of Washington's parochial resistance to fiscal responsibility.

I sensed at the time that Musk was disappointed in what he had found in Washington among the political class. I just had no idea how close he was to boiling over and completely blowing up his relationship with the president of the United States, whom he had helped elect and enthusiastically worked for over the last several weeks.

Even so, Republican politicians for years have sounded the alarm on wasteful spending, only to be met with a hail of rhetorical bullets from bureaucrats, the media, and the subject matter's dedicated constituency. And make no mistake: the constituencies of individual government programs are incredibly vicious and smart. They can tug heart strings or smack a congressman with a tack hammer, whichever is most effective.

Occasionally, Republicans would strike a blow against some incredibly wasteful program. But there is a difference between going after government waste with a scalpel, picking out programs to cut and carefully negotiating with Democrats about how and when you can cut them, and slashing through wasteful government programs with a chainsaw. Up until the second Trump administration, the political will to take the *Texas Chainsaw Massacre* approach simply wasn't there. Most Republican politicians would have told you they *wanted* to do it, but in private would admit that the Washington swamp has a way of swallowing up the will and the testicles of those in a position to act.

All the while, the federal government continued to grow larger and spend more—unimaginably more. Finally, in the aftermath of the 2024 election, at long last, the American people delivered a mandate to finally go for it. In addition to securing the border, renegotiating trade deals, and signing a mountain of executive orders, President Trump added "eliminate government waste" to his already long list of commonsense priorities. And he wasn't going to do it alone. Instead, he would enlist the help of two men from outside the government, neither of whom had been on the Trump Train from the beginning. The first, Vivek Ramaswamy, was a young Indian American biotech entrepreneur who'd risen to fame for critiquing the woke drift of corporate America. After the success of his book *Woke, Inc.* Ramaswamy ran a 2024 presidential campaign that Trump easily dispatched.

According to reporting in *The New York Times*, the seeds of DOGE were truly sown in September 2023, when tech investor Chamath Palihapitiya held a dinner in support of Ramaswamy's presidential campaign. In attendance was Tesla and SpaceX founder Elon Musk. As the *Times* tells it, Musk spoke to a crowd of about twenty people about many things: his companies, electric cars, and his reluctance to get into politics. Then, when the subject of making the government more efficient came up, he told a few stories about what he'd done when he took over Twitter, now called X. Musk was rumored to have said that when he was figuring out how to strip Twitter down to its essentials and make it work more efficiently, "the key was getting access to the company's servers."[14]

He then suggested doing the same thing with the federal government.

But the question is: How to start? Trump turned to a familiar Republican punching bag: former president Barack Obama.

THANKS, OBAMA (NO, SERIOUSLY)

Even when you have the power of the presidency behind you, cutting government spending can be a nearly impossible job. First, there is the matter of the US Constitution, specifically Article I, Section 8, Clause 1:

"The Congress shall have Power to lay and collect Taxes, Duties, Imposts and Excises, to pay the Debts and provide for the common Defence and general Welfare of the United States; but all Duties, Imposts, and Excises shall be uniform throughout the United States; . . ."

This "Spending Clause" has long been interpreted by the Courts to mean that Congress has the power of the purse. But, of course, the money appropriated is spent by the executive branch. What discretion does the president have when it comes to spending less, cutting programs, or eliminating programs altogether? Trump and Musk were determined to test the limits, and felt they had a political mandate to do so.

Over the course of the twentieth century, the federal government grew to a size that would've made our Founders blush, adding three- and four-letter agencies at an astounding rate, a vast, unelected bureaucracy becoming less accountable to the American people with each passing year. Just before President Trump took office a second time, approximately 3 million people were working for the federal government (an additional 1.3 million are active-duty military). Our national debt was rapidly approaching the $40 trillion mark, and almost no one in Washington seemed to feel any urgency about it. Whenever anyone suggested cutting government programs, most politicians folded in the face of negative press and intense lobbying campaigns.

For the second Trump administration, bad press wasn't going to be a problem. The first four years Trump spent in the White House (and certainly the 2024 campaign as well) had taught his team that Trump is more or less invulnerable to the howlings and manufactured narratives of the political information distribution complex. Trump, with the exception of the period after January 6, has been one of the most stable political figures in history when it comes to public opinion polling, no matter the undulations of the news cycle. And his loyal base of supporters tends to give him a long leash when it comes to policy decisions. So there was no need for the Trump White House to worry about potential negative press impacts of the DOGE effort. Democrats were going to howl about anything Trump proposed, anyway. So why not just do the right thing?

But the not-so-small matter of logistics remained. When someone wants to do something to the federal government, that person needs legal authority. And that authority is not as easy to come by as you might think, even when you've just won a popular mandate at the ballot box. If Elon Musk wanted to have any real power, he needed to move quickly; otherwise, he risked getting stuck in the same Washington quicksand that had befallen previous efforts to cut waste, fraud, and abuse. Musk was not interested in overseeing a simple commission and writing yet another report. No, he came to do to Washington what he had done in his corporate life: enforce ruthless efficiency in pursuit of better outcomes.

The answer, again according to the *Times*, was a little-used government office founded by none other than Barack Obama. In 2014, when the Obama administration was having trouble with the Affordable Care Act website (the failure of which is legendary), they set up a kind of tech support office for the federal government. This office, which was (quite blandly) called the US Digital Service, has been around ever since, helping federal agencies solve specific problems with computers and data management. Crucially, the office was able to reach every layer of the federal government. It was exactly what Elon Musk had in mind when he mused about having access to the government's servers.

Of course, he still physically needed access. To get it, he went to the Office of Personnel Management (also known as OPM). According to *The Wall Street Journal,* Musk was helped by Chuck Ezell, who'd just become acting director of the agency. This happened on January 20, Trump's first day in office.

For the next few weeks, Musk brought together a small team of engineers, mostly people he'd worked with at his other companies. He'd also put out a call for employees on X, noting that anyone hoping to join the Department of Government Efficiency would need to work long hours for little pay. He'd issued a similar directive when he took over Twitter, all but ensuring that the people working with him would be headstrong and dedicated. Musk's government team, which numbered between fifty and a hundred people, depending on the day, went to work with the access they'd been granted, hunting for waste and getting rid of whatever bloat they could.

When Musk took over Twitter in 2022, he cut the company's staff from about 7,500 down to just 1,500. Critics called it reckless. But inside the company, something unexpected happened: operations kept running and, in some cases, improved. As former X CEO Linda Yaccarino later put it, "We're leaner, we're faster, and we're scrappier." That mindset—cut the fluff, move fast, and let talent thrive—became the model for Musk's work in government.

As Musk set about optimizing the federal government the way he did at X, the evidence of waste, fraud, and abuse came oozing from every corner of the bureaucracy. During a press conference in the Oval Office, Musk enumerated just a few of the discoveries. There was, according to a summary posted later by the DOGE X account, "$6.9 million for 'smart toilets' that scan users anal prints, $2.3 million to inject beagles with cocaine, and a $118,000 study to determine if a robotic replica of Marvel's Thanos could actually snap its fingers. And that's just the tip of the iceberg."

In late February, Musk sent a few emails that raised hackles across Washington and made him the object of liberal media scorn. One email demanded that all federal employees simply send weekly progress reports to prove they were doing something useful (or that they were checking their emails at all. A "pulse check" Musk called it). Another required every agency to provide a detailed breakdown of its budget—line by line—and justify each expenditure in plain English, without bureaucratic doublespeak. The response was immediate and furious. Career government officials, apparently unaccustomed to even basic oversight, called the initiative "draconian." *The Washington Post* ran a story describing it as a "mass purge," and by the end of the first month, multiple federal employee unions filed lawsuits. But the administration didn't back down. Instead, Musk—with Trump's full backing—doubled down.

As you can imagine, Musk's request for a basic pulse check from federal workers sent liberal politicians and media personalities into a tailspin. One particularly over-the-top exchange took place on *NewsNight with Abby Phillip*, where I squared off against Ana Navarro and Tara Setmayer—two of the most reflexively anti-Trump voices on television.

Navarro called the email "abusive" to federal employees. When I pointed out that it was, in fact, just an email, she doubled down. Setmayer followed by asking if I'd ever received a message from someone who wasn't technically my boss—at which point I reminded her that, yes, the White House is the boss of every federal employee.

The whole exchange underscored just how detached the resistance had become. Anything Trump or Musk touched was going to be treated as a threat to democracy, no matter how mundane. And a thread to most anti-Trump punditry was clear: even though he won the election, Trump and his agents should not be allowed to actually manage the federal government.

But Trump and Musk were undeterred. The president himself, recognizing the political value in exposing the most absurd government expenditures, elevated the matter of ridiculous spending during his March 4 address to Congress. With the timing of a veteran comedian, Trump unleashed some all-time one liners, laying out one DOGE-identified wasteful program after another. Here's a sampling of the president's best hits, straight from the night's transcript:

+ $40 million to improve the social and economic inclusion of sedentary migrants. Nobody knows what that is. (Laughter.)
+ $8 million to promote LGBTQI+ in the African nation of Lesotho, which nobody has ever heard of. (Laughter.)
+ $8 million for making mice transgender. (Laughter.) This is real.
+ $1.9 billion to recently created decarbonization of homes committee, headed up . . . by a woman named Stacey Abrams. Have you ever heard of her?
+ $47 million for improving learning outcomes in Asia. Asia is doing very well with learning. (Laughter.) Don't know what we're doing. We should use it ourselves.[15]

Beaming in the House gallery, Musk saluted Trump as the president thanked him for his work on the DOGE effort; the roaring Republican majority gave him a standing ovation. Known for his casual attire around the White House complex, Musk sported a dark suit and blue tie to a congressional affair and caused a stir when video circulated of him offering a bottle of water to an attractive woman who was standing in a nearby section.

And then came the backlash. In March, the Government Accountability Office (GAO)—normally focused on rooting out waste—released a report accusing Musk of destabilizing the federal bureaucracy. Never mind that Musk was acting on the authority of the duly-elected president who had appointed him. Democrats flooded cable news to accuse him of gutting their favorite programs, firing longtime staffers, and supposedly putting lives at risk. One recurring refrain: if Musk keeps cutting, people will die.

During one of the more absurd CNN debates that month, a

progressive commentator insisted Musk's reforms were endangering public health—citing everything from measles to bird flu. When I pressed her on whether she was blaming Elon Musk for infectious disease outbreaks, she backtracked, but not before the moment had gone viral.

(One of the underrated joys of my job is simply repeating what my liberal counterparts say back to them—verbatim—and watching them deny it.)

In Musk, Trump made an unprecedented and extremely valuable hire—an advisor with the ability to instantly activate grassroots pressure at a scale and speed that no president had ever had before. Musk was wielding a chainsaw on the federal bureaucracy, just as conservatives had always dreamed of. As I said on CNN, Musk was Trump's "instrument of destruction" against the bloated federal bureaucracy.

President Trump did have to mitigate a few growing pains between Musk and the appointed members of his cabinet. Calling a meeting on March 7, Musk and the cabinet members had some adult conversations about how the DOGE effort would proceed now that the president's cabinet was fully formed. Afterward, Trump issued a statement praising DOGE and promising a more cohesive effort between the White House and cabinet leaders.

"Over the past six weeks, our Administration has delivered on promises like no Administration before it, always putting America First! DOGE has been an incredible success, and now that we have my Cabinet in place, I have instructed the Secretaries and Leadership to work with DOGE on Cost Cutting measures and Staffing. As the Secretaries learn about, and understand, the people working for the various Departments, they can be very precise as to who will remain, and who will go. We say the 'scalpel' rather than the 'hatchet.' The combination of them, Elon, DOGE, and other great people will be able to do things at a historic level."

Trump added that it was important "that we cut levels down to where they should be, but it's also important to keep the best and most productive people . . . The relationships between everybody in that room are extraordinary."

It was to be expected that cabinet members, confirmed by the US Senate after their presidential appointments, would want some say in how their departments were to be organized and streamlined. Trump recognized the need to bring people together to meet his goals—a smaller, cheaper, more efficient government.

The meeting paid off. Within weeks, cabinet secretaries began to come forward with evidence of wasteful spending they'd uncovered with the DOGE team. On March 25, Agriculture Secretary Brooke Rollins unfurled at a cabinet meeting three ridiculous contracts she had just ended, including "a $300,000 contract educating on food justice for queer and transgender farmers in San Francisco."[16]

"I'm not even sure what that means," Rollins quipped, "but apparently the last administration wanted to put our taxpayer dollars towards that." She also canceled a similar contract in New York. Another USDA DOGE discovery: $600,000 sent to Louisiana to study the "menstrual cycles of transgender men."[17]

The rot ran deep in the federal government, and it was apparent that Elon Musk—at the direction of Donald Trump—had finally imbued in the political leadership the fighting spirit needed to rip it out, root and branch.

ELON DERANGEMENT SYNDROME

The cabinet room of the White House sits just a few feet from the Oval Office. It's empty most of the time, because the cabinet doesn't meet that often and presidential meetings often take place in the Roosevelt Room, which is across the hall. If you happened to walk by the cabinet room on a White House tour, you'd see a long wooden table polished to a high shine with about twenty high-backed chairs tucked neatly into it (the president's chair, incidentally, is just a little bit taller than the rest). Depending on the president, there might be historic portraits or sweeping landscapes on the walls or small white boxes of presidential M&Ms laying around. But there'd be no people.

On February 26, 2025, though, lots of people crowded into this room for Trump's first full cabinet meeting. So many, in fact, that extra chairs were placed along the walls to accommodate the overflow. Around ten o'clock in the morning, the members of President Trump's second cabinet began arriving. The faces at the table reflected the ideological diversity of the coalition that had formed during Trump's 2024 campaign. Traditional Republicans could rest easy knowing that Marco Rubio, the former senator from Florida, had just returned from his first two trips abroad as America's top diplomat. The more excitable, mostly young members of the "new right" who wanted to expose intelligence agencies for their various misdeeds over the years had a champion in Tulsi Gabbard, the former Democratic congresswoman who'd just been confirmed by razor-thin margins in the Senate.

In between them were people who never would have been in the same room with one another just four short years ago. Not far from Governor Kristi Noem, the South Dakota governor turned director of Homeland Security, sat Robert F. Kennedy Jr., another Democrat who'd become fed up with his party and embraced Trump over the president's willingness to investigate our obviously broken health and food system. The fact that all these people had been confirmed by the Senate without much trouble is yet another testament to President Trump's political clout. Just four weeks into his administration, he'd had his entire cabinet confirmed with almost none of the setbacks his critics had predicted.

For a president, coalition building is important. That's true with the electorate, but it's also true within the administration. Trump was reelected to a second term because he built one of the most ideologically and racially diverse coalitions for a winning GOP campaign since Richard Nixon in 1968. And he constructed a cabinet and senior staff designed to reflect and represent that diversity. Contrast this against Biden's cabinet, which was made up of people who checked DEI boxes and were more than happy to focus their time on the pet issues of the fever swamps of the American left, like the time Transportation Secretary Pete Buttigieg spent one billion dollars to ensure that highways aren't racist.

In the Trump White House, on the other hand, focused and decisive action was an everyday occurrence—or, more accurately, an every-*hour* occurrence. Everyone understood that the orders came from the man at the top, and they were there to carry them out. Republicans were largely thrilled with the president's cabinet and senior staff, and each seemed to understand the top-down nature of a Trump-run organization. There's one Boss, and freelancing will not be tolerated. During an interview for this book, Treasury Secretary Scott Bessent said, "We have fun. Marco Rubio is one of the funniest people I've ever met, and you'd never know it."

And six months into the term, the cabinet—as a team—was getting glowing reviews from "the most powerful woman in the world," as Trump calls her, Susie Wiles—the White House Chief of Staff. Wiles is revered in the building, respected across the Republican Party, and deserves enormous credit for Trump's well-run second term.

"It is an amazing group of people that he put together. . . . There is not one who I would say is not a complete success in what they're doing," Wiles said on "Pod Force One" podcast.[18]

Back at the February cabinet meeting, an energized Musk delivered a progress report to the assembled officials and media, all while wearing a black T-shirt reading "Government Tech Support."

He gave a quick update on his progress, then said, "I'm getting a lot of flak and a lot of death threats, by the way. I can, like, stack them up. But if we don't do this, America will go bankrupt. That's why it has to be done."

In one of thousands of hysterical comments uttered in the media, the ever-insightful Joy Behar, co-host of *The View*, said, "[Trump] can take a nap while this guy, who's not born in this country, who was born under Apartheid in South Africa, so has that mentality going on, he was pro-Apartheid as I understand it."

This comment, which would have been ripped apart and viewed as racist if it had been about anyone else—especially a Democrat—didn't even make it off the set of *The View* without a little pushback. Alyssah Farah Griffin, who served as a communications director to the Trump White House in the first term before turning against her old boss, pointed out that Musk is, in fact, a naturalized citizen. After the commercial break, Behar apologized, ending her discussion of whether Elon Musk was "pro-Apartheid" (he wasn't) by saying, "Don't be suing me, okay, Elon?"

Representative Maxine Waters of California ramped up the rhetoric against Musk in a shocking way. "Send him back from wherever he came from," Waters said, engaging in a level of xenophobia that usually draws howls from the media.[19]

But not this time. Think about it—a Democratic member of Congress demanded that a legal citizen of the United States be sent "back" to Africa! And it was met with yawns from a press corps that was itself in full "Get Elon" mode. Democrats and their media allies turning into nasty, nativist hacks simply because a Republican had become president was one of the strangest yet revealing features of Trump's second term.

The next day, Mark Halperin summed up my feelings on Waters's rant when he said, "I think when historians write about this first month of the Trump administration, they're going to be bewildered by just the rank inability of the opposition to figure out how to talk about what's going on. And you saw there in sharp relief, just making claims about Elon Musk that have nothing to do with the real lives of people in real America, but also just ripping on things that—it's just hard to know where she was headed."

During President Trump's first term, we had a name for this kind of thing: Trump Derangement Syndrome, or TDS. Formerly sane people would go nuts on television, ranting and raving about things they might have otherwise supported all because Donald Trump was involved. Today, Trump Derangement Syndrome is still common, although it has mutated into a new variant: Elon Derangement Syndrome, which began running rampant early in Trump's second term and shows no signs of slowing. The symptoms are similar to TDS. Normally sane pundits—and, of course, the ones who were never all that sane to begin with—will hate anything that involves Elon Musk, even when it's a good thing. When announcements come down about how much government waste we're cutting, their first reaction is to blurt out that Musk is not an American (which is false, he has been a citizen for over twenty years), or that he wasn't elected by the American people (all presidents have un-elected advisors). Many of them don't like the fact that he was success-ful, fussing about "the oligarchs." Some demand that his companies be stripped of all government contracts, despite the fact that, among other things, the federal government hired his company to rescue NASA as-tronauts Suni Williams and Butch Wilmore, who were stranded in outer space for 286 days before Musk's SpaceX company returned them safely to earth on March 18.

I had dinner with a close friend in New York City on March 3. He told me that he and his wife had recently gone to the Tesla dealership in town to trade in their old electric vehicle for a new, larger model to accommodate their two kids. Upon arriving, the entire family was greeted by a mob of anti-Elon protestors who were screaming at the children. My friend remarked: "It is amazing how Elon has completely exposed the insanity of the entire left-wing environmental movement." My buddy made his vehicle trade and went about his business, but not before having to explain to his children why their fellow New Yorkers were going insane in the streets.

On March 24, the FBI launched a task force to investigate nearly fifty attacks on Tesla vehicles and charging stations, including firebomb-ings, shootings, and vandalism. Numerous arrests were made around the country of vandals being caught on camera keying Tesla vehicles.

Perhaps no one suffered from Elon Derangement Syndrome more acutely than Jimmy Kimmel, the late-night talk-show host on ABC who long ago abandoned comedy in favor of partisan invective. In multiple monologues, Kimmel not-so-subtly celebrated the attacks on Tesla deal-erships and car owners. His studio audience howled as he egged on the vandals who had targeted dozens of locations across North America.

This wasn't satire. It was incitement dressed up as entertainment.

"The message from the American Left to conservatives is unmistak-able: silence yourselves, or we will do it for you. This isn't comedy—these are marching orders," I posted on X in response to Kimmel's remarks.

The message was hateful and corrosive: we are willing to destroy an American company, tens of thousands of American jobs, and one of the most important entrepreneurs in modern history—all because he supported the wrong candidate. Musk's only sin was backing Donald Trump. And for that, the Left tried to grind him into dust.

As Trump dismissed reporters covering a cabinet meeting on March 24, Musk stopped them to express gratitude to "all the DOGE team who are getting death threats on a daily basis. They're just trying to do the right thing for the American taxpayer for the American people.

"The DOGE team are literally getting death threats and being accosted . . . " Musk lamented. "A lot of them are just kids you know. They're just trying to help out and they're very talented. They could get jobs [paying] millions of dollars a year. Instead, they come here, earn peanuts, and get death threats. So, thanks to the DOGE team. Thank you."

To me, this reveals a great deal about the way the Left thinks about government. If they don't want successful private sector people involved in it, then they must, almost by definition, want people with less experience running things in perpetuity. These people will say they want to modernize the FAA's computer systems, and then when a man who *literally* sends rockets into space on a regular basis offers to do just that, they're not happy because he's a little eccentric.

Over the years, I've read many biographies of great Americans: Thomas Edison, Benjamin Franklin, George Washington. None of them would have been considered "normal" by the elite liberal media. As Musk himself put it when he hosted *Saturday Night Live*: "Look, I know I sometimes say or post strange things. But that's just how my brain works. To anyone I've offended, I just want to say: I reinvented electric cars and I'm sending people to Mars in a rocket ship. Did you also think I was going to be a chill, normal dude?"

Elon Musk's leadership of DOGE became a defining feature of President Trump's second term—a bold, unapologetic effort to dismantle the entrenched bureaucracy that has long burdened the American people. In just a few months, DOGE identified and eliminated billions in wasteful spending, streamlined federal operations, and challenged the status quo of Washington's administrative state.

Musk's approach is as unconventional as it is effective. By deploying teams of engineers and technologists across federal agencies, DOGE uncovered inefficiencies that career bureaucrats either overlooked or ignored. For instance, the revelation that the federal government maintained approximately 4.6 million credit cards for its 2.3 million employees highlighted a staggering level of fiscal irresponsibility. Similarly, DOGE's audits exposed redundant IT systems within agencies like the National Institutes of Health, which operated with seven hundred different systems and twenty-seven chief information officers, hindering effective research and collaboration.

These findings are not just bureaucratic anomalies, they are symptomatic of a government that has grown complacent and disconnected from the principles of efficiency and accountability. Musk's mission with DOGE is to realign the federal government with the values of productivity and fiscal responsibility, ensuring that taxpayer dollars are spent wisely and effectively.

Despite facing legal challenges and criticism from various quarters, the impact of DOGE's initiatives is undeniable. The department's aggressive cost-cutting measures have not only saved money but have also restored public confidence in the government's ability to self-correct and improve. Musk's tenure, though temporary, has set a precedent for how private-sector innovation can be harnessed to reform public institutions.

At a bare minimum, Elon Musk finally reminded us that hard things could be done if we are willing to break the shackles of Washington's usual prison of mediocrity.

Reviewing the Musk effort now, it is safe to conclude that the principles of DOGE represent perfectly Trump's "revolution of common sense"—a return to the foundational belief that government should serve the people efficiently and transparently. That questions should be asked and answered clearly by the people who spend our tax dollars. Even if the DOGE effort didn't always live up to Trump's stellar public relations instincts, it certainly started a conversation that won't be ending anytime soon.

CHAPTER THREE

Empire Strikes Back

"The United States will once again consider itself a growing nation . . . and we will pursue our Manifest Destiny into the stars."

—PRESIDENT DONALD J. TRUMP,
SECOND INAUGURAL ADDRESS

"Sorry about yesterday," said Secretary of State Marco Rubio. "That was a busy day for us."[1]

I couldn't help but laugh. It was Friday, May 2, and Secretary Rubio had been kind enough to carve out forty minutes to speak with me. We'd been scheduled to conduct the interview the previous day, but scheduling conflicts had gotten in the way.

Well, "scheduling conflicts" is a rather mild way of putting it. Just twelve hours earlier, President Trump had announced that Rubio would be taking on a second title: national security advisor. He would serve in both roles after Mike Waltz was nominated for ambassador to the

United Nations. Not since Henry Kissinger had a single official assumed such sweeping authority over American foreign policy.

Rubio wasn't daunted. "There's a lot of overlap between the two," he told me. "The core function of this job is to operationalize the president's policy directives across various agencies. That's what I was doing anyway. We'll streamline it, straighten it out, and make it functional—then the president can decide on a permanent setup."

If the former senator from Florida had proven anything during the early months of the second Trump administration, it was his ability to get things done. He wasn't interested in theory. He was interested in delivery. And the organizing principle guiding him—like the president—was common sense.

"What the president has returned to in foreign policy is common sense," Rubio said. "We are going to make foreign policy decisions on the basis of what is good for America. If it makes America stronger, if it makes America safer, if it makes America more prosperous, we are going to do it."

Under Joe Biden, that had rarely been the standard. America's foreign aid system, and the State Department more broadly, had become a bloated apparatus focused on symbolism, social engineering, and globalist signaling. Billions of dollars were funneled to NGOs, many of them based in Washington or Brussels, to run programs that had more to do with Western guilt than with US national interest.

Rubio moved fast to change that. He dismantled the sprawling bureaucracy of USAID, pulled its core functions under his office, and began reorienting foreign aid toward outcomes that aligned with America's strategic priorities. That meant fewer redundant contracts and fewer $10 million initiatives that delivered just $1 million worth of food or supplies. It also meant asking hard questions: Was a given program actually helping a regional partner? Or just propping up the foreign aid industrial complex?

Cutting red tape was only part of it. The bigger shift was in the worldview—how America defines its interests and why they should come first. "Only Western Civilization," Rubio told me, "has elements within it actively trying to destroy itself." From his perch at State, he saw how a deep discomfort with Western values had infected not only America's institutions, but those of our closest allies. And he believed it was time to stop apologizing for a civilization that had given the world democracy, free speech, and individual dignity.

There's no question that Rubio's appointment changed the tone and trajectory of US foreign policy. The resistance from entrenched interests was real. But the machinery was starting to bend in a new direction—one more responsive to the president, more aligned with the public, and more focused on results.

That shift had already begun to take hold by early spring. But to understand just how much it mattered—and how far the administration was willing to go—you have to look back a little further.

A BREATH OF FRESH AIR

In the weeks following his election, and even before he was sworn in, Donald Trump immediately filled the vacuum of international leadership left by his vanishing predecessor.

"Biden has effectively disappeared from the radar in the wake of Democrats' bruising electoral loss," *Politico* wrote on December 9, when Biden still had forty-two more days in office. "Biden's low profile since the election has contributed to the sense of rudderlessness that's taken hold across swaths of Washington, as lawmakers, aides, and party officials brace for Trump's return to power and seek a new direction and vision ahead of the midterms and 2028."[2]

A former White House official told *Politico* that Biden was "cavalier and selfish about how he approaches the final weeks of the job."[3]

On December 7, Trump traveled to Paris, France, for the reopening of the Notre Dame cathedral, which had shockingly caught fire and was heavily damaged on April 15, 2019, during Trump's first term.

During the trip, he met with President Emmanuel Macron of France, with Ukrainian president Volodymyr Zelenskyy joining as well. Trump also sat down with Prince William of Great Britain on the trip.

At the cathedral, all eyes were on Trump and First Lady Jill Biden, who attended instead of her husband, a self-described devout Catholic. The odd couple created a viral moment when a photo appeared of the two seated near each other, with the First Lady smiling broadly at the president-elect as he chatted her up. Social media went nuts for it, and Trump himself hilariously used it in an advertisement for his personal brand of cologne.

"A fragrance your enemies can't resist" read the advert.[4]

The world's most lovable rascal (or troll, if you prefer) was back, and the trip gave an unmistakable impression that Trump, and not the vanishing Biden, was already in charge.

Against this backdrop, *Washington Post* columnist Josh Rogin, Texas Republican representative Tony Gonzales, and I sat down with CNN's Abby Phillip on January 7 to discuss Trump's transition. For a while, Abby led us through a chat on the latest personnel developments and rumors of cabinet appointments.

But there was one subject that we couldn't possibly avoid.

Empire.

Specifically, the burgeoning American Empire that President Trump seemed to be envisioning through increasingly provocative statements. The previous day, President Trump had made headlines (something he seems genuinely incapable of *not* doing) by suggesting that the United States should take over Greenland. He'd also mused a few weeks earlier about retaking the Panama Canal, which the United States had given over to Panama in 1999 as part of the Torrijos-Carter Treaties of 1977. The treaties, negotiated by President Jimmy Carter, transferred control of the waterway to Panama after nearly a century of US ownership, despite strong opposition from many conservatives at the time (the treaties barely passed the Senate, in fact). That February, in the middle of a lengthy thread about potential US-Canada trade negotiations, President-elect Trump mused that he might annex Canada as America's "beloved 51st state."

I had to laugh a little. If the idea of Justin Trudeau, a prissy woke moralist of the highest order, having to sign over his country to Donald Trump doesn't make you chuckle, I'm not sure what would. Can you imagine? A red-cheeked Trudeau (who once infamously donned black-face) hoisting the American flag above Parliament Hill in Ottawa?

I was always lukewarm on the Canada idea, if only because we don't need another liberal state sending Democratic senators and congress-men to Washington, a sentiment I expressed to the president in the Oval Office in February. But I didn't mind Trump's tweaks, as they tended to enrage his most hysterical media haters and made the point that Canada depends on the United States far more than we depend on them.

But on the other two propositions—Panama and Greenland—I was more than intrigued. I encouraged the president on these fronts when we first met.

The idea of acquiring Greenland wasn't new. President Trump had raised it during his first term, although it was just a back burner idea. And the Panama Canal seemed reasonable enough to me because I believed—along with several others—that Panama was violating its treaty obligations to keep the canal operating in a neutral fashion. It was obvious that Panama allowed China to exert far too much con-trol over the canal's operations and fee structures, opening the door for American intervention.

In his March 4 joint address to Congress, President Trump made his intentions and US policy clear, saying that "to further enhance our national security, my administration will be reclaiming the Panama Canal."[5]

The proposal sparked debate on CNN and elsewhere, with critics accusing Trump of saber-rattling and downplaying the threat posed by Chinese control of key ports on either end of the canal. When Abby Phillip asked if the US was planning to invade Panama, I clarified that military action wasn't the goal—Southern Command was simply evalu-ating all strategic options. The real issue was China's growing influence in the region, and whether America was prepared to confront it.

Later in the discussion, the topic shifted to Greenland, and

Representative Gonzales noted that everything should be on the table from a foreign policy standpoint. Josh Rogin fired back that "America is not an expansionist military power."

"Why not?" I asked, keeping my voice level and honestly attempting to convey genuine curiosity about the issue.

From there, things got heated, as they sometimes do (and I should disclose that I like Josh even though we argue from time to time on TV). Rogin demanded to know whether I would support attacking Greenland using the United States military. I rattled off a few strategic reasons for the United States to purchase Greenland—an idea that had been raised before by presidents of both parties. Lincoln's secretary of state William Seward, in fact, promoted Greenland as being rich in "whale, walrus, seal and shark, cod, salmon, salmon-trout and herring; foxes, wolf, reindeer, bear, a myriad of birds. Good coal is found on the western coast at various points, extending far north, most cheaply mined and close to good harbors."

Today, the landmass would fortify the United States against an attack from the Russians. And we already have a base there—Pituffik Space Base, which supports missile defense, space surveillance, and satellite command and control.

There are valuable rare earth minerals there, not to mention that Greenland is actually closer to the United States than it is to Denmark, the country that currently controls it. The population is roughly 56,000—4,000 fewer than the fourth largest city in my home Commonwealth of Kentucky (hello Owensboro, home to some of the best barbecue on planet Earth).

Almost none of it broke through. At least not in the moment.

My sparring partners were obsessed with the supposed "rules" Trump was breaking. The United States was not *supposed* to be interested in expanding its territory, they condescended. The American president was not *supposed* to suggest during press conferences that we retake canals or turn neighboring nations into new states. He certainly wasn't *supposed* to long for an expanding American *empire*, one that was better equipped to resist Chinese and Russian aggression.

However, I challenge you to ask yourself the same question I asked my fellow panelists back in January (a question, it bears mentioning, to which I have yet to receive a good answer . . .)

WHY NOT?

If you asked a random person on the street, Democrat or Republican, to list a few of President Trump's key attributes, I'm not sure any of them would say "curiosity." But just because he's not known for it doesn't mean he doesn't have it in spades. In some sense, curiosity—combined with a healthy dose of audacity—is one of the qualities that has enabled the man to score some of his biggest wins. This is especially true when it comes to foreign policy.

Israel is a good example. For decades, presidents of both parties had made promises to the Israeli government. Some had been better than others about keeping those promises. But it wasn't until President Trump, who had less direct experience in international diplomacy than almost any president before him, that the paradigm completely shifted. On the podcast *Honestly*, historian Victor Davis Hanson recalled an off-the-record conversation with a high-level member of the Israeli government. As Hanson tells it, this official and his compatriots were concerned when Trump, who had little experience and no in-depth academic knowledge of the region and its history, took office.

"The most sophisticated people in the biparty, uniparty . . . had always told Israel there were certain things they'd never do," this person is reported to have said. "And then Donald Trump came along and it was very clear to a lot of these leaders, military and civilian, that he didn't know anything about 1947, or the Seven Day War, or the intricacies and terms of Green Line." And yet when these same leaders came to President Trump and presented their arguments for why certain things should be done—things, by the way, that had been promised by many presidents before them—he was able to analyze the evidence with fresh eyes and take action.[6]

Hanson says the Israeli official asked him, only somewhat rhetorically, how a man who was supposedly so inexperienced in Middle East affairs had managed to do more in one year than very sophisticated people in both parties had done in the last seventy years.

Hanson's answer was "a kind of animal cunning. If you had to survive in Manhattan with pressure groups, crooked politicians, environmentalists, minority groups, community groups and build Trump Tower, you have to be pragmatic. He understood that Israel was an asset and he wanted to help them."[7]

That's probably true. But it misses something more important: President Trump's willingness to sit in a room with experts, listen to their advice, and then ask the questions no one else dares to ask—something I've personally witnessed in the Oval Office. When someone tells him not to move the US embassy to Jerusalem, he says, "Why not?" When they tell him not to recognize Israel's sovereignty over the Golan Heights, same response: "Why not?" And when no one can give a good answer, he trusts his gut and makes the call.

That instinct for decisive leadership—free from the paralysis of conventional wisdom—set Trump apart from Joe Biden, whose presidency was defined by delay, appeasement, and moral confusion. With Trump, voters corrected that flaw in a serious way.

Israel saw the difference immediately. In his first term, Trump brokered the Abraham Accords, normalized relations between Israel and multiple Arab nations, withdrew from the disastrous Iran nuclear deal, and reinstated crushing sanctions on Tehran. He recognized Israeli sovereignty over contested territories and moved the US embassy to Jerusalem, finally delivering on a promise Congress made in 1995 but no president had kept.

But those achievements were only the beginning. In 2025, as Iranian missiles rained down on Israeli cities and the world watched in horror, Trump made clear he hadn't changed. I saw it firsthand in the early days of this new war, traveling through Jerusalem and the Galilee as Iranian rockets triggered the Iron Dome and civilians fled for cover. Israel struck military targets. Iran targeted hospitals. That contrast—between civilization and barbarism—could not have been starker.

This is the fight Trump has been preparing for. He knew from the start that the mullahs in Tehran weren't interested in peace. And he's the only president who had the courage to act on that knowledge. When I think about fighting for the future of Western Civilization, a concept I speak about often, Trump's resolve against Iran marked a key moment in this conflict.

From killing Qasem Soleimani in 2020 to backing Israel's right to self-defense in 2025, Trump has stood firm. His strategic posture— peace through strength, deterrence through certainty—has helped Israel decimate Iran's terrorist proxies and brought America and Israel to the brink of a decisive victory.

On June 21, after a few days of public debate and conjecture, President Trump made a courageous and fateful decision—to order American air strikes against Iran's nuclear facilities. He sent B-2 bombers from Whiteman Air Force Base in Missouri to hit Iran's nuclear facilities with "massive ordnance penetrators," otherwise known as bunker buster bombs. These bombs can destroy targets deep underground, which is exactly what was required to defang Iran's nuclear ambitions.

Each of the B-2 bombers carried two GBU-57 "MOPs." Over about a half-hour window, a total of 14 MOPs were dropped on the nuclear sites of Fordo and Natanz, while Tomahawk missiles from a US submarine targeted a nuclear site in Isfahan. More than 125 aircraft in total participated in the mission, which was one of the most precise and successful military engagements in American military history.

Trump made the decision to bomb Iran over the objections of some of his MAGA allies, including Steve Bannon and Tucker Carlson. But for years, Trump had been perfectly clear—there can be no peace if Iran has a nuclear weapon. Trump was absolutely clear-eyed and consistent on this point for a very long time, so it should have come as no surprise that he would take the opportunity to strike Iran when it became necessary and advantageous to do so.

And this was the genius of Trump's move—the timing. He

supported Israel in its war against Iran and watched as Israel pummeled Iran's air defenses. Once the field was plowed, Trump dropped the explosive seeds. Iran never even knew the American bombers were there, let alone fired a shot in retaliation.

"Tonight, I can report to the world that the strikes were a spectacular military success. Iran's key nuclear enrichment facilities have been completely and totally obliterated. Iran, the bully of the Middle East, must now make peace. If they do not, future attacks would be far greater and a lot easier," Trump reported to the nation from the White House, with Vice President JD Vance, Secretary of State Marco Rubio, and Secretary of Defense Pete Hegseth flanking him.

"For 40 years, Iran has been saying Death to America, death to Israel. They have been killing our people, blowing off their arms, blowing off their legs, with roadside bombs. That was their specialty. We lost over 1,000 people and hundreds of thousands throughout the Middle East, and around the world have died as a direct result of their hate in particular. So many were killed by their general, Qasem Soleimani. I decided a long time ago that I would not let this happen. It will not continue," Trump said.

Of course, Democrats and some media commentators immediately sided with the Iranian regime against Trump, once again proving that even the most righteous of Trump's decisions will always be met with reflexive and thoughtless criticism.

"He has impulsively risked launching a war that may ensnare us for generations," said Representative Alexandria Ocasio-Cortez in a post on X. "It is absolutely and clearly grounds for impeachment."

There was even an effort by Democrats and some media outlets to argue that somehow 420,000 pounds of bombs didn't do much damage to Iran's nuclear capabilities, a ridiculous assertion. Israel, the International Atomic Agency, and most of the US intelligence apparatus agreed that yes, in fact, Trump's decision had proven highly successful in seriously setting back Iran's nuclear ambitions. And everyone who predicted that his actions would lead to World War III or some prolonged "boots on the ground" conflict were also proven wrong.

Shortly after the bombing, someone leaked preliminary, top-secret intelligence from the Pentagon that was labeled "low confidence" to the media. Trump speculated it came from Democratic members of Congress who had obtained the report from a secure system. The leak was designed to make it seem that Trump had lied when he said that Iran's nuclear sites were "obliterated." Almost immediately, other intelligence agencies debunked this ridiculous assertion—yes, the strikes were a success. But it was an important reminder that no matter what Trump does, no matter how righteous or successful his actions are, there are malign actors in and around the federal government who will stoop to unethical and perhaps illegal actions to hurt him politically.

Despite the leak, this episode was one of the most triumphant moments of the early part of Trump's second term. While he does listen to a disparate number of voices, he has a way of cutting through the clutter and seeing the big picture. He doesn't mind defying even his biggest political and media allies if it means making a righteous decision that enhances American national security.

Before he made the decision, I publicly stated that I believed Trump should be awarded the Nobel Peace Prize should he stop Iran from obtaining nuclear weapons and help Israel pummel the butchers into submission. And as of the writing of this book, it appears that Trump's move may in fact bring more security to Israel, greater stability to the Middle East, and peace to a region that has long been stabilized by the religious fanatics in Iran who chant "Death to America" and "Death to Israel" as a governing mantra.

On a visit to the White House in July 2025, Israeli prime minister Benjamin Netanyahu announced he had personally nominated Trump for the Nobel Peace Prize. Following the US air strike, Iran offered nothing more than a weak retaliation and quickly agreed to a ceasefire with Israel.

The commander in chief, Donald Trump, had in fact brought the war to an end with decisive action and a swift move toward a ceasefire, which both parties ultimately accepted.

Standing at the White House early in President Trump's second term, long before the 12-Day War with Iran, Netanyahu had already said it best: "You are the greatest friend Israel has ever had in the White House."

Netanyahu went on to list Trump's achievements: recognizing Jerusalem as Israel's rightful capital, moving the American embassy there, recognizing Israeli sovereignty over the Golan Heights, pulling out of the Iran deal, and brokering four historic peace agreements in a span of months after a quarter century of diplomatic stalemate. "It speaks loudly for common sense," Netanyahu said. "Just looking at things and seeing them as they are."[8]

Greenland was no different. And he was hardly the first president to have the idea. As far back as 1868, the aforementioned Secretary of State William Seward, famous for acquiring Alaska, tried to acquire Iceland and Greenland from Denmark for $5 million. And a few years earlier, he'd also attempted to negotiate with Denmark the purchase of two Caribbean islands, St. John and St. Thomas. As you can see, this kind of thinking was common during the first hundred years of the United States. Expanding for strategic reasons has always been part of America's greatness. Whether you are Thomas Jefferson making the Louisiana Purchase; James K. Polk annexing Texas; Abraham Lincoln acquiring Alaska; William McKinley annexing Guam, Puerto Rico, and the Philippines after the Spanish-American War; or Harry Truman snagging several island groups from Japan, America has a long history of expanding its reach for national security and economic reasons.

Despite what you may have heard in history class about how unpopular the purchase of Alaska was—in some newspapers, it was called "Seward's Folly"—recent reviews of popular opinion have revealed that most voters liked the idea of adding to the territory of the United States. A professor of Alaskan history who reviewed newspaper editorials from the time wrote that the idea that Americans did *not* support the purchase is "one of the greatest myths in American history."[9] Even as far back as the late 1800s, media institutions had a tendency to believe that *their* opinions stood in for the opinions of the public at large, even when those opinions were wildly out of step with popular opinion. (Sound familiar? We'll explore our crumbling media in a future chapter.)

Sadly, Seward's Greenland-Iceland plan fizzled out. In decades to come, however, the idea percolated again. In 1946, a secret plan was drawn up for the United States to acquire Greenland for about $100 million worth of gold bars. This plan wasn't discovered until about fifty years later, when declassified documents revealed details of the negotiations. Former president Harry Truman knew the strategic value of using Greenland to fortify the United States against the Soviet Union.

The next year, *another* proposal to purchase Greenland was reported by *Time* magazine, which showed an overhead map displaying just how close Alaska and the world's largest island are to one another. With the Cold War underway, the United States was beginning to realize that Russia, which had been our reluctant ally during World War II, wasn't going to remain a friend for long. Military conflict with the Soviets wasn't entirely outside the realm of possibility. According to the report in *Time*, the purchase of Greenland would have given us a key strategic advantage against Russia.

"Greenland's 800,000 square miles," according to the article, "make it the world's largest island and stationary aircraft carrier. It would be as valuable as Alaska during the next few years, before bombers with a 10,000-mile range are in general use. It would be invaluable, in either conventional or push-button war, as an advance radar outpost. It would be a forward position for future rocket-launching sites. In peace or war it is the weather factory for northwest Europe, whose storms must be recorded as near the source as possible."

Almost eighty years later, Greenland's strategic value and our geopolitical rivalry with Russia remain cold hard facts. Despite what you might read in hysterical editorials from left-wing media outlets, the Trump administration is well aware of the threat posed by President Vladimir Putin and his violent, expansionist government. Oddly enough, it's the people who claim to be the *most* fearful of Russia who are most likely to pretend they don't understand why acquiring Greenland might give us a military advantage against the Putin regime. This group includes Democrats who, until President Trump took office, were hell-bent on supporting Ukraine at any cost.

The reasons for their opposition are usually hazy, such as "the post-war neoliberal world order." Rules and norms put in place after World War II discourage countries from expanding their territories for any reason. Critics usually elide the distinction between Putin-style military expansion versus the kind of peaceful, mutually beneficial acquisitions President Trump proposes with Greenland. To them, expansion always means war. It never involves the kind of deal-making for which Trump is famous.

But the world order they presume is falling apart. In the last year of the Clinton presidency, Democrats and free-trade Republicans granted the People's Republic of China most favored nation trade status based on expectations of open markets, human rights, and the development of democracy. Instead, China has only become less liberal and its leaders are openly hostile to the United States. While skeptics wring their hands about the evils of territorial expansion, the Chinese government is growing its Belt and Road initiative, coercing "partnerships" (a charitable word) all over the world, particularly in Latin America, to widen its reach and build a new kind of global empire. As Anthony Kleven wrote for the nonpartisan Lowy Institute, China's actions have "already turned into a Chinese neo-colonialist project."[10]

I told my fellow CNN panelists that Chinese influence over the Panama Canal is real—and that we need to get it back under control. China is violating its treaty obligations. We cannot allow Beijing to run roughshod over one of the most strategically vital shipping routes in the world.

A few days later, President Trump laid aside criticisms of woke Blackrock CEO Larry Fink to celebrate the asset management company's agreement to acquire the ports at each end of the Panama Canal from Hong Kong's CK Hutchison company.

"The president always appreciates efforts from American companies to advance our nation's national security interests," White House press secretary Karoline Leavitt said in a statement to *The Wall Street*

Journal. The newspaper reported that Trump welcomed Fink to the White House where they met for more than an hour with Elon Musk, National Security Advisor Michael Waltz, and Vice President JD Vance to discuss the Panama ports deal and the economy.[11]

But China balked. Days after the April 2 target date passed without a finalized deal, Reuters reported that pro-Beijing media was "criticizing CK Hutchison's deal, depicting it as a betrayal of China and a 'perfect cooperation' with the U.S. strategy to contain China."[12]

Every day, China inches closer to a full-scale invasion of Taiwan. Russia has already invaded Ukraine. Meanwhile, President Trump's critics insist that the United States is wrong to consider new strategic ideas to fortify our nation in a changing, unpredictable world. They seem to believe that if we follow the old rules, everyone else will, too. But that is not the world we live in. Right now, the global order is in a precarious position and American foreign policymakers must be nimble and creative enough to react to it.

In late March, Vice President JD Vance took a trip to Greenland to reinforce the seriousness of the Trump administration's interest in an acquisition. Vance visited American troops at Pituffik Space Base, enjoying lunch and making some pointed comments. "Let's be honest. This base, the surrounding area, is less secure than it was 30, 40 years ago, because some of our allies haven't kept up as China and Russia have taken greater and greater interest in Greenland, in this base, in the activities of the brave Americans right here," Vance said, as reported by *The New York Times.*[13]

Vance continued his critique of Denmark's stewardship, arguing that, much like the rest of Europe, "Denmark has not kept pace in devoting the resources necessary to keep this base, to keep our troops, and in my view, to keep the people of Greenland safe from a lot of very aggressive incursions from Russia, from China and from other nations."[14]

Those tough words from Vance kept the cold island on the front burner. While some in Greenland's political leadership remained resistant to the idea of becoming part of the United States, the argument for doing it, from an American perspective, is as sound today as it was during Lincoln or Truman's time.

Throughout this process, the enduring phenomenon of reflexive opposition to anything backed by Trump reared its head. Many people threw cold water on the idea of acquiring Greenland simply because it was Trump's idea (they obviously don't know their history). Remember when Trump's Operation Warp Speed delivered the COVID vaccine in record time in 2020? Leading Democrats, including Kamala Harris, then a candidate for vice president, were actively telling people not to trust it. But once Trump was out of office and she and Biden took over, Harris was all for the Trump-driven vaccine.

In addition to reflexive Trump resistance, some of the opposition to the president's Greenland ambitions comes from the entrenched foreign policy establishment that is about as creative as dry toast. This kind of advice is common in Washington. Things tend to move slowly, if they move at all. Before anyone takes action a proposition needs to be studied by twenty committees and historical commissions. Professors and policy wonks need to weigh in. When the final verdict comes down, it's usually some variation of "*Sorry, Mr. President. You can't do that.*" And until recently, we didn't have a president who was willing to get together with his team, examine the evidence, and chart their own course . . . even if that course deviated from Washington's well worn "do nothing" path.

As for those who assumed that Trump meant he wanted to take Greenland by force, Vice President Vance deescalated such talk during his visit. "We do not think that military force is ever going to be necessary," Vance said. "We think the people of Greenland are rational and good, and we think we're going to be able to cut a deal, Donald Trump–style, to ensure the security of this territory, but also the United States of America."

When it comes to foreign policy, a good group of close advisors is important. That's true in every aspect of a president's agenda, of course, but it's especially true here. After all, a president of the United States can set policy, but he can't travel around the world to implement that policy and negotiate every little detail, especially when he has so many important domestic issues to deal with back home. I'm told that early in the campaign, President Trump understood the importance of a good foreign policy team, placing particular emphasis on the secretary of state. By all accounts, he wanted someone who was knowledgeable, decisive, and willing to communicate and execute the president's commonsense agenda on the world stage.

Welcome to the show, Senator Marco Rubio.

"FLORIDA MEN" REWRITE THE RULES

In early July 2024, when President Trump was still running a campaign against Joe Biden, he held a small rally at his golf club in Doral, Florida. Appearing with him was a former rival from the 2016 Republican presidential primary.

"Together, we're not just going to make it great again. We elect this man as president, we will together make America greater than it has ever been," said Florida senator Marco Rubio, whose hometown of Miami was just a few miles away.[15]

The two had certainly come a long way since the 2016 campaign, when Trump and Rubio famously traded harsh jabs on the debate stage. Since then, according to an account President Trump would give during his own speech, Rubio had become "really a friend." Over the course of President Trump's first four years in Washington, Senator Rubio had proven himself to be a loyal Republican who responded to the will of his party by advancing the president's agenda. Rubio's willingness to absorb the movement in his own party as his constituents responded to Trump's new leadership style was smart politics. And the two worked together on many bills, including the Tax Cuts and Jobs Act of 2017, where Rubio fought to expand the child tax credit; the Hong Kong Human Rights and Democracy Act of 2019, which imposed sanctions on China for suppressing pro-democracy protests; and the VERDAD Act, which strengthened sanctions against the Nicolás Maduro regime in Venezuela. Rubio was also a key ally in shaping Trump's Latin America policy, pushing for stronger action against socialist regimes in Cuba and Nicaragua.

Now, with only a few months to go before election day, Rubio found himself on a shortlist of potential vice presidential picks, along with Senator JD Vance of Ohio and Doug Burgum of North Dakota. During his speech in Doral, President Trump looked to the back of the crowd, where more reporters than usual had gathered. He said, "Look out there. They probably think I'm going to be announcing that Marco is going to be vice president." Later in the speech, when discussing his proposed policy to eliminate taxes on tips for service workers, President Trump turned to Senator Rubio, who was standing at the side of the stage.

"Marco, you're going to vote for it, I hope," he said, then paused. "Well, you may or may not be there to vote for it. But you'll be involved."

On its face, this is yet another example of President Trump's tendency to build suspense, turning major decisions into tension-filled cliffhangers worthy of a reality television show. The skills that made him such a great host of *The Apprentice* have made him a master political showman.

In the end, a legal quirk might have kept President Trump from selecting Rubio as his vice president. They both lived in Florida, which would have run afoul of a little-known provision of the United States Constitution that states electors cannot vote for both a president and vice president from their own state. Trump had an embarrassment of riches of possible running mates, and his choice of Senator JD Vance of Ohio turned out to be an inspired pick. But it did leave many political commentators wondering whether Trump had just been teasing the crowd when he said Rubio might not be in the Senate to vote on legislation much longer.

Despite not being on the ticket, Rubio turned in one of the best speeches of the 2024 Republican National Convention. He's always been a gifted speechmaker and communicator, and he brought the house down in Milwaukee.

"By giving voice to everyday Americans, President Trump has not just transformed our party, he has inspired a movement. A movement of the people who grow our food and drive our trucks, the people who make our cars and build our homes, the people whose taxes fund our government, and whose children fight our wars," Rubio smoothly intoned from the Milwaukee podium.[16]

As it turned out, Trump wasn't teasing when he said Rubio might not be in the Senate much longer. During the campaign, Senator Rubio had let Trump know that he would do anything he could to help him during his administration. "I'll do whatever you think I can to be helpful," he recalls saying, "assuming it's a fit for both of us."[17] Then, after the election, Rubio was sitting in a Senate lunch when he got a phone call from the president-elect.

"He said, 'I'd like you to be Secretary of State,' and I said, 'Of course I'll do that.' And it was kind of as straightforward as that," Rubio said.[18]

Although he told me he'd never had clear aspirations to hold this position, Secretary Rubio noted that his experience in the Senate prepared him well for the job. He'd served on the Senate Foreign Relations Committee and dealt with many high-level national security issues during his term in office. And clearly, people in both parties were impressed by him as Rubio was confirmed for the position 99–0.

Rubio is well regarded across the broad GOP spectrum, from the old-guard establishment to the newer senators who have come along in the Trump era. Time and again during the first months of Trump's second term, Rubio earned praise for his steady, calm articulation of the administration's views on everything from the Panama Canal to revoking student visas from those who hate our country. He was brilliant on the case of Kilmar Abrego Garcia, the illegal alien and suspected MS-13 affiliate from El Salvador the Trump administration deported back to his home country over the howls and objections of Democrats and the media.

As the son of Cuban immigrants, Senator Rubio was well educated on the chaos wrought by communist regimes and violent despots. He was perhaps the Republican Party's most articulate and passionate advocate for keeping order in the Western hemisphere, where numerous countries had fallen into chaos because of socialist takeovers.

In February 2025, on the same day I saw him in the Oval Office with President Trump, I interviewed Secretary Rubio on Sirius XM radio. Rubio had just wrapped up his first trip abroad as the Trump administration's top diplomat on a trip that included stops in Panama, El Salvador, Costa Rica, Guatemala, and the Dominican Republic.

He was full of good news. Several of the countries he'd visited had agreed to take back dangerous migrants expelled by the United States (which would become increasingly important over the next few weeks). Guatemala agreed to increase the number of flights it would take by 40 percent. Panama, a country that became a hotbed of controversy when President Trump brought up the canal issue, agreed to pull away from a 2017 agreement it had made with China called the "Silk Road" memorandum, taking an important step toward curbing the influence of the Chinese Communist Party in the region. When I asked specifically about Chinese influence, Secretary Rubio delivered a cold assessment of the facts.

"China is a rich and powerful country," he said, "and that's what they're going to be. That's not going to change. They've got over a billion people and the second-largest economy in the world. We're going to be competing with them for the rest of the century, and beyond. I think the story of the twenty-first century is going to be defined by what happened between the US and China. What we can't allow is for a dangerous imbalance to develop—where they become more powerful than we are and we become dependent on them. That danger is already here."[19]

A few months later, speaking with me by phone, he said, "What the president has returned to foreign policy is common sense—we're going to make decisions based on what's good for America. If it makes us stronger, safer, or more prosperous, we'll do it. If it doesn't, maybe we shouldn't do it at all."[20]

Listening to Rubio, you got the sense that the world had entered a new era and that Trump's people were taking it seriously. He didn't mention the "postwar global order" by name, but his critique of it was unmistakable. For decades, he explained, America's foreign policy had been driven by abstract ideals—supporting the "international community," upholding global norms, funding development for the sake of diplomacy—without regard for actual American interests. "Only Western Civilization," he said, "seems embarrassed by its own principles."

China had mastered the art of exploiting that weakness. As Rubio put it, the global trade system had become "a Cold War relic . . . never corrected," and it left America deindustrialized and vulnerable. "It should've been reset a long time ago," he said. "Now it finally is."

That vulnerability extended well beyond trade. In places like the Panama Canal, China had entrenched itself by buying up key infrastructure and leveraging its command-and-control economy to deny access to American firms. "It's reckless and irresponsible," Rubio told me, "for the US not to respond with strength when a geopolitical adversary takes control of strategic land and critical infrastructure in our own hemisphere."

We had made progress. In early March, Secretary Pete Hegseth traveled to Panama to deliver a blunt message to the Chinese Communist Party: "The era of capitulating to coercion by the communist Chinese is over. [China's] growing and adversarial control of strategic land and critical infrastructure in this hemisphere cannot and will not stand."

While attending a three-day security conference in Panama City, Hegseth announced a major new partnership between the United States and Panama. "The Panama Canal is key terrain that must be secured by Panama, with America, and not China," he said at a joint press conference with Panama's public security minister Frank Abrego.[21]

Just prior to that press conference, the two nations signed a memorandum of understanding, or MOU, focused on regional security cooperation. A second declaration was forthcoming, Hegseth explained—one that would give US warships and auxiliary ships priority passage through the canal. "These documents reaffirm our historic ties and outline how we will deepen our relationship and strengthen bilateral canal security cooperation."

The MOU also paved the way for a renewed American military presence in Panama. Former US bases like Rodman Naval Station, Howard Air Force Base, and Fort Sherman were being reactivated for joint training and operations. The agreement included cyber cooperation, intelligence sharing, and infrastructure improvements.

"Our countries reaffirmed our shared commitment to protecting Panamanian sovereignty from malign influence," Hegseth said. "And we recognize the foundational importance of our constitutional governments—including respect for our neutrality treaty."

Asked whether the US still recognized Panama's sovereignty over the canal, he responded, "Protecting Panamanian sovereignty from malign influences in the region is essential. When President Trump says, 'We're taking back the Panama Canal from Chinese influence,' that involves partnership with the United States."

At the time of the announcement, two US Navy guided-missile cruisers, a Coast Guard cutter, four F-18s, and more than a thousand American service members—including a Marine infantry company—were conducting joint training with Panamanian forces. The US Navy hospital ship USNS *Comfort* was also preparing to deploy to Panama to provide medical assistance and build goodwill.

Calling the expanded partnership "a golden age of clear-eyed Americanism," Hegseth said, "We want this to be a golden age for our countries, together, and for this hemisphere. We want—not only to make America great again—but to make the Americas great again."

Recounting his trip for me a few weeks later, Secretary Hegseth remained confident that America was on the right track in Panama because of President Trump's focus on restraining China. And it turns out that, despite the hysterical claims of the anti-Trump punditocracy, good old-fashioned diplomacy and reasoning were the tools Trump used to solve his Panama problem, not a full-scale invasion. Once again, common sense prevailed.

Meanwhile, Secretary Rubio went about dismantling that old order on the home front, ensuring that the United States would not find itself in another Panama Canal situation. In late April, he announced a full reorganization of the State Department. The real plan, as Rubio put it, was a policy exercise, not a budget one. "This is not a cost-cutting exercise, although it certainly will provide savings to the American people."

The key change would be a new balance between pragmatism and idealism. "We're going to stop telling other countries what we think they need and start listening to what they actually ask us for," Rubio explained. "There were places where we were sending millions to fund puppet shows while local officials were begging us to help build up their police forces."

Radical ideologues had captured key offices in the department and used them to sabotage the administration's priorities. The most glaring example was the Global Engagement Center, which Rubio shut down after discovering it had been working with media outlets to suppress political speech—including attacks on Trump himself. "Even after Congress voted to shut it down, they just renamed it and kept going," he said. "That era is over."

Under the new structure, regional bureaus regained operational control, while duplicative offices were eliminated. Security assistance and arms control functions were consolidated under one undersecretary, and the left-wing human rights bureaus collectively known as the "J Family" were dismantled.

In the early days of Donald Trump's second term, one of the clearest signs that the "revolution of common sense" had arrived in Washington was his move to dismantle the bloated and outdated US Agency for International Development (USAID). For decades, USAID operated as a global piggy bank for left-wing ideologues and international NGOs. With almost no accountability, it had become a vehicle for exporting progressive values under the guise of humanitarian aid.

Trump and Rubio weren't against helping people abroad. What they were against was stupidity—specifically, the kind that sent billions in taxpayer dollars to corrupt regimes, anti-American organizations, and pet projects that had nothing to do with national security or Western values.

"Every dollar we spend, every program we fund, every policy we pursue, must be justified by the answer to one of three questions: Does it make America safer? Does it make America stronger? Or does it make America more prosperous?" Rubio said, adding that "placing our core national interest above all else is not isolationism."[22]

That approach marked a return to common sense in American foreign policy. Gone were the days when bureaucrats in Washington funneled millions to absurd projects like a $40 million "gender equity" program in Pakistan or a $20,600 grant to promote drag shows in Ecuador.

Even the mainstream media couldn't ignore the absurdity.

Enough was enough.

By shutting down USAID as it had existed for decades, Trump and Rubio sent a loud and clear message: American strength was back—and the era of funding those who hate us was over. Months later, in May 2025, President Trump embarked on a whirlwind tour of the Middle East, ushering in a new era of American foreign policy. During one stop at Al Udeid Air Base in Qatar, he spoke before a banner reading PEACE THROUGH STRENGTH. This, it seems, will be the overriding message of the Trump administration as we move forward. The United States will no longer attempt to remake the world in its own image; instead, it will deal with the world as it is, acknowledging political realities and forging alliances with anyone who is committed to keeping peace.

THE GULF OF AMERICA

President Trump's second inaugural address contained many memorable moments. Watching from CNN's Washington, DC, studio alongside Anderson Cooper, David Axelrod, Alyssa Farah Griffin, and Van Jones, I marveled at the straightforward nature of it. As I found out from his key advisors in private conversations on the previous evening, Trump was not shooting for sweeping oratory. Indeed, he was going for a workmanlike speech that would send a clear signal:

Trump plans to restore confidence in America and restore the nation's collective swagger.

To that end, one moment stood out, and not just because of what President Trump said.

It came about twenty minutes into the address. There had already been many applause breaks. The president had announced that he would reimplement several policies from his first term, including one stipulating that migrants wait in Mexico, not the United States, while their claims were being processed. In front of him, several key American political figures—former presidents, their spouses, and many future members of the Trump cabinet—sat with serious faces on. Some applauded; others, mostly Democrats, tried to remain as still as possible.

Then came this line: "A short time from now, we are going to be changing the name of the Gulf of Mexico to the Gulf of America."[23]

More applause broke out. But just before it did, former secretary of state Hillary Clinton let out a cackle. This sent a clear message—that she found the idea instantly repulsive or at least unworthy of being mentioned in a president's inaugural address. I believe the incident illustrates better than perhaps anything else just how strong the divide between liberal elites and everyone else still is in this country. Why had an expression of American pride been met with such immediate derision? Liberals like Clinton rushed to embrace changing genders and pronouns, but changing the words on a map was a bridge too far?

As it turned out, the idea had been popular online for a while. According to reports published in *The Washington Post*, of all places, President Trump had picked up the idea from a few conservative influencers on X. Although it's rumored that the president doesn't actually *follow* many people on X, he does rely on a small team of aides to print out people's posts and show them to him at various points during the day.

If nothing else, the Gulf of America change (as well as some of the others President Trump included in his "Restoring Names That Honor American Greatness" executive order) gives the Left a little taste of its own medicine. After all, they were the ones who've spent the past two decades or so telling us that the names of our sacred national institutions needed to change. In moves that enjoyed broad support among Democrats, the Washington Redskins became the Washington Commanders and the Cleveland Indians became the Guardians. Aunt Jemima syrup was rebranded to the Pearl Milling Company. The Dixie Chicks became The Chicks. Statues of Thomas Jefferson, George Washington, and Teddy Roosevelt—three of the most important and consequential figures in American history—were torn down or removed from public spaces, all in the name of "progress." Christopher Columbus was sent swimming in Baltimore Inner Harbor by unhinged leftists during a protest. Even the federal government got in on the renaming spree when Biden administration's interior secretary Deb Haaland announced the removal of the word "squaw" from over 650 US geographical landmarks. In 2021, Democrats including Elizabeth Warren—the last person who should be weighing in on the misuse of Native American names—introduced a bill that would rename more than a thousand places in the United States because they had names that were considered offensive by modern standards.

Compared to all that, renaming the Gulf of Mexico—which, it bears mentioning, borders about 1,700 miles of American coastline—was nothing! But to the people who had supported the idea online, it confirmed that the president was willing to listen to ideas from real Americans that were generated outside of a three-block radius of the White House. Once again, I was struck by how quickly President Trump and his team jumped on the idea and made it actionable, and how closely they keep their ear to the ground of public opinion. In any other administration, this name change—as well as the others, including Mount McKinley—would have been studied to death and discussed in committees for years. In the second Trump administration, it was done in a matter of days. Just as he had been during the campaign, Trump was displaying a nimbleness in his leadership style that eludes most politicians.

Of course, not everyone was happy with the change. Some people refused to use the new name—which, in the United States, is perfectly fine. We do have a First Amendment, after all. People are entitled to their opinions, and they're entitled to express those opinions using any language they see fit, provided their language does not immediately incite violence. If you want to refer to a banana as an apple, go right ahead. It's a free country, and you are more than welcome to make yourself look like a moron in front of your fellow citizens.

Which is exactly what happened, as we will soon find out.

CHAPTER FOUR

Briefing Room Battles

"In order to Make America Great Again, it is very important, if not vital, to have a free, fair, and open media or press."[1]

—PRESIDENT DONALD J. TRUMP

When you work for a news organization, as I do, you tend to spend a great deal of time looking at printed copy. People send you reports from within the organization, and you read through them before you go on the air. If you look closely, you'll notice that all the periods, commas, and quotation marks are arranged in a certain way. Sometimes a report will spell out a number—say, *"nine,"*—and sometimes, they'll just use the digit. If you're a normal human being, you may not think twice about stuff like this. Or maybe you have, and you never knew the answer.

But I'm going to tell you anyway.

These are small examples of a news organization's "house style." Some publications have their own. Writers at *The New Yorker*, for instance, are told they must do funky things like place umlauts over the letter *o* in some long words. They're also instructed to use hyphens in ways that look odd to general readers in the twenty-first century. Next time you find yourself in a dentist's office or your liberal relative's house, pick it up and marvel at the sight of words like *"coordinator"* and *"reëlec-tion."* HarperCollins, the publisher of the book you're now reading, uses the *Chicago Manual of Style*, which means that all my references are in endnotes at the back of the book and the names of all the publications I've just mentioned will be in italic font.

These might seem like trivial things. And in most cases, they are. (No disrespect to the copy editors who help ensure my own writing hits the world without typos and dumb mistakes.) But when it comes to news organizations, other matters of style can have far more devastating consequences. In some cases, they can change the way the American people think, often without anyone even noticing it's happening.

Here's how.

AP ENGLISH

On January 23, 2025, just a few days after President Trump announced that the Gulf of Mexico would now be called the Gulf of America, the Associated Press issued a statement on the matter.

"President Trump has signed an executive order to rename the Gulf of Mexico to the Gulf of America," it read. "The body of water has shared borders between the U.S. and Mexico. Trump's order only carries authority within the United States. Mexico, as well as other countries and international bodies, do not have to recognize the name change. The Gulf of Mexico has carried that name for more than 400 years. The Associated Press will refer to it by its original name while acknowledging the new name Trump has chosen."[2]

You can imagine how that went over in the Oval Office.

When the Associated Press was founded in 1846, the news traveled slowly. Most people found out what was going on via newspapers, of which there were many. New York City alone had more than two dozen daily papers at the time, all of which employed numerous reporters covering the local scene. But these papers needed news from other places, too. So a group of five newspapers collaborated to form the AP, the world's first wire service. AP members received ready-to-publish articles from around the world, covering everything from war in Europe to the latest developments in Washington.

Over time, the AP built a reputation for being credible and fair. The AP's journalists were told to report only the facts, leaving aside personal opinion. They held on to this reputation for some time, distributing stories that were written in a plain, unadorned style. The "inverted pyramid" template, which started every article with the most important facts, allowed newspapers the flexibility to print what they could fit without any editing. The AP "stylebook" became the journalist's bible on how to write their own stories.

During my high school and college years, I worked in a few radio stations in my home Commonwealth of Kentucky. My first professional encounters with the AP came through a dot matrix printer, where the AP wire stories would print out endlessly (for readers of a certain age, feel free to close your eyes for a moment and recall that beautiful, rhythmic sound). Broadcasters like me would sometimes "rip and read" these printouts for our newscasts. Using AP copy for several years, I became quite familiar with the AP stylebook and the organization's reputation. If it came from the AP, you could take it to the bank. Or so I was taught.

But times eventually changed for the worse. The Associated Press began showing signs of left-wing bias in its reporting in 2013, when it made the controversial decision to ban the terms "illegal immigrant" and "illegal alien" from its stylebook, a move that reflected political correctness rather than journalistic objectivity. This change marked a turning point in the AP's editorial direction, as it appeared to align itself more closely with progressive ideology.

Over time, the AP increasingly adopted terminology and framing favored by the political left, particularly in its coverage of race, gender, climate, and law enforcement, raising concerns that the once neutral outlet had begun injecting ideology into its reporting of the facts. This trend deepened during the Trump era, when AP's coverage often mirrored Democratic talking points and relied on selectively framed facts, further eroding its reputation for balance.

According to Jonathan Tobin of *The New York Post*, the Associated Press exhibited significant left-wing bias in its coverage of the 2020 George Floyd protests. The AP's stylebook advised journalists to avoid terms like "riots" and "looting," even when describing violent events that definitely included looting, suggesting that such language could be perceived as racist. Instead, reporters were encouraged to focus on the "underlying grievance" of those involved in "rioting and property destruction."[3] This guidance was seen as an attempt to reframe the narrative in a way that aligned with progressive perspectives, downplaying the severity of the unrest.

In his scathing critique titled "Who Radicalized the Associated Press?," columnist Becket Adams outlines how the AP had abandoned traditional journalistic neutrality in favor of progressive activism.

Adams cites numerous instances where the AP lost its way:

+ **FLORIDA SHOOTING BLAME:** AP suggested that Florida governor Ron DeSantis's stance against racially charged curriculum somehow contributed to a racially motivated shooting, without evidence.
+ **HUNTER BIDEN INVESTIGATION:** AP tried to equate Hunter Biden's alleged large-scale influence-peddling with Representative James Comer's partial land ownership through an LLC, creating a false equivalence.
+ **KETANJI BROWN JACKSON NOMINATION:** AP portrayed Republican opposition to Jackson as being based on her having "too much empathy," instead of focusing on concerns about her political biases.
+ **LAKEN HOPE RILEY MURDER REPORTING:** AP referred to the illegal immigrant suspect as an "Athens man," avoiding mention

of his illegal immigration status, and framed the story as a warning for "solo female athletes" rather than addressing immigration enforcement failures.

+ **MOLLIE TIBBETS MURDER OMISSION:** In a story referencing Mollie Tibbets's murder, AP did not mention that she was killed by an illegal immigrant.

+ **BAN ON THE TERM "ILLEGAL IMMIGRANTS" (2013):** AP officially stopped using the term "illegal immigrant," choosing instead language that obscures the legal status of individuals.

+ **BORDER CRISIS LANGUAGE (2021):** AP instructed staff not to use the word "crisis" to describe record illegal border crossings under President Biden, despite previously describing smaller events under President Trump as a "humanitarian crisis."

+ **GAZA HOSPITAL EXPLOSION REPORTING (2023):** AP initially reported that an Israeli airstrike killed hundreds at a Gaza hospital, when in fact it was a misfired Palestinian rocket that hit a parking lot, and the death toll was far lower.[4]

During the first Trump administration, the Associated Press joined most other news organizations in covering the president negatively. After President Trump left office, the organization continued its strange leftward slide, once posting this tweet, which was roundly mocked on X:

@APStylebook: We recommend avoiding general and often dehumanizing "the" labels such as the poor, the mentally ill, the French, the disabled, the college-educated. Instead, use wording such as people with mental illnesses. And use these descriptions only when clearly relevant.[5]

People had a field day with this, as you might expect. The official Twitter account of the French embassy changed its name to "Embassy of Frenchness in the US." Some journalists sarcastically suggested using "People Experiencing Frenchness" instead of "the French." A few months later, having learned exactly nothing, the AP cautioned people against using the word "woke" in stories, writing:

@APStylebook: Use quotes around the slang term "woke," which originally described enlightenment or awakening about issues of racial and other forms of social justice. Some people and groups, especially conservatives, now use it in a derogatory sense implying what they see as overreactions.[6]

On issue after issue, the AP seemed to be morphing into a left-wing advocacy group. Take transgender issues as an example, where the AP recommends avoiding referring to a trans person as being born a boy or girl at all. The AP is now instructing reporters to refrain from using harmful terms such as "biological sex," and to avoid saying things like "both sexes."

This is the kind of thing that confuses regular folks and flies in the face of how a vast majority of Americans view many issues. But this is, sadly, the state of large swaths of our nation's media institutions—the forced installation of fringe views into what is supposed to be straight-forward news coverage, and the use of tortured language instead of just facts and plain talk that matches the cultural norms of the vast majority of news consumers.

What was a useful product for most news readers had become nothing more than a vehicle for extreme progressive ideologues to shape American culture. If you can't trust a news organization to tell the difference between a man and a woman, why would you trust them with any other basic fact on any story at all? For instance, during the 2024 election, the Associated Press ran the ridiculous headline "Biden at 81: Often sharp and focused but sometimes confused and forgetful."[7]

Over time, the Associated Press has been more than happy to change the names of things and enforce new names when it suited the organization's preferred political narrative. So it is notable that when President Trump's executive order in January renamed the Gulf of Mexico to the Gulf of America, the AP refused to adapt.

On February 11, in retaliation for the AP's refusal to acknowledge reality (and lawful US policy), the Trump White House temporarily restricted the AP from access to certain presidential events—including Oval Office sessions and flights aboard Air Force One. The wire service responded with a lawsuit, claiming First and Fifth Amendment violations. A Trump-appointed judge, Trevor McFadden, ultimately ruled in the AP's favor, stating that the White House could not exclude a media outlet based on viewpoint.

The incident underscored the Trump administration's willingness to challenge legacy media institutions it viewed as hostile, while sparking renewed debate over the limits of press freedom and executive authority.

In February, Press Secretary Karoline Leavitt strode into the briefing room and put the legacy media on notice.

"As you all know, for decades, a group of DC-based journalists, the White House Correspondents Association, has long dictated which journalists get to ask questions of the President of the United States in these most intimate spaces. Not anymore," Leavitt stated. "I am proud to announce that we are going to give the power back to the people who read your papers, who watch your television shows, and who listen to your radio stations. Moving forward, the White House press pool will be determined by the White House press team. Legacy outlets who have participated in the press pool for decades will still be allowed to join. Fear not. But we will also be offering the privilege to well-deserving outlets who have never been allowed to share in this awesome responsibility."[8]

The White House restructured the press pool, removing AP from its rotating access and emphasizing broader inclusion of new media voices in the briefing room (journalists such as Matt Boyle of *Breitbart*, Mike Allen of *Axios*, and John Ashbrook of the *Ruthless* podcast).

On February 27, a Gallup poll illuminated the difficult relationship that Americans have with mass media. The number of Americans who say they trust the media "a great deal" or "a fair amount" has declined from 68 percent in 1972 to just 31 percent in 2025. The number of people who say they have "no trust" in the media at all, however—the number that we should probably consider the most important—has risen from 6 percent to 36 percent over the same period.

For reference, consider that President Trump's approval rating in February 2025 was sitting around 50 percent. In other words, the man the media had attacked for close to a decade as an untrustworthy fascist liar was actually more trustworthy to the American people than the media itself.

The issue at hand is credibility. A media industry hell-bent on destroying Trump at all costs destroyed itself in the process, while Trump rose again in 2024 stronger and more influential than ever.

The media pushed hundreds of lies about President Trump, including several very big ones. And even before the Trump era, it always seemed to Republicans as if the media existed to defend Democrats at all costs, and disprove Republican claims no matter what. Let's take a trip down memory lane of some of the bigger anti-Trump whoppers.

1. Trump-Russia Collusion

CLAIM: Trump colluded with Russia to win the 2016 election.
REALITY: After a two-year investigation, the Mueller Report found no evidence of criminal conspiracy or coordination between Trump's campaign and the Russian government.

2. The "Very Fine People" Hoax

CLAIM: Trump called neo-Nazis and white supremacists "very fine people."

REALITY: In the same 2017 press conference, Trump explicitly condemned white nationalists, clarifying he was referring to peaceful protesters on both sides of the debate over Confederate statue removal. The news media dishonestly leaves that part out of Trump's sound bite.

3. Lafayette Square Tear Gas

CLAIM: Trump ordered peaceful protesters to be tear-gassed for a Bible photo-op.
REALITY: A Department of the Interior inspector general report concluded the park was cleared for preplanned security fencing—not for the photo-op.

4. The Russian Bounties Story

CLAIM: Trump ignored intelligence that Russia offered bounties to kill US soldiers.
REALITY: Intelligence agencies later assessed the claim with "low to moderate confidence," and no corroborating evidence was found.

5. Injecting Bleach

CLAIM: Trump told Americans to inject bleach to treat COVID-19.
REALITY: Trump did not instruct anyone to inject bleach. The media exaggerated his remarks. Even the incredibly biased *Politifact* found that Trump didn't tell people to "drink bleach," a phrase still used by supposedly credible journalists and commentators to this day.

6. Steele Dossier Credibility

CLAIM: The Steele dossier contained credible intelligence linking Trump to Russian blackmail.
REALITY: The dossier was largely discredited, with major claims unsupported. Its use by the FBI was later criticized by the DOJ inspector general.

7. Overfeeding Koi Fish in Japan

CLAIM: Trump rudely dumped fish food into a koi pond during a state visit.
REALITY: Japanese prime minister Shinzo Abe did it first, and Trump followed. The media selectively edited the footage to mislead viewers.

8. The "Muslim Ban" Narrative

CLAIM: Trump implemented a blanket ban on Muslims entering the US.
REALITY: The policy targeted countries flagged as high-risk by the Obama administration. Several non-Muslim-majority nations were also included. The Supreme Court upheld the order.

9. USPS Mailbox Sabotage

CLAIM: Trump ordered USPS mailboxes removed in 2020 to disrupt mail-in voting.
REALITY: The mailbox removals were part of routine USPS operations and cost-cutting measures that predated Trump's presidency.

Clearly, when it comes to Donald Trump, narrative often overtakes the facts. While legitimate criticisms of any politician exist, the frequency of inaccurate or exaggerated stories about Trump should make it clear to anyone that the press has always had it out for our 45th and 47th president.

And the media colluded with more than fifty so-called intelligence experts in 2020 to claim that Hunter Biden's laptop was a "classic Russian disinformation campaign." Looking back on this episode now is crazy. You had the son of a former vice president and Democratic nominee for president's laptop containing a treasure trove of evidence of bad deeds and corruption. Instead of taking it seriously, the mainstream media decided to suppress it in the days leading up to the presidential election. And if they dealt with it at all, it was to parrot the idea that it was a Russian disinformation campaign! NPR even issued a now infamous statement justifying the suppression of this information from the voters: "We don't want to waste our time on stories that are not really stories, and we don't want to waste the listeners 'and readers' time on stories that are just pure distractions."[9]

Hunter Biden, of course, was later convicted of gun charges and indicted on charges of tax evasion.[10] It is evident he violated numerous drug laws. According to a congressional investigation led by Kentucky's James Comer, chairman of the House Oversight Committee, Hunter and James Biden "lied to cover up President Biden's involvement in their family's international influence peddling schemes that have generated millions of dollars." President Joe Biden granted his son a blanket pardon on December 1, 2024, covering potential offenses from January 1, 2014, to December 1, 2024, just before leaving office.

But sure, let's call Hunter a distraction, shall we?

President Trump, meanwhile, maintained his innocence on all the charges lobbed against him. He tweeted about stories he thought were bogus, and he attacked people who attacked him, just trying to get the truth out. And he turned out to be correct on just about everything. There was no collusion, no obstruction, no pee tape, and no secret plot to overthrow the government. Those who insisted that the FBI and DOJ were out to get President Trump, many of whom had been called "conspiracy theorists" by the media for years, were proven right as well. As Senator John Kennedy of Louisiana so eloquently put it during the confirmation hearing of Kash Patel in February 2025, "Sounds to me like we need to get some new conspiracy theories because all the old ones turned out to be true."

If I've learned one thing during my career in politics, it's that the American people aren't stupid. The media and the Democratic Party might *treat* them that way—saying, for instance, that a president who can't seem to finish a sentence or get himself off a stage is "sharp as a tack" behind closed doors, or that the woman they selected to replace him was "eminently qualified" despite having accomplished exactly nothing while in office—but they're not. Americans can smell horse manure from a mile away.

On November 5, 2024, the American people had a choice of whom to believe. They could believe the people who told them that Donald Trump was a fascist who was going to march minorities into camps and install neo-Nazis as the heads of government positions, or they could believe the evidence of their eyes and ears, which clearly told them that President Trump (a guy who genuinely seemed to have fun on the campaign trail) was *not* a racist, a sexist, or a Nazi.

And we all know what they decided.

What we don't yet know is what this means for the media industry, which has taken perhaps the longest series of *L*s in modern political history.

But I think I have an idea.

RIP: THE POLITICAL INFORMATION DISTRIBUTION COMPLEX

During CNN's election night broadcast, I said that the results of the 2025 election represented "an indictment of the political information complex." Because I only had a few minutes to speak, I didn't get to elaborate on exactly what I meant by that.

Allow me to do so now.

When I say "political information distribution complex," I don't just mean liberal news organizations. I don't just mean the PR departments of political campaigns. I'm talking about the entire network of pundits, columnists, party operatives, and supposedly objective political reporters who feed the American public's appetite for political coverage—especially in the run-up to a major election. These are the people whose job it is to keep voters informed on the key issues of the day. And in the lead-up to the 2024 election, the collective proved that it was no longer capable of doing that effectively. More importantly, they made the American public question whether they ever had been.

The tense relationship between the press and politicians is nothing new. As someone who has advised many Republican candidates over the course of my career, I know that better than most. I also know that the media—which has always tilted heavily to the Left—has consistently gone after conservatives far more aggressively than liberals.

I will never forget my stint as a campaign operative for Mitt Romney's failed presidential bid in 2012, when the national media worked itself into a frenzy over two so-called scandals: that Romney said he wanted to hire a record number of women for his administration, and that he identified Russia as America's number one geopolitical foe.

Despite Romney having, clearly, the best ideas on both topics, the press berated him anyway because it was October and President Obama had to be defended at all costs.

By the end of the Obama era, Republicans had become so used to biased coverage that complaining about it wasn't even interesting anymore. People would roll their eyes and say, "Yes, we know." The political information distribution complex was biased against us—everyone knew it.

"All the reporters . . . are traumatized for having to cover a Republican president . . . they have covered Republican presidents, particularly this one, hostilely for decades . . . the double standard is so strong," famed political journalist Mark Halperin said on Megyn Kelly's podcast.

And the numbers backed it up. According to a study by Syracuse University's Newhouse School of Public Communications, just 3.4 percent of full-time journalists identified as Republicans by the end of 2022. In 2002, that number was 18 percent.[11] The trend wasn't subtle. Over the course of two decades, the media had shifted from left-leaning to overwhelmingly left-aligned—and anyone who worked in Republican politics could feel it every day.

This was surprising to everyone but those of us who'd been working in politics and media for years. We had seen firsthand how Democratic talking points flew from party offices straight to the nation's largest newspapers (and to influential smaller outlets where key races were taking place). Calling out this obvious left-wing bias was fine, but it didn't do much good. Sometimes it worked against you by making you sound like a sore loser. In Republican politics we have a saying: "The talking points have gone out." A cursory scan of major media X accounts, news articles, and public utterances during a major political uproar shows just how efficient and insidious the political left is when disseminating biased political messages. The Democrats tend to get everyone on the same page quickly, because the people who control the pages, as they were, sympathize with them. Or worse, they view journalism as just another tool to drive an ideological viewpoint or grind an axe against their political enemies.

Talking with a Republican senator, he said it succinctly: "I'm always amazed at how authoritarian the Democrats are. They live to take orders." I think that's true in governing situations, but certainly, 100 percent true in messaging. When the talking points go out, everyone—and I mean everyone—is expected to get on and stay on message. Or else.

There seemed to be hope when social media came along. Finally, it seemed, there was a way for politicians to speak straight to the American people without the filter of news organizations to twist their words and subtly inject their left-wing, neo-Marxist opinions into the fabric of what people were reading. I was pleased, for instance, to see that Donald Trump had managed to build a considerable following largely by giving his thoughts out directly, not even bothering to rely on news organizations to filter his words.

But soon it became clear that conservative voices were being throttled by social media companies just like they had been in the traditional media. It just took the social media companies a few years to catch up. But by the middle of the first Trump administration, it had become crystal clear that companies such as Twitter, Facebook, and YouTube were run completely by small bands of left-wing ideologues, and this time they had more power than ever before. Now, rather than simply writing stories with a left-wing slant, these people could control what information was allowed to be seen at all. They could "shadow ban" people whose views they didn't like, boosting their friends in the liberal media while severely limiting the reach of conservative commentators.

It came as no surprise to most of us that the figures in social media companies were just as bad—worse, in some cases—as the old guard of news organizations. According to campaign finance data from the 2022 midterm elections, Twitter employees donated over $234,000, with more than 99 percent of those contributions going to Democratic candidates and committees. Of course, you didn't need to read that study to know that the content policies of Twitter had a left-wing authoritarian flavor to them. As Elon Musk put it during an interview on the *Joe Rogan Experience*, the platform was essentially broadcasting the ideology of San Francisco to the world.

The censorship regime began to crumble almost from the moment Elon strode into the building with a kitchen sink in his arms at Twitter headquarters. Immediately, he fired more than 50 percent of the staff, including significant cuts to the trust and safety team responsible for content moderation. These actions were part of Musk's broader strategy to overhaul the company's operations and policies.

The censorship policies were soon replaced by "Community Notes," a function designed to provide context to tweets through user-contributed notes. This feature aims to empower users to collaboratively add context to potentially misleading tweets, enhancing the platform's commitment to transparency and free speech.

Amid all these changes, the legacy media let out a few final gasps. They dialed up their rhetoric about Donald Trump, assuring us that his election would mean the end of democracy and freedom of the press. On the weekend after President Trump narrowly survived an assassination attempt, *The New York Times* dedicated an entire section to a series of articles titled "UNFIT," more than one of which implied he was a fascist. But it was clear that these tricks, which were already tired by the end of the president's first term in office, were no longer working. Most of the energy in the campaign came from social media sites such as the newly reinvigorated X, and a great deal of it came from young people tuning in to new media content on YouTube and elsewhere.

In fact, when historians look back at the election of 2025, they might be surprised at the extent to which President Trump was able to build support among people between the ages of eighteen and twenty-five. Once viewed as a soft, participation-trophy-collecting, woke-beyond-all-reason bunch of lunatics, Gen Z proved to be far less susceptible to Democratic messaging than most people had predicted. An uprising of young people that lived through the Left's draconian school closures during COVID provided massive enthusiasm to the Trump campaign effort in 2024.

It's no accident that members of this key demographic report that trust in traditional media is declining rapidly. They get their news straight from the source, expertly combing through posts on X, Instagram, and TikTok and making decisions about what's true for themselves. While the rest of the world was fighting over whether *60 Minutes* had intentionally doctored an interview with Kamala Harris to make her appear more knowledgeable on certain issues (which, clearly, they did), members of Gen Z weren't even watching. Instead, they were looking at raw footage of Joe Biden tottering around like a blind man after speeches, mocking Kamala Harris online for her word-salad answers to questions, and showing up to support President Trump in droves. They played on a loop musical mashups of Donald Trump, including the famous "dance party with Beyoncé" remix.

On election night in November 2024, more young people were shown to have migrated to the Republicans than in any other race in recent memory. In part, we have influencers such as Charlie Kirk, Joe Rogan, and Theo Von to thank for that. We also have a slew of stand-up comedians and podcasters who decided that after four years of being terrified about what to say, they were going to embrace the free-speech attitude of Donald Trump, Elon Musk, and the rest of the incoming Trump team. By the time President Trump began unveiling his first executive orders and policy propositions, the political information distribution complex that had tried so hard to keep him out of office was effectively on its last legs. Its members had risked all their credibility on opposing Trump (by pushing false narratives and sometimes outright lies), and nothing had worked—not lies about Joe Biden's competency, not hagiographic profiles of Kamala Harris, and certainly not the breathless coverage of the nonsensical felony charges brought against President Trump in New York City. The pipeline, once secret, that ran from Democratic campaigns straight to the newsrooms of major media organs had been revealed, largely thanks to the small army of people on X and other social media platforms willing to call it out every day.

I believe strongly in a free press and its role in a democratic republic, but how "free" is "the press" when one party has a stranglehold on the content creators and the distribution hubs? The democratization of our political media (Musk says "you are the media" now) has created new avenues for people to get information, and new competition for the old guard. Competition is a good thing; the traditional media will either adapt and realize there's a market for information beyond just progressive audiences or it will die.

And media competition during President Trump's second term has been stiff. During those first months, many new faces appeared in the White House briefing room. They asked questions the American people wanted answers to. They filed stories that revolved around key issues rather than puff pieces about the latest group chat snafu at the State Department. And they seemed to have a good time doing it. According to a profile of eight new "MAGA media" stars published in *Politico* in mid-April 2025, the new media people tended to gather in a "conservative corner" of the briefing room. They "cut a sharp contrast to their seated colleagues: Many of the reporters in the gaggle are younger than the average White House correspondent, and a handful of them tote around hand-held cameras or other DIY live-streaming equipment. Their fashion choices—flashy ties and steep high heels—stand out in the sea of grey suits and sensible flats."[12]

As of this writing, the White House has announced plans to reorganize the seating chart in the briefing room to give these people better opportunities to ask questions and get the White House's message out to the people, which is a welcome development after so many years of misleading stories by the legacy White House press corps.

I think *all* conservatives should be grateful for these developments in alternative media. Working in politics and public relations, I know better than almost anyone how unlevel the playing field has been for years. Something needed to happen. And it's no surprise that President Trump, a true disruptor who seems to be ushering in a complete realignment of American culture and politics more generally, made it happen. As time goes on, it appears that Henry Kissinger, the former secretary of state and elder statesman of American politics, was correct in 2018 when he said President Trump was "one of those figures in history who appears from time to time to mark the end of an era and to force it to give up its old pretenses."[13]

The era of the political information distribution complex is now over, and that's largely thanks to President Trump. There is no longer a monolithic, all powerful media that purports to deliver the whole, unspun "truth" to the American people. Supposedly, centrist organizations that allowed themselves to drift too far to the Left over the past few years are attempting to reverse course. During the early months of President Trump's administration, Jeff Bezos announced in a letter to staff at *The Washington Post* that the editorial page would now stand up for "personal freedoms and free markets," an edict that followed the paper's decision not to endorse Kamala Harris (or anyone) in the

2024 election.[14] The uproar from some members of the paper's editorial board was predictable. And in the short run the *Post* did lose thousands of subscribers. But isn't that the point? The *Post* had become a home for readers who only wanted one thing—Trump hate and bias against the Republican Party. It's too early to tell if Bezos's experiment will pay off, but he, along with Dr. Patrick Soon-Shiong of the *Los Angeles Times*, are trying to reorient major news outlets to be a haven for every American, not just progressive Democrats.

After all the battles and the bitter back-and-forth jabs, is there any way to return to a normal relationship between the press and the president? More importantly, what is it about President Trump that makes the press so deranged, and can they ever get over it?

The answer to both questions, I think, is: *maybe, though probably not.* Although you can't fault Trump on the issue of transparency.

ACCESS JOURNALISM

In principle, the press should love President Trump.

For one thing, he sells newspapers. According to figures compiled in 2021, the nation's top papers saw enormous spikes in subscriptions during Trump's first term. *The New York Times* grew from around 2 million digital subscribers in early 2017 to more than 7 million by November 2020. The growth at *The Washington Post* was even steeper, with subscriptions rising from an estimated 100,000 to 200,000 in early 2016, to 1 million by the end of 2017, and reaching 3 million by late 2020. Cable news networks saw similar bumps in ratings.[15]

Which brings me to the *real* reason the press and Trump should get along great.

Access. Donald Trump is the most transparent president we've ever had, and by miles is more transparent than his predecessor.

Never in American history has a president made himself so accessible to reporters. All the press pool has to do is shout a question and

President Trump will speak to them for almost a full hour, weaving in and out of topics that viewers and readers want to hear about. The copy is usually so interesting and so densely packed with quotable material that the stories practically write themselves. During his first term, President Trump answered thousands of questions from reporters, taking them even outside the confines of traditional briefings. And that's not even counting all the off-the-cuff interactions he had with reporters, or the many one-on-one interviews he gave for magazine profiles and books (many of which went on to become bestsellers simply because they had Trump's name on the cover).

During the first few days of his second term, the president beat that by a mile. In a story he posted to X on February 25, political analyst Chris Cillizza, a former colleague at CNN, pointed out that President Trump took an amazing 1,009 questions from the media during his first month in office. He also pointed out that during this same period, Joe Biden took 141.[16] That night, I found myself on a panel with a few people who were trying to tell me that President Trump was "a dictator." Peter Baker, a reporter at *The New York Times*, had sparked this conversation by comparing President Trump to Vladimir Putin in another post on X, apparently unable to give up his paper's debunked obsession with the Trump-Putin connection.

"Having served as a Moscow correspondent in the early days of Putin's reign," he wrote, "this reminds me of how the Kremlin took over its own press pool and made sure that only compliant journalists were given access."[17]

This post, an apparent reference to Trump's revocation of the AP's credentials, failed to mention that during Joe Biden's four years in office, his administration revoked the hard passes of 442 journalists (something else I pointed out on the air). It also didn't take into account the irony that Peter Baker—a journalist who, as far as I can tell, has not been "compliant" with the Trump White House, whatever *that* means—still had access to the press pool, as did many other hard-hitting reporters who'd been critical of the Trump administration.

Yet I'm sure that within a few days of sending that message, Peter

Baker probably found himself in the same room as President Trump. If he shouted a question, the president would probably have answered it. This had not been the case during the Biden administration, when White House staffers worked overtime to keep their boss out of sight of the media (and, as it turned out, out of sight of his own cabinet and virtually anyone else with a functioning pair of eyes). If they didn't, everyone would have seen just how incapacitated the man truly was, and how strenuously the most powerful people in our nation were working to cover it up.

The White House Press Corps didn't mind this, of course. They liked having Joe Biden in office even though they barely had any access to him. In truth, it probably made their jobs easier. They could take anonymous quotes from White House officials and write up their stories, counting on the fact that the people who read those stories wouldn't be able to fact-check them in real time. If a White House aide said that Joe Biden had just played a full game of chess while juggling chainsaws behind closed doors, a reporter could put that in a story knowing that no one (certainly not Joe Biden) was going to come out and contradict it.

The same went for issues of foreign and economic policy. With Joe Biden effectively sleepwalking most of the day, the press was free to work with his staff to invent a version of Biden that didn't really exist: a virile, energetic dealmaker who knew the ins and outs of policy and was (we *swear*) still very much aware of his surroundings. As long as they kept "the Big Guy" hidden, there wouldn't be much evidence to suggest this wasn't true.

With President Trump, the situation is different. He's about as "out there" as a president has ever been, taking shouted questions from the press pool and getting face-to-face with the people who cover him. This past year, he became the first sitting president ever to attend a Super Bowl, where he received a giant round of applause when they announced his name.

Every time there's an anonymously sourced story about him in the media, he can get right out and prove it isn't true. You might not remember, for instance, that the liberal press attempted during President Trump's first term to say that *he* had some kind of dementia, selectively editing videos of him during speeches to make him appear confused and old. Many liberal outlets seriously suggested that it might be appropriate to invoke the Twenty-Fifth Amendment against him because he walked slowly down a wet ramp before a speech and held a glass of water with two hands!

But these rumors were put to rest every time President Trump escaped the White House and gave a speech, speaking off the cuff for hours at a time and then taking questions. They were *certainly* put to rest during the campaign of 2024, during which he did more long speeches and media appearances than any candidate in history (and ran circles around Kamala Harris's comparatively light schedule). Slowly, as internet platforms became less censorious and support for the president among young people continued to build, the anonymously sourced stories became even less credible than they had been. Reporters came to realize that when you have a president who is effectively an open book, you can't really lie to people about what's in that book.

During a press briefing on May 1, 2025, White House deputy chief of staff Stephen Miller delivered a stirring rebuke to the reporters gathered in the briefing room. Responding to a question about tariffs, he pivoted forcefully to the larger issue of media accountability. "Most of your papers never covered the brutal murder of Jocelyn Nungaray when it happened," he said. "To the extent that you covered it at all was because President Trump forced you to cover it by highlighting it repeatedly over and over again. He had to shame you into covering it. And each one of you that sides over and over again with these MS-13 terrorists, to the extent that you have the financial means to do so, you all choose to live in condos or homes or houses as far away from these kinds of gangbangers as you possibly can. If I offered any one of you a rent-free home with no taxes to pay in any of these gang neighborhoods and I said your neighbors are MS-13 terrorists or Mexican Mafia or Sinaloa Cartel or Tren de Aragua, I couldn't pay you to live there. But yet, you with your coverage are trying to force innocent Americans to have these people as their neighbors. And that one day their daughter may be abducted from their home and raped and murdered."[18]

Moving forward, I hope journalists can learn to use the incredible access they are given to keep the American people informed. We need more facts and fewer narratives. Less conjecture and more concrete news.

If what we've seen during the early stages of President Trump's second term is any indication, some news outlets are no longer up to the job. But I hope that the next few years bring the rise of organizations, whether they be online, in print, or on television, that are. When it comes to politics, things are moving more quickly now than ever before. Every day brings a dozen new developments that people need to know about. And the American press is not the only force President Trump is up against. Speaking of which . . .

CHAPTER FIVE

Bad Faith Actors

*"Every time I speak of the haters and losers I do so with
great love and affection."*

—PRESIDENT DONALD J. TRUMP, 2014

Something my close associates and I discuss often: Donald Trump
broke a lot of people. Like, broke them. Absolutely shattered them.
Experienced people in politics that we used to think of as being generally levelheaded became functionally crazy. And their mania never sub-
sides; it only seems to get worse, no matter what's going on in the world.
No Trump accomplishment can ever be acknowledged. No conspiracy
theory can ever go unexpressed. All Trump ideas must be reflexively
opposed.

Some used to be Democrats who could at least make a reasonable
argument. Others used to be Republicans who made millions working
for the GOP (often in losing campaigns) before they cashed in on the
anti-Trump grift.

And others still used to be respected journalists who contracted Trump Derangement Syndrome to the point of cashing in all their credibility chips in a never-ending search for online clout. Some days I hate spending so much time thinking about these people, because most have absolutely beclowned themselves and there's not much more I can do to help them. But understanding the Trump 2.0 presidency—and why Republicans and his loyal supporters will not abandon him—runs right through this group of people who are constantly melting down on your television and in your social media feeds.

Throughout this book so far, I've focused primarily on the people inside the White House. That is, after all, where the action happens. What I haven't done is check up on the opposition. And by "opposition," I don't mean Democrats. At least, I don't mean *only* Democrats. I mean the vast network of writers, political consultants, and left-wing academics who've made careers out of opposing President Trump in public. When Trump launched his presidential campaign in 2015, little did he know he was starting a professional anti-Trump boom that would build untold numbers of beach houses for this new industry's most dedicated hacks.

As soon as Trump secured the nomination in 2016, these people began crawling out of the woodwork, realizing they could get extremely high engagement figures by tweeting negative, usually false, things about President Trump. No matter their pedigree, they all wound up speaking the same deranged, conspiratorial language. A former professor of English named Seth Abramson, for instance, found that he could suddenly sell books by doing unbearably long tweet threads about all the "proof of collusion" he had seen between the Trump campaign and Russia. Within a few months, his follower count soared into the hundreds of thousands. Then there were the two skinny social media grifters, Brian and Ed Krassenstein, who found themselves trending on Twitter every day of President Trump's first term for embarrassing social commentary such as this, which was posted on the day of the 2019 Super Bowl:

@krassenstein: "While many of you are likely yelling "GO
PATRIOTS" or "GO RAMS!" I'm yelling "GO ROBERT MUELLER
and the rule of law!"[1]

Of course, you expect this kind of thing from idiots on the internet, particularly liberal idiots on the internet. After all, their lives are largely ruled by emotion and emotional outbursts. But you don't expect it from seasoned political operatives who are supposed to know better. And yet during President Trump's first term, we saw dozens of formerly reasonable people hop on the #Resistance bandwagon. Some, I assume, did it for money and fame. Others did it because they really believed that President Trump, a man who has been duly elected president twice now (against some of the longest odds in American political history, by the way) posed a unique threat to democracy.

I don't doubt that some people who oppose President Trump fall into the second camp. I think they're wrong, but I don't doubt their sincerity. That is why, when I debate with good faith actors on CNN and other venues, I don't call them liars or accuse them of saying what they're saying for money and fame. For the most part, the people I spar with on television are basically honest, and I like them despite having profound differences of opinion.

But there are members of the political information distribution complex who *absolutely* lie through their teeth to the American people. Sometimes they call themselves members of the #Resistance; other times, they stick with other labels such as "Never Trumper" or "principled conservatives." Or even "journalist." But whatever they call it, their act is transparently dishonest. I used to know and respect many of these people. Some of them were once my friends and colleagues. We worked on Republican campaigns together, and we tried to figure out how to implement many of the policies that President Trump is implementing right now. And yet twenty years later, while I'm more than satisfied with a Republican Party that has a champion who fights back and puts ordinary Americans at the center of his politics, these people are complaining. They're joining ranks with Democrats who hate President Trump because it's lucrative. They have turned Trump Derangement Syndrome into an industry—and sadly, business is still pretty good.

We lost many good men and women to the TDS epidemic, among them Bill Kristol, Sarah Longwell, Tim Miller, and the insufferable Stuart Stevens, to name a few. Stevens might be the most extreme example: after spending his career banking millions working for Republican campaigns, he turned on his party late in his comfortable, wealthy life. All these people gave up their Republican and conservative credentials just to oppose Trump.

In one of the dumbest arguments ever made in political campaigns, these people argued that, to save conservatism, Republicans needed to vote for Harris in the 2024 election, this after all that she and Joe Biden had done to jerk the country radically to the left. After her career as a flimflam artist of the highest order. And after her embarrassing performance in the 2024 campaign, these folks were *still* asking Republicans like me to vote for her over Trump to save the conservative movement?

Just galaxy brain stuff, to be honest. Even if you are a Republican or conservative who dislikes 30 percent of what Trump does or says, that leaves you satisfied 70 percent of the time versus another round of Biden/Harris policies that would've left you downright mortified 100 percent of the time!

I knew from the minute I heard that argument that it wouldn't work. And I was proven right on election night, of course. But I also knew the people making it were professional plate spinners who just needed to say something to keep the money rolling in.

And roll in it did. It turns out that the one thing super rich Democratic donors love more than liberal politicians are former Republican consultant grifters who tell them fanciful tales of all the votes they can buy if only they send over a few million more dollars.

Their hatred for their fellow Americans—anyone who voted for Trump over Clinton or Harris—is palpable every time they appear on cable news. Their hateful attitude hurts Democrats more than it helps them, and 2024 exit polls backed it up.

"The vice president [Harris] did not pull Republicans from Trump, and the percentage of voters identifying as Democrat declined, according to exit polls," reported *Rolling Stone*.[2]

The Lincoln Project is a prime example of just how much of a fiasco the Never Trump industry became—for the Democratic Party and for the country.

Founded by a group of former Republicans who realized there was money to be made by vociferously attacking President Trump during his first term, the Lincoln Project raked in tens of millions from liberal donors who thought slick ads would topple Trump once and for all. Instead, the group imploded in scandal, financial mismanagement, and humiliation.

They produced overwrought emotional ads and proclaimed themselves defenders of decency. And yet Rick Wilson, one of their founding members, is fond of posting tweets such as the following: "We will remember Biden well and fondly, even when Donald Trump's gravesite reeks of piss for a hundred generations and his name is reviled in every history of these times."[3]

In 2021, the Lincoln Project staged one of the most infamous political stunts in recent memory, sending five people dressed in khakis and carrying tiki torches to stand outside Republican Glenn Youngkin's campaign bus in Charlottesville, Virginia. According to *The Intercept*, "The tiki torch stunt was meant to echo the far-right show of force in the city in 2017 and visually tie Youngkin's campaign for the Virginia governorship with former President Donald Trump—a manifestation of Democrats' ultimately doomed strategy not to attack Youngkin on his own terms but to tar him by his association with Trump. Instead, when local media painted the stunt as a real demonstration by white supremacists, and it was amplified by the campaign of Democrat Terry McAuliffe, a former governor of the state, it spiraled out of control, with the Lincoln Project only claiming credit for it much later in the day."[4]

In other words, the folks at the Lincoln Project, blinded by their anti-Trump rage, actually staged a white supremacist rally—which backfired badly against the Democratic campaign.

Obviously, these people came to believe that Twitter was real life, and that the insane people who'd been liking their tweets for the past five years were representative of the American electorate. But it turned out that the #Resistance was nothing more than a bunch of strange, borderline mentally ill people with nothing better to do than tweet hateful, unhinged things about the president all day. The American public was still basically reasonable, which was why they had problems with the strange demonstration the Lincoln Project staged in Charlottesville.

It's also why they had problems with the leaders of the Lincoln Project covering up for John Weaver, one of their founding members, who, according to *Tablet Magazine*, "admitted to sending sexual propositions via text and Twitter to numerous young men over the course of several years, sometimes with promises of jobs and professional advancement attached."[5] According to *The New York Times*, Weaver was accused by twenty-one young men of sending lewd texts and offers for sex. All the while, his supposedly virtuous colleagues covered for him even as they attacked Trump as a sexual predator.

The fact that these people were willing to attack President Trump on moral grounds is sickening. It only proves that, for many of President Trump's biggest detractors, their cynicism is outstripped only by their hypocrisy.

The Lincoln Project wasn't an isolated case. The broader Never Trump movement—the #Resistance Republicans who found themselves overbooked on cable news and showered in Democratic donor money—collapsed in much the same way.

Bill Kristol, the godfather of Never Trumpism, went from editing *The Weekly Standard* to launching a series of ill-fated grift machines: *The Bulwark*, Defending Democracy Together, and countless donor-funded panels that served more as group therapy for political losers than as vehicles of real influence. Kristol and his peers raised millions, spent lavishly, and accomplished nothing. Well, not nothing—they did help elect Joe Biden, a man whose presidency spiraled into economic stagnation, foreign policy humiliation, and cultural rot. What a legacy for a so-called conservative like Kristol to leave behind.

Consider the reality: *The Bulwark*, originally a project underlined by solemn proclamations of saving the soul of conservatism, now regularly publishes screeds indistinguishable from Democratic National Committee press releases. In one article, Mona Charen described Trump's policy on Ukraine as "morally bankrupt," ignoring how Biden's weakness and strategic missteps opened the door for Russia's invasion in the first place.

Sarah Longwell, George Conway, and others carved out similar niches—polishing their MSNBC résumés while building little media empires off Trump hatred. Longwell's podcasts became echo chambers of elite Beltway angst, while Conway's transformation from conservative lawyer to liberal resistance hero was rewarded with glowing media profiles, but not much else. Longwell's polling shop, the Republican Accountability Project, produced slick charts and graphs that always seemed to support whatever anti-Trump narrative was trending in the news cycle.

Tim Miller, another *Bulwark* mainstay, built his brand around smirking derision toward the very voters he once claimed to understand. A former Jeb Bush flack turned Resistance keyboard warrior, Miller now spends his days podcasting, tweeting GIFs, and offering hot takes that land somewhere between cynical defeatism and liberal fan fiction. It's sort of funny that the Bush family once relied on the likes of Miller and MSNBC's Nicole Wallace to explain their policies to conservative audiences—and now they offer the most ridiculous drivel to partisan liberal fanatics. No wonder Republicans constantly suffered in the press during the Bush years.

These Never Trumpers never seemed to grasp that their message had no audience outside of the Beltway and maybe Brooklyn and San Francisco. Middle America never bought the idea that a party of elites, lobbyists, and failed consultants knew better than they did. The farther these figures drifted from conservative voters, the more irritating—and irrelevant—they became.

They mistook being overbooked on cable news for actual influence with voters. To the liberal media, it filled their desire to force a narrative that Republicans had given up on Trump. But using these Never Trump voices to create a funhouse mirror image of the Republican Party couldn't have been further from reality.

FRIENDS AND ENEMIES

If you believe what you read about President Trump in the liberal press, you probably think he's brutal to his enemies no matter what. You probably assume he gets up every morning, checks his list of people he hates, and then schemes about how to make their lives miserable that day.

Nothing could be further from the truth.

In fact, President Trump is unique among the American politicians I've known in just how quickly he'll forgive those he's sparred with. In April 2025, he welcomed comedian Bill Maher to the White House for dinner despite nearly three decades of trading vicious insults with the guy. During his monologue on *Real Time* after the meeting, Maher noted that he'd asked his staff to print out every insult President Trump had ever leveled at him so he could bring it to the White House and have the president sign it. Which, of course, President Trump did.

Speaking about the meeting on his show, Maher said, "Just for starters, he laughs. I've never seen him laugh in public, but he does! And it's not fake. Believe me, as a comedian of forty years, I know a fake laugh when I hear it . . . I'm just taking it as a positive that this person exists, because everything I've ever not liked about him was, I swear to God, absent. At least on this night, with this guy . . . I never felt like I had to walk on eggshells around him. And honestly, I voted for Clinton and Obama, but I would never feel comfortable talking to them the way I was able to talk to Donald Trump. That's just how it went down. Make of it what you will. Me? I feel it's emblematic of why the Democrats are so unpopular these days."[6]

Maher faced immediate backlash from the Left for his sin of eating a meal with Trump and then speaking positively about the experience. Fellow comedy writer and actor Larry David took to the op-ed pages of

The New York Times and penned a ridiculous op-ed comparing Trump to Hitler and slamming Maher over the episode. As I wrote for *The Daily Mail*:

> Mr. David's night wheezes were, more than anything, a warning. A message to any other public figure on the Left who might dare to deviate from the approved script: Break bread with Trump, and we'll break ties with you.
>
> Mr. David didn't write that op-ed because Maher's actions hurt him personally. He wrote it because the Left operates like a mafia—and these days unhinged Boomers like Mr. David feel empowered to play the role of enforcer. This isn't about policy. It's not even about Trump, really. It's about control.
>
> We've seen this game before. In today's liberal circles, social punishment isn't meted out for committing crimes. It's dished out for breaking narrative discipline. You're allowed to vandalize a Tesla in Minnesota and get a soft-on-crime D.A. to shrug it off. But have a glass of wine with Trump at a nice restaurant? You'll be hunted like a war criminal by a relatively famous person on the pages of the nation's supposed paper of record.

One of the main reasons President Trump was able to beat the odds and win the White House a second time is that he doesn't let old arguments get in the way of useful alliances. After all, his secretary of state is a man he once traded schoolyard barbs with on a stage in front of millions of people. His cabinet is filled with former opponents who became Trump supporters. Eventually, these people realized that Trump had leadership qualities they could support, and Trump knew their help could be invaluable in winning the election and then governing.

Still, some people refuse to believe the evidence of their eyes and ears. One of the golden rules for political punditry is *don't die on every hill*. Sometimes, when you realize you've been wrong about something, you should concede the point—or, at the very least, stop talking about the issue until you get a better handle on the truth. Yet when the foaming-at-the-mouth anti-Trump crowd is proven wrong, they die on the hill over and over again. Then they come back to life as zombies, repeating the same tired slogans until they go blue in the face. President Trump, they assure us, is going to turn into a third-world dictator any day now. The fascist armies are coming.

James Carville is a good example. Long ago, Carville helped get Bill Clinton elected president, which made him relatively famous. Every election season, he'd come out to deliver sermons in a barely understandable Cajun accent, always predicting that Democrats would win and Republicans would lose. Because his chances were pretty much fifty-fifty on that, he was right some of the time.

During the 2024 campaign, Carville stooped to new lows. He wrote a widely mocked column in *The New York Times* confidently declaring that Kamala Harris would win the election—based not on polling or turnout models or anything resembling serious analysis, but on vibes. He cited Trump's past loss, Harris's fundraising, and his own emotional instincts. In a race that every serious observer recognized as a toss-up, Carville managed to convince himself that the outcome was preordained.

He didn't just get it wrong. He got it laughably, embarrassingly wrong. And when the dust settled and Harris had lost, Carville didn't retreat quietly to lick his wounds. Instead, barely a month into Trump's second term, he was back at it again, declaring that the administration was already collapsing.

Trump wasn't the one collapsing. Carville was. His credibility had evaporated. His instincts were hopelessly outdated. His analysis was a joke. And yet he kept coming back to shout predictions into the void while hoping no one remembered the last ten times he'd been wrong.

As I said at the time: the next time he felt the urge to weigh in, he would have been better off screaming into a pillow.

In some cases, these people used to love Donald Trump. Take *The View*, for instance. Back in the early 2000s, when he was still a billionaire real estate developer, the future president was a guest on the show. The hosts, including Joy Behar herself, would gush about what a great guy he was. They'd ask fun questions, and they'd laugh at all his jokes. Today, they talk about him as if he is the second coming of Adolf Hitler.

The late-night shows do the same thing. As David Letterman has said recently, Donald Trump was always the guest he'd call when they didn't know where else to turn. He was willing to talk about anything, and the audience loved him. Now, hardly a day goes by without Stephen Colbert or Jimmy Kimmel delivering a canned, hackneyed, unfunny screed about President Trump to please their deranged (and shrinking) liberal audiences.

Both of them are a street corner and a sandwich board short of the loony bin.

TDS: AN EVER-MUTATING VIRUS

I spoke a little about Trump Derangement Syndrome earlier, as well as the new variant Elon Derangement Syndrome. You should know the warning signs in case you, or a member of your family, becomes afflicted.

One of the first symptoms is an overreliance on left-wing social media accounts for news. If you glance over the shoulder of your friend or loved one and find they're viewing posts from The Lincoln Project, *The Bulwark*, or some kind of Brooklyn Dad influencer account, take the phone away and throw it out the window. It's only a matter of time before your loved one opens an account on BlueSky, and once that happens, you may just lose them forever.

The second symptom is a kind of blindness. Those suffering from advanced TDS will celebrate the misfortunes of President Trump even if it means rooting against the success of our own nation.

Consider Governor Tim Walz of Minnesota (who, if you don't remember, once ran for vice president). During his frequent public appearances after his election loss, Walz reveled in the volatility of Tesla's stock. During one appearance, he pulled out his iPhone and said, "They've got that little stock app. I added Tesla to it to give me a little boost during the day—$225 and dropping."[7]

Apparently, this man's hatred for Elon Musk blinded him to the fact that his home state of Minnesota, whose people he was supposed to be governing, was heavily invested in the stock he was rooting against. The state of Minnesota owned more than 1.8 million shares of Tesla stock through its retirement and non-retirement funds. But this was a hit he was willing to take just to see his political enemies suffer in public. This is classic Trump Derangement Syndrome, and it's probably incurable.

Here's a quote from Tim Walz about Elon Musk: "I'm not a vindictive person . . . but I take great pleasure in the fact that this guy's life is going to get very, very difficult."[8]

Walz embodies the buffoonery of the modern Left, which roots against American entrepreneurs whose only sin is having the wrong politics. Tesla employs tens of thousands of American workers, whom I assume Walz believes should be in the unemployment line.

As the case count of TDS continues to rise in the United States, the Democratic Party keeps throwing up stranger and less likable spokespeople. A recent example is Representative Jasmine Crockett of Texas, who should probably go on television ten times as much as she does. If she did, Republicans would never lose an election again. Asked how to beat Republicans in late March 2025, Crockett said, "I think you punch . . . It's Ted Cruz. I mean, like this dude has to be knocked over the head hard, right?"[9] Shortly before that, she had suggested that the Left should "take down" Elon Musk. In response, her voters went nuts, and she raised nearly $1.7 million in a single quarter—which, I believe, should tell you something about the radical donor base of the Democratic Party. Her increasingly unhinged rants created viral moments during a period when Democrats in Congress, in one poll, had a 21 percent approval rating.

But to ordinary Americans, this kind of rhetoric is shocking and off-putting. It's exactly the kind of thing that could well have made two insane people feel that President Trump was such a big threat that they needed to assassinate him. And yet the overblown rhetoric continues, despite repeated warnings from the Left that we need to "cool things down."

Senator Chris Murphy of Connecticut, a frequent cable news presence and one of the most unhinged people in the US Senate, styled himself as the intellectual conscience of the anti-Trump left. But while he bemoaned Trump's foreign policy, it was under Biden—and with Murphy's full support—that America saw its global standing crater. From Afghanistan to Ukraine to the Red Sea, the chaos mounted. And when Trump returned and swiftly imposed order, Murphy was left sputtering conspiracy theories on the Sunday shows.

Governor JB Pritzker of Illinois, flush with inherited wealth and progressive platitudes, spent the Trump years posturing as a warrior for democracy. In truth, his policies led to population loss, rising crime, and economic stagnation in a once-great state. His attacks on Trump in 2024 felt more like auditions for MSNBC than actual leadership. It was hilarious to watch the billionaire speak on the stage of the Democratic National Convention in 2024, having just listened to Vermont senator and socialist Bernie Sanders excoriate the "billionaire class" to the assembled delegates. As he readies a 2028 presidential campaign, I can't help but laugh at Pritzker—a modern oligarch himself—tangling with Alexandria Ocasio-Cortez and Bernie Sanders over the future of the progressive movement.

Gavin Newsom, the coiffed governor of California, perfected the art of sanctimonious hypocrisy. While attacking Trump for "authoritarianism," he imposed some of the harshest COVID-era lockdowns in the country, attended maskless dinners at luxury restaurants, and watched as Californians moved out in record numbers.

Adam Schiff and Chuck Schumer, two of the highest-ranking Trump antagonists in Congress, led investigations, press conferences, and leaks that promised bombshells but delivered duds. Schiff's predictions of imminent legal doom never materialized, and Schumer's breathless floor speeches failed to inspire anyone beyond his own staff. Meanwhile, Trump, unbothered, marched back into power.

And of course, no accounting of the failed resistance would be complete without mentioning some of the professional scolds from the think tank, cable news, and "defend democracy" industrial complex.

Jennifer Rubin, once billed as *The Washington Post's* "conservative" columnist, fully abandoned any pretense of ideological consistency in her quest to oppose Trump at all costs. Over the course of a few years, Rubin managed to reverse herself on virtually every major policy position she had once claimed to hold—from foreign policy hawk to Biden apologist, from tax cutter to big-government enthusiast. Her social media feed, once a source of center-right commentary, became a relentless stream of progressive talking points, hysterical anti-Trump rants, and Biden White House press releases dressed up as "analysis." When Trump returned to power in 2025, Rubin's frantic attempts to will another "resistance" into existence looked more like performance art than punditry.

Norm Ornstein, the perennial Beltway "institutionalist," spent years masquerading as a neutral political scientist while lobbing increasingly unhinged attacks at Trump and his supporters. He warned that Trump would destroy American democracy, yet when Biden weaponized federal agencies against political opponents and presided over a culture of censorship, Ornstein offered little more than a shrug. By 2025, his credibility was in tatters—another self-appointed guardian of democracy exposed as nothing more than a partisan hysteric. Rather than admit error, he retreated into the same tired social media tirades about "authoritarianism," blind to the irony that Trump's return marked not the end of American freedom, but the restoration of it.

Joy Reid, MSNBC's resident conspiracy theorist, continued her transformation from cable host to carnival barker. Throughout Trump's comeback, Reid spun increasingly ludicrous tales of Russian plots, insurrections, and authoritarian takeovers, all while ignoring the real-world failures of the Biden era that fueled Trump's return. Her nightly sermons became loud, theatrical, and utterly disconnected from the concerns of ordinary Americans. Ultimately, she became too crazy for even MSNBC to platform, no small feat.

Norm Eisen, another self-styled defender of the "rule of law," had spent years filing endless ethics complaints, leading impeachment efforts, and warning that Trump was moments away from becoming a dictator. Yet when real legal abuses unfolded under Biden—ranging from censorship collusion with tech companies to politically motivated prosecutions—Eisen's voice curiously softened.

Figures like Rubin, Ornstein, Reid, and Eisen weren't just wrong, they were spectacularly, historically wrong. Yet even after the 2024 election shattered their narratives, they clung to their illusions, refusing to grapple with why common sense—and not their smug, mean-spirited elitism—carried the day.

Trump's willingness to defy this orthodoxy, to take the slings and arrows and keep going, proved once again that courage in the face of elite scorn resonates with the American people.

CHAPTER SIX

Fighting for Peace

"Stop the bloodshed, now. We will be wherever is necessary
to help facilitate the end to this cruel and senseless war!"

—PRESIDENT DONALD J. TRUMP

Donald Trump inherited a mess when he took the oath of office on January 20, 2025.

On the economy. Immigration. The federal budget.

And perhaps there was no bigger mess left behind by the Biden administration than the war between Russia and Ukraine. One month after President Joe Biden virtually invited Russia to invade Ukraine with a "minor incursion," Vladimir Putin launched the massive attacks on Kyiv. Biden slow-walked US military support, further setting the stage for a protracted battle. Biden's actions on reversing Trump-era sanctions against Russian oil and gas exports via the Nord Stream 2 pipeline, it can be argued, led directly to Putin's decision to invade Ukraine.

During the campaign, Trump often promised to end the war "in twenty-four hours" if he won. Of course, this was a rhetorical device to draw a line between himself and the "forever war" establishment in Washington, and underscored Trump's keen interest in brokering a peace deal between two leaders (Putin and Zelenskyy) who have both proven extremely difficult to deal with.

However it turns out, one thing is true: Donald Trump desires peace, and his rhetoric on the issue represents a pivot away from the foreign policy establishment in Washington that seemed, during the Biden years, content with an open-ended conflict in Europe.

From day one, President Trump made it clear that the policies of the Biden administration would not continue.

Sometimes, things got messy.

THE BLOW-UP

The first hour went fine.

On a bright, unseasonably warm afternoon in February, Ukrainian president Volodymyr Zelenskyy visited the White House for what was to be a perfunctory lunch and signing of a mineral rights deal with the United States. The talks, according to sources I spoke to in the building, were planned down to the minute (albeit not easily, as the Ukrainian leader had been difficult to deal with in the days leading up to the meeting).

In the grand scheme of things, the meeting in the Oval Office was supposed to be the least important part of the day. This is not uncommon when foreign dignitaries visit the White House. In front of the press, everyone is supposed to stick to their scripts. It's generally believed that matters of foreign policy and national security are too important to ad-lib. By all accounts, Zelenskyy and President Trump planned to say a few words about how important it was to both countries (and the world) that they work together to find a quick solution to end the war. When the cameras were gone they could argue all they wanted. But in front of the press—and the world—a united front was everyone's primary concern.

When I worked in the Bush 43 White House in his second term, we hosted several high-level meetings. In 2006, both Prime Minister John Howard of Australia and Prime Minister Junichiro Koizumi of Japan came by for state visits, complete with the pomp and circumstance you'd expect for welcoming close allies to the United States. Bush also got along with both men personally, and it showed in the public interactions they had while answering media questions. And, for their part, neither of them yelled at the president of the United States during their press conferences.

Volodymyr Zelenskyy was a different kind of world leader, a former comedian whose unlikely presidency came to be defined by his heroic resistance to the Russian siege. He wasn't afraid to make bold demands of American presidents. According to NBC News, Zelenskyy's demands were so harsh and frequent that even Joe Biden lost his temper with him sometimes. It happened most notably during a phone call in June 2022, just a few months after the initial invasion. As NBC reported, "Biden had barely finished telling Zelenskyy he'd just greenlighted another $1 billion in US military assistance for Ukraine when Zelenskyy started listing all the additional help he needed and wasn't getting. Biden lost his temper, people familiar with the call said. The American people were being quite generous, and his administration and the US military were working hard to help Ukraine, he said, raising his voice, and Zelenskyy could show a little more gratitude."[1]

The story about this call, which was published in late October 2022, didn't cause a massive freak out that the president of the United States had a difficult conversation with the leader of Ukraine. And following the call, many billions more were funneled into the Ukrainian war effort, even as questions mounted about what exactly the endgame would be and where the money was going. During this time, it became almost forbidden, at least in left-wing and media circles, to point out that Ukraine is one of the most corrupt countries on earth. A few years ago, this fact was common knowledge and was at the center of President

Trump's first impeachment! Just a few years later, though, simply suggesting that Ukraine's political leaders were anything other than virtuous warriors was forbidden in liberal media.

President Zelenskyy, who had leaned hard on those outlets to get his message out to the world, seemed to enjoy this protection. On February 28, 2025, with a new president in the White House and several new reporters in the press corps, that changed. About twenty minutes after one testy exchange, where Brian Glenn of Real America's Voice asked Zelenskyy why he wasn't wearing a suit, Vice President JD Vance spoke up. Leaning forward on the couch in full view of the American press and Treasury Secretary Scott Bessent, among other administration officials, the vice president said, "For four years, the United States of America, we had a president who stood up at press conferences and talked tough about Vladimir Putin, and then Putin invaded Ukraine and destroyed a significant chunk of the country. The path to peace and the path to prosperity is, maybe, engaging in diplomacy. We tried the pathway of Joe Biden, of thumping our chest and pretending that the president of the United States' words mattered more than the president of the United States' actions. What makes America a good country is America engaging in diplomacy. That's what President Trump is doing."[2]

Rather than simply nodding, smiling, and moving on, Zelenskyy challenged the vice president, apparently hoping that the resulting argument would rally the media to his side. In part because of the language barrier but mostly because of Zelenskyy's unwillingness to follow the script, things devolved quickly.

Finally, after a few more minutes of painful back-and-forth, Zelenskyy said, "First of all, during the way everybody has problems, even you. But you have nice ocean and don't feel it now. But you will feel it in the future. God bless—"[3]

"You don't know that," President Trump finally said. "You don't know that. Don't tell us what we're going to feel. We're trying to solve a problem."

"I'm not telling you. I am answering on these questions," Zelenskyy said.

"Because you're in no position to dictate that," President Trump said.

From there, it got worse, and it happened in full view of the American people.

Later, Secretary Marco Rubio told me, "You know, before that meeting, we had sort of advised the Ukrainians of what we thought a good meeting would look like and what we thought a bad meeting would look like. And I frankly just sat there sort of stunned that it took the direction that it took because he began to do all the things we asked him not to do."[4]

In the final minutes of that meeting, Zelenskyy looked about as shell-shocked as I've ever seen a foreign leader as he left the Oval Office, the minerals deal (which would've also been a de facto security deal with the United States, his biggest ally) now in serious jeopardy. As the uproar began on X and the liberal media lost its collective mind (a daily occurrence in the Trump era) it became clear that President Zelenskyy had made a serious miscalculation.

What we didn't know was *how* serious it was.

RARE AGREEMENTS

That night, I joined *Laura Coates Live* on CNN to discuss the fallout. With me was a friendly media acquaintance, Josh Rogin, a columnist for *The Washington Post*.

Laura asked how badly Zelenskyy had blown it, and I told her the truth: President Trump needed him to understand the reality of the situation. She asked me to spell it out, so I did.

"We're their patron," I said. "We're their best shot at stopping the killing, at coming out of this sovereign and stable. And we're their best economic partner going forward. All Zelenskyy had to do today was put on a tie, show up, smile, say thank you, sign the documents, and have lunch. That's it. And he couldn't manage it. After ten days of being a pain behind closed doors, now we get one day of him being reckless in public. This didn't have to happen like this. No matter how it started—who's right, who's wrong—we have the power to help them come out of this in one piece. And he's making it harder."

I leaned back, bracing for Rogin to go on the attack—to bash Trump and, by extension, me—like every other liberal pundit had since the meeting.

But he didn't.

Josh, who calls it like he sees it even when he's dead wrong, said, "I can't believe I'm saying this, but I actually agree with Scott. He's basically right. I'll take the heat online for admitting that. So be it."

I don't say this to spike the football. I'm sure there will come a day soon when Josh gets one over on me, and when that day comes, I'll tell him so on the air. And I'll be happy to do it. When people ask me what makes a good political pundit, I tell them there are two rules. First, don't take it personally; and second, (as I've already stated), don't die on every hill. Still, the fact that Josh was willing to break with the liberal media narrative that Zelenskyy is infallible let me know that things were changing on the issue of Russia-Ukraine. The American people wanted this conflict to end, and they had responded to Trump's clear desire to end it. They were disappointed when Zelenskyy failed to sign the minerals deal that would have served as the first step to peace.

As I noted later in that same program, the minerals deal—and going into business with the United States in general—would be a tremendous guarantee of security for Ukraine. When the interests of other countries become the interests of the United States, we protect those interests. I'm sure Zelenskyy knew this before he stepped into the Oval Office, which makes his blow-up all the more tragic. To my surprise, Josh didn't disagree with this point either.

But others did.

In the two or three days following that fateful meeting in the Oval, the left-wing went at Trump hard—so hard, in fact, that I had to check to make sure I hadn't stepped into a time warp that put me back in 2017. Even the accusations were the same. According to *The New York Times*, President Trump was spitting out Vladimir Putin's talking points. The most liberal outlets suggested that this one meeting was all the proof we needed that Trump and Vance wanted Putin to win and Ukraine to lose.

The myth of President Trump's allegiance to Russia—which really reached a fever pitch during the doomed Russia collusion investigation that took up so much time during his first term—has come back. And since it has, I think it's worth pointing out just how *not* friendly to Russia the president has been since he first took office. Trump was the president who armed Ukraine in the first place after Barack Obama refused to do it. As Glenn Greenwald of *The Intercept* pointed out on X in early March, President Trump "flooded Ukraine with lethal weapons" during his first term.[5] As evidence, he posted an article from *The New York Times* by Peter Baker entitled "Obama Said to Resist Growing Pressure From All Sides to Arm Ukraine." The March 2015 article reported that Obama resisted pressure from the intelligence community and Senate Democrats to arm Ukraine because he believed "arming the Ukrainians would encourage the notion that they could actually defeat the far more powerful Russians, and so it would potentially draw a more forceful response from Moscow."[6]

In other words, it was the Obama administration that shied away from supporting Ukraine after Russia annexed Crimea. It wasn't until December 2017, when President Trump had been in office for almost a year, that he and his administration lifted Obama's de facto restrictions. According to an article from this time published in *The Washington Post* (and written, as it turns out, by none other than my friend Josh Rogin), the Trump administration's approach to the situation was "measured." In the article, Josh notes that President Trump "didn't approve everything the Ukrainians asked for but nonetheless crossed the line of approving lethal sales, a significant shift in his administration's approach and U.S. policy overall."[7]

Whether you think this is the right move or not, you have to admit that sending lethal weapons to Ukraine is not something a secret agent of the Kremlin would have done. And yet the lie that President Trump was somehow in league with Putin persisted. It was reported with the utmost seriousness in every one of our nation's major newspapers, and it became the focus of a lengthy (and outrageously expensive) federal investigation that went nowhere. Among other things, the conspiracy theorists ignored just how hard President Trump lobbied European nations to end their reliance on Russian energy. At the time, he was lambasted for this by the media, not to mention the representatives of the countries themselves. During an address to the United Nations that he gave in September 2018, he said, "Germany will become totally dependent on Russian energy if it does not immediately change course. Here in the Western hemisphere, we are committed to maintaining our independence from the encroachment of expansionist foreign powers."[8]

At this, the German delegation broke up laughing. Apparently, the idea that silly things like the availability of energy or an expansionist Putin regime might ever trouble them was ridiculous. Late-night host Seth Meyers got a few minutes of programming out of it as well, mocking President Trump for being "detached from reality." A little over seven years later, the situation is dire on all fronts. Russia is three years into its attempted takeover of Ukraine, and it's generally liberals like Seth Meyers who are the most upset about it. Germany even increased its use of coal because of its overreliance on Russian oil.

President Trump was correct, but more importantly, this proves his allegiance was always to America (and the West overall) and not Russia. If anything, he was a primary antagonist of the Putin regime on the world stage. But the media, which had fallen in love with the fanciful story about secret collusion, a pee tape, and a British spy who uncovered the whole thing, forced a made-up narrative that President Trump was somehow beholden to Putin. By the time he returned to office in January 2025 and began attempting to end the war in Ukraine, that theory was right there, waiting to be picked up again.

President Trump is more or less an open book, perhaps the most transparent president we've ever had. In the aftermath of his disastrous meeting with President Zelenskyy, Trump made it clear what the Ukrainians needed to do to achieve peace.

Trump was willing to apply pressure, as anyone who negotiates for a living must be. In early March, he ordered a pause on all funding to

Ukraine, then instructed his intelligence agencies to cease information-sharing operations. These actions were part of a broader strategy to bring both sides to the negotiating table. Trump emphasized that the goal was to facilitate a swift resolution to the conflict, noting that he had received strong signals from Russia indicating a readiness for peace.

Through it all, the guiding light was peace. As he said during his address to a joint session of Congress on the evening of March 4, "It's time to stop this madness. It's time to halt the killing. It's time to end this senseless war. If you want to end wars, you have to talk to both sides."[9]

As he has done on tariffs, Trump, at least in disposition and rhetoric, has supplanted the formerly dominant hawkish voices that led the Republican Party for years with a new ethos of peace through strength. Of course, Trump is not averse to using military might when needed. Just ask the Houthi rebels who took a pounding from the US military beginning in the spring of 2025, or the Iranian regime that watched helplessly as American B-2 bombers destroyed its nuclear ambitions in June.

I mentioned talk about President Trump and the Nobel Prize. At the very least, he will have earned it with an astonishing accomplishment: he helped broker a historic ceasefire between Iran and Israel. After a series of targeted US strikes on Iranian nuclear infrastructure in response to escalating threats, Trump announced that both sides had agreed to stand down. The deal came together quickly and quietly, through a mix of public pressure, private diplomacy, and Trump's willingness to use force while signaling openness to peace. The fighting stopped. The missiles stopped. And, for the first time in years, a fragile calm settled over one of the most volatile flashpoints in the world.

It was a bold, high-wire act of diplomacy—unconventional, risky, and exactly the kind of thing that makes Trump, well, Trump. And though the ceasefire remains delicate, it's progress. It's movement. It's more than most people thought possible.

So yes—he deserves the Nobel. He's shown a rare willingness to engage directly, to talk to both sides, and to use every tool of statecraft to create openings for peace. In a world that rewards delay and punishes risk, he chose action. During an interview for this book, Treasury Secretary Scott Bessent—who, as the former manager of a hedge fund, knows a thing or two about risk—said, "[President Trump] has incredible risk tolerance, but he also has an incredible survival instinct. Most people who have a high survival instinct don't want to take risk. Most people who take a lot of risk don't think about survival."

"TRUMP'S SUPERPOWER"

At the beginning of President Trump's second term, Americans were leery of another open-ended foreign quagmire. Most people understood that Ukraine was the victim in the war, but that the war had become a stalemate with no clear end in sight. The European people, according to contemporaneous polling, were feeling the same way. According to *The Guardian*, more than 50 percent of Europeans believed Ukraine should be getting more money. However, fewer than 25 percent believed *their* country should increase financial support.[10]

This presented President Trump with a problem. He wanted Europe to pick up most of the tab for the Ukrainian war effort. After all, the war was happening in their backyard. So he took the strategic step of halting US funds completely, publicly rebuking the president of Ukraine. At the time, public opinion toward the Ukrainian war effort was shifting even further away from Zelenskyy and his government. Exactly 50 percent of Americans, according to a CBS News/YOUGOV poll, said they supported ending the war even if Russia kept the land it captured from Ukraine.[11]

In other words, Europe had no choice but to pick up the slack on Ukraine's defense. And that's exactly what they did. In early March, with Zelenskyy still cleaning up the mess from his disastrous visit to the United States, European leaders declared they would "double down" on their support for Ukraine. *The Washington Post* reported that Europe's aim was to "arm Ukraine sufficiently so that it could begin any peace talks from a position of strength."[12]

Watching this play out brought to mind a post on X that I'd seen just a few days earlier. In the post, a popular user who goes by the moniker "Cynical Publius" wrote:

> @CynicalPublius: Here's the thing about Trump.
>
> Trump says or does something that antagonizes some group of people who don't like him.
>
> Then that group of people say, very spitefully, "OH YEAH???? We'll show him!!!"
>
> Then they do exactly what Trump wanted them to do.
>
> It happens over and over, and they never see it.
>
> It's Trump's superpower.[13]

I'm not sure I agree with this in every case, but it certainly seemed to be true during the early phases of negotiations with Ukraine. However, a little over two months after that first disastrous meeting in the Oval Office, President Trump met with Zelenskyy again. This time, the occasion was solemn: the funeral of Pope Francis, who passed away in late April. The two leaders were photographed sitting side by side in St. Peter's Basilica, their expressions calm and reserved. There was no audio, no press availability, no fireworks. But those who knew the backstory understood what the image meant. The anger was gone. The frustration had passed. The American president was calmly explaining to Zelenskyy the way things had to be.

Behind the scenes, diplomacy had resumed. Negotiations restarted. And after some last-minute hiccups, the United States and Ukraine signed a closely watched minerals agreement on April 30. The deal, finalized at the US Treasury Department in Washington, granted the United States preferential access to Ukraine's rare earth minerals, oil, and gas. It also created a joint investment fund—50 percent US-funded, with future military assistance counting as part of the American contribution. The revenue from the partnership would be split evenly between the two countries.

"This agreement is a win-win, and it is written in friendly language," said Ukraine's deputy minister of economy. "It is about investments, investments, and investments."[14]

More importantly, the deal marked a turning point in the relationship. "It signals clearly to Russia that the Trump administration is committed to a peace process centered on a free, sovereign, and prosperous Ukraine over the long term," Treasury Secretary Scott Bessent said.

With Russia proving resistant to President Trump's peace overtures, Zelenskyy made the right decision. The deal showed President Trump to be a peace-minded American president who understands the reality of what it takes to end a war between two very difficult leaders even if, at times, they both do things that vex him.

Trump's frustrations with Putin became more publicly known as spring gave way to summer. On July 8, in fact, just as this book was headed to the printer, Trump said at a cabinet meeting: "We get a lot of bullshit thrown at us by Putin, if you want to know the truth. He's very nice all the time, but it turns out to be meaningless."

In every theater, the strategy is the same: stabilize the world by making America stronger. That means working with difficult partners when it serves our interest. It means ending wars on our terms. It means securing the release of hostages not with hashtags, but with pressure. And it means reasserting the idea—long forgotten under previous administrations—that peace is not a gift handed out at conferences. It's earned, enforced, and defended.

Trump is doing what his critics said was impossible: reshaping a chaotic world order without surrendering American values. Not by retreating from the world, but by leading it—with the clarity, force, and moral seriousness that only come from knowing exactly what's at stake.

CHAPTER SEVEN

Alien Enemies

The Immigration Fights

"As commander in chief, I have no higher responsibility than to defend our country from threats and invasions, and that is exactly what I am going to do. We will do it at a level that nobody has ever seen before."

—PRESIDENT DONALD J. TRUMP,
SECOND INAUGURAL ADDRESS

Of all the challenges Donald Trump took on in the first hundred days of his second term, none produced more immediate results than his actions to stop illegal immigration. His return to the Oval Office—paired with decisive executive orders and aggressive enforcement—effectively closed the southern border and reminded the country just how disastrous his predecessor had been.

Trump restored something that had vanished under Joe Biden:

common sense. After four years of record-breaking illegal crossings, fentanyl flooding across the border, and asylum laws twisted beyond recognition, the American people demanded change. Trump's election wasn't just a political victory, it was a mandate to end the madness and reassert the most basic truth of national survival: a country without borders is no country at all.

He delivered.

In just weeks, illegal crossings plummeted. Remain in Mexico was back. Deportations surged. Asylum loopholes closed. And under Secretary of State Marco Rubio, the administration began rooting out pro-Hamas agitators embedded in US universities. For the first time in years, the federal government was acting like it's on the side of the American citizen (even if Democrats were fighting tooth and nail to retain the various illegal aliens Trump was trying to deport).

What's more, the American public supports President Trump's immigration agenda. Despite the screaming of progressive activists, legacy media, and activist judges, support for Trump's agenda is over-whelming. Polls show Americans backing tougher border enforcement, faster deportations, and even mass removals of foreign nationals who flout our laws and values. Immigration is no longer a wedge issue for Democrats—it's one that splits them, as independents and working-class voters drift away from a party that invites chaos into their neighborhoods, schools, and ERs.

Trump stands with American families. Democrats, meanwhile, send congressional delegations to El Salvador to protest the deportation of suspected gang members.

This is not xenophobia. It's not cruelty. It's common sense. Washington forgot that; Trump didn't. For decades, leaders in both parties allowed the system to rot and told Americans to live with the consequences. Trump refused. He enacted the policies that he had campaigned on, refusing to soften his message once he got elected. He understood that if you don't have borders, you don't have a country.

The administration has also pushed the message that this is not just an American issue. During a historic speech in Munich, Vice President

JD Vance warned that "of all the pressing challenges that the nations represented here face, I believe there is nothing more urgent than mass migration."[1] He condemned Europe's crackdown on free speech, its loss of democratic confidence, and its retreat from shared values. "If you are running in fear of your own voters," he said, "there is nothing America can do for you."[2] But he also offered hope: the Trump administration would fight to preserve the voices and conscience of ordinary people across the Western world.

Two months later, sitting in the Oval Office, President Giorgia Meloni of Italy told Trump, "I know when I speak about the West mainly, I don't speak about geographical space. I speak about a civilization, and I want to make that civilization stronger." She said Trump's visit to Rome—recently accepted—was not just about strengthening ties with Italy, but about "all of Europe." And the goal they shared, she said plainly, was to "make the West great again."[3]

But the work on immigration, like so much else, began at home. From the moment they took office, they began undoing the disaster they'd inherited, once again sending a message to the world that borders mattered.

JUST LIKE THAT

"The media and our friends in the Democratic Party kept saying we needed *new legislation*. We *must* have legislation to secure the border." Trump reminded a joint session of Congress on March 4, "But it turned out that all we really needed was a new president."[4]

In a hundred-minute speech lengthened by 120 applause breaks and nearly as many standing ovations, that line was the most memorable. Trump brought Republicans to their feet while laying waste to the tiresome Democratic talking point that the border could not be secured without legislation from Congress (specifically legislation proposed in 2024 by the Biden White House and Republican Senator James Lankford as it scrambled to contain the political fallout from his failure on the issue).

During his last year in office, President Joe Biden belatedly signed executive actions designed to stem the bleeding after three and a half years of surging mass migration. Clearly, the people running his re-election campaign had finally prevailed upon him that the immigration crisis caused by his policies was a major political problem for the Democratic Party.

But it was too late. Voters knew the Democrats couldn't be trusted on the issue because open borders are embedded in their party's DNA. Last-ditch conversions in a campaign could always be reversed after the election.

Biden's record was a disaster. During his four-year term, the United States experienced an unprecedented surge in illegal border crossings, with US Customs and Border Protection (CBP) reporting over 10.8 million encounters nationwide from Fiscal Year 2021 through Fiscal Year 2024. That's more than triple the approximately 3 million encounters recorded during the four-year period from FY2017 to FY2020, during Trump's first term.[5]

The Biden administration's lenient immigration policies not only overwhelmed border enforcement agencies, but they also had tragic consequences for American citizens. In August 2023, Rachel Morin, a thirty-seven-year-old mother of five from Maryland, was brutally murdered while jogging on a local trail; the suspect, an illegal immigrant from El Salvador, had previously been arrested at the border and released into the US.

As previously mentioned, twelve-year-old Jocelyn Nungaray from Texas was found dead in June 2024 after being assaulted; two illegal immigrants from Venezuela were charged with her murder. In February 2024, twenty-two-year-old nursing student Laken Riley was killed in Georgia by another illegal immigrant from Venezuela who had been arrested and released under Biden-era policies. These devastating incidents underscore the dire consequences of the administration's failure to secure the border and protect the American people.

Despite the obvious reasons for the surge in illegal immigration and ensuing crime spree (Biden's open-border attitude, executive actions, and lax enforcement disposition), the Biden White House insisted that the only way to fix the problem was with a bill—something they knew was extremely unlikely to happen. When President Trump claimed he could limit the flow of illegal migrants—as well as the flow of the illegal drugs they often carried with them—Democrats dismissed it as bluster.

Then, over the course of a few short weeks in January and February 2025, Trump did it. Working primarily with Deputy Chief of Staff Stephen Miller and Tom Homan, the new border czar who ran Immigration and Customs Enforcement (ICE) during President Trump's first term, the new Trump administration swung into action.

The first and most obvious step was an executive order titled "Securing Our Borders." Signed on day one, the order, in conjunction with other executive actions, declared a national emergency at the southern border, allowing for the rapid deployment of military forces to assist Border Patrol, the resumption of border wall construction, and the reinstatement of the "remain in Mexico" policy. The administration also expanded detention facilities and designated MS-13 and Tren de Aragua as foreign terrorist organizations, giving law enforcement broader authority to crack down on the violent criminals entering the country. A separate executive order sought to end birthright citizenship for children of illegal immigrants, a move that faced instant legal challenges.

The impact was immediate. In February 2025, illegal border crossings dropped to 8,300—the lowest monthly total on record.

Then in March, the number fell even further. According to Customs and Border Protection data, just 7,181 people were apprehended crossing illegally between ports of entry—a 95 percent drop compared to March 2024 and the lowest total ever recorded for that month. Simply put, Donald Trump effectively closed the southern border—and not even the mainstream media could ignore it:

"The number of migrants caught illegally crossing the U.S.-Mexico border in March fell to the lowest level ever recorded, according to initial figures released by the U.S. government on

Tuesday . . . The data shows a dramatic shift from the previous administration, when illegal crossings routinely topped 150,000 per month."—Reuters, April 1, 2025[6]

"Since Trump began implementing—and broadcasting—his sweeping immigration crackdown, border apprehensions have plunged. Officials say the impact is visible not just in arrest figures but in deterrence metrics, with cartels and smuggling networks adjusting operations."—*Axios*, March 4, 2025[7]

"In President Trump's first full month back in office, illegal border crossings dropped to levels not seen in a generation. Border Patrol recorded just 8,450 apprehensions in February—lower than any month since the Clinton administration. Officials say the speed and clarity of Trump's actions left no ambiguity for would-be crossers."—CBS News, March 3, 2025[8]

Like it or not, Donald Trump is one of the most decisive men ever to hold the office of the presidency, a drastic departure from his notoriously wishy-washy predecessor. And on immigration, this personality trait has paid off in spades. Politically, the issue propelled him to the White House in 2016 and again in 2024. And as a governing matter, Trump's night-and-day record compared to Biden's is one for the history books.

"OOPSIE . . . TOO LATE"

Late in the presidential race, President Trump held a rally in his hometown of New York City. Thousands of people poured into Madison Square Garden to hear a lineup of speakers who'd go on before the man himself. One of these speakers, a shock-jock comedian named Tony Hinchcliffe, ended up making most of the headlines with a joke about Puerto Rico. The media uproar over this joke was so overblown, in fact, that it somewhat overshadowed the *actually* shocking and newsworthy things that President Trump said during his speech that evening.

One of them came about halfway through the speech, when the president launched into a familiar section on immigration. By this point, he'd given some variation of his stump speech hundreds of times, always with slight alterations for the crowd he was speaking to. This time, however, there was a line that he'd been working into his speeches over the past two or three weeks, including at a rally in California. Looking out into the sea of faces in the arena, President Trump said:

> On day one, I will launch the largest deportation program in American history to get these criminals out. I will rescue every city and town that has been invaded and conquered, and we will put these vicious and bloodthirsty criminals in jail. We're going to kick them the hell out of our country as fast as possible.
>
> And to expedite removals of Tren de Aragua and other savage gangs like MS-13, which is equally vicious, I will invoke the Alien Enemies Act of 1798. Think of that. That's how far back. That's when they had law and order. They had some tough ones. Think of the Alien Enemies Act of 1798.[9]

There was a round of applause. Most people probably didn't think much of the semi-obscure law the president had cited. I'm sure a few of them had trouble hearing that year—*1798*—above the clamor of the crowd. If elected, President Trump planned to use a law passed under John Adams, our second president, to deport criminal illegal aliens who were causing harm to American citizens during wartime. The Left, predictably, freaked out, noting that the law (passed as part of the Alien and Sedition Acts during a quasi-war with France) had not been viewed favorably by historians. It had also paved the way for the shameful internment of Japanese Americans during the Second World War by President Franklin Delano Roosevelt.

This rough history would have been enough to make most presidents hesitant to use it for modern purposes, even though it is, in my opinion, perfectly suited for the times. After all, the invasion of this country by criminal illegal gangs was roughly tantamount to war. This was particularly true of Tren de Aragua, a group that had established a reputation as one of the most violent transnational criminal organizations in the Western hemisphere. Originally formed inside a Venezuelan prison, Tren de Aragua spread rapidly across Latin America and into the United States, bringing with it a bloody trail of extortion, human trafficking, arms smuggling, and murder.

In early 2024, law enforcement in Aurora, Colorado, responded to growing alarm over the presence of Tren de Aragua, a violent transnational gang originally from Venezuela. Surveillance footage that went viral showed armed men entering an apartment complex, sparking public outcry and a wave of media attention. Local officials confirmed that criminal elements had effectively taken over parts of multiple buildings, prompting the city to shut down entire sections of the complex and launch a criminal nuisance case. Police arrested several suspects, and residents described widespread intimidation, vandalism, and fear. Mayor Mike Coffman stated that the gang had "infiltrated" apartment buildings, and federal authorities soon joined the investigation.

At the outset, we heard little about the president's plans to use the Alien Enemies Act against these people. And given how much else was going on—deportations, tariff fights, executive orders, and more—no one in the media bothered to check in and ask about what had happened with it. All the while, two small teams were working within the White House to make something amazing happen. One was led by Stephen Miller, the architect of many of President Trump's most strident and effective immigration policies. After working for Senator Jeff Sessions, Miller had joined Team Trump from the beginning, helping to turn the president's campaign promises into policy that would withstand legal challenges from the Left. He'd been brought back for the second administration to continue that mission. The second team was led by Kristi Noem, who'd been confirmed as President Trump's secretary of homeland security just a few months earlier.

By March 13, CNN broke the news that the administration finally planned to follow through on its promise to deport criminal illegals using the Alien Enemies Act of 1798. Almost as soon as our anchors rushed to the air to report it, we learned that 261 people with ties to various Central American gangs were being loaded onto planes bound for El Salvador, 137 of whom were removed under the Alien Enemies law. The deportations were well underway when attorneys with the American Civil Liberties Union and a group called Democracy Forward filed suit in Washington, DC, to prevent them. The flights were over international waters when the judge who got the case, an Obama appointee named James Boasberg, issued an order that attempted to block any further immediate use of the Alien Enemies Act. In this order, he wrote that any flights that had taken off carrying migrants who'd been deported needed to turn around.

Another administration might have turned the planes around in midair to comply with the strict language of the order. But this, as we would learn on numerous fronts, was not an ordinary administration. They were willing to pick big fights with anyone—even federal judges—if it meant fulfilling promises they'd made to the American people. So they decided to let the flights land, relying on the legal argument that the flights were already out of the United States when the order came down.

This was by design. According to sources in the White House, the administration sought to get the planes in the air before a federal judge could intervene, thus setting up a legal battle that was all but guaranteed to go up to the Supreme Court. The administration knew this, and they were, as one official put it, "going to win." Over the next few days, representatives for the administration argued to media outlets that they had not set out to deny a court order; they had simply refused to halt actions that were already in progress.

This was yet another example of a trend that has come to define the first part of President Trump's second term. In those first crucial months, the battle lines of a war were drawn. It wasn't between the executive branch and the judiciary per se; it was between President Trump

and left-leaning district court justices who sought to stop his most ambitious policies from the bench. It was a fight President Trump had
been personally prepared for, especially in the past few years. After all,
he managed to run his successful 2024 campaign while fighting at least
four different serious lawsuits, any one of which would have crippled
another candidate both politically and financially.

As soon as the court order came down, the president of El Salvador
posted an image on X of one of the planes, which had just landed in
his country. The caption was "Oopsie . . . too late." Secretary of State
Marco Rubio reposted the image, sending a message to the world that
the administration would not be backing down or shying away from a
fight, especially over illegal immigration.

And in a stunning photo op of her own, Secretary of Homeland
Security Kristi Noem traveled to El Salvador to appear at the prison
where the recently deported people were being held. It almost didn't
look real—here was a member of the president's cabinet standing feet
from glowering prisoners, many shirtless and featuring various tattoos
on their chests.

"I also want everybody to know, if you come to our country illegally, this is one of the consequences you can face," Noem intoned on
a video she posted to her X account. Broadcasting from the CECOT
prison, Noem said: "Know that this facility is one of the tools in our
tool kit that we will use if you commit crimes against the American
people."

The video was instructive, because it signaled a sea change in communications strategies from Biden to Trump. Under Biden, the message to illegal aliens seemed to generally be *just get here and things will
probably work out for you.*

But under Trump, the message was unmistakable—illegal immigration will not be tolerated. Violence against Americans will not be
tolerated. And your rear end might wind up in an El Salvadorian prison
if you come here. The change in attitude and public communications
undoubtedly was part of why Trump succeeded in effectively closing
the southern border.

THE MANUFACTURED MARTYR

Why does the political left always choose the worst heroes?

Hamas terrorists? Check. Harvard elites who looked the other way on campus antisemitism while sitting on a $53 billion endowment demanding several billion more from the federal government? Check. Biological males trying to invade women's sports? Check. Luigi Mangione, the accused killer of UnitedHealthcare CEO Brian Thompson, a fifty-year-old father of two? Check. Karmelo Anthony, the seventeen-year-old teenager who stabbed fellow teenager Austin Metcalfe in the heart, murdering him at a high school track meet? Check.

And there are others. So many others. And during President Trump's first weeks in office, perhaps none encapsulated how much the Democrats had lost their way on the issue of immigration than their latest cause célèbre: Kilmar Abrego Garcia.

In March 2025, Garcia, a Salvadoran national illegally residing in Maryland, was deported back home to El Salvador by the Trump administration. Despite what you might have heard at the time, Garcia was not a "legal" resident of the United States. He entered the country illegally in 2011 and lived here for fourteen years as an illegal alien until the Trump administration deported him in 2025.

During that time, he was, in fact, given due process and an immigration judge ordered him to be deported. Just not to El Salvador, where he claimed—ridiculously—that he was in danger. So, for many years, Garcia continued to live in the United States as an illegal alien. He married an American citizen who then took out protective orders against him claiming he had been violent toward her (there was photographic evidence of it at the time). On top of that, he was pulled over by the Tennessee State Highway Patrol under suspicion of human trafficking in 2022, but federal officials ordered him to be released, despite his illegal alien status and not having a valid driver's license.

So, by 2025, after fourteen years of living illegally in the United States, Garcia was swept up in the Trump administration's aggressive deportation policies and found himself on a plane to El Salvador, where he was sent to the CECOT prison. The Trump administration defended the action, citing alleged affiliations between Abrego Garcia and the MS-13 gang. Trump had designated MS-13 as a terrorist organization, which, in their eyes, made Garcia instantly deportable under the Alien Enemies Act.

Democrats seized upon this incident to challenge President Trump's immigration policies, and the political left again lost its mind over another terrible hero. They complained of a lack of due process and demanded that Garcia be returned to the United States. The optics could not have been worse for Democrats and better for Trump—one party trying to rid the country of a suspected MS-13 gangbanger who had been in the country illegally for fourteen years while the other was fighting to "bring him home."

As legendary investor Bill Ackman posted on X at the time: "A nation in which one administration can allow millions of unvetted illegal migrants into the country but requires that a court vet each deportation decision in an individually adjudicated case will soon lose the values our democratic system was intended to preserve."

Spot. On.

And Elon Musk agreed, telling me for this book that illegal immigration—combined with low birth rates—would eventually "break" the United States of America. "Criminals and murderers," he said to me, "must be deported immediately.

"It's not that every person who comes here is unproductive. But many people who do come here are violent criminals and murderers," Musk said.

The news media lost its mind during this case, repeatedly referring to Garcia as a "Maryland man" in headlines and reports despite the fact that he was a citizen of El Salvador!

Then Trump's opponents escalated the matter, and it cost them dearly.

Senator Chris Van Hollen of Maryland traveled to El Salvador to meet with Garcia, positioning himself as a defender of constitutional rights. But pictures of the meeting between the two emerged, showing them sitting at a table having margaritas! Van Hollen claimed El Salvador's government staged the margaritas, but as I said on CNN on April 18: If you are explaining how you came to be sitting at a table with an MS-13 gang member while sipping margaritas, you are losing the political argument. As it turned out, House Democratic Leader Hakeem Jeffries may have agreed with me. He pleaded in late April with his conference to stop their pilgrimages to El Salvador in the hopes of bringing MS-13 gangbangers back to the United States. Jeffries later denied having said this.

Democrats downplayed Garcia's ties to MS-13, a transnational gang that Trump had designated as a terrorist organization. They kept up the fiction that he was some mild-mannered suburban father even as evidence emerged that he was a pretty bad dude illegally inhabiting our country. Courts had previously found that Garcia was a probable MS-13 gang member, a fact that Democrats tried to sweep under the rug.

After Van Hollen returned from his trip, Trump twisted the political knife even further. A photograph of Garcia emerged with a clear image of his tattooed fingers of which the symbols left little doubt that he was part of MS-13. Trump himself took the image to the Oval Office and released a photo of himself holding up the evidence of Garcia's MS-13 gang affiliation.

And a subheading to the affair came when it was revealed that Van Hollen had used taxpayer money to take the trip to El Salvador. Here you had an administration working to eliminate waste, fraud, and abuse of taxpayer dollars versus a political opposition spending taxpayer money for a trip designed to reimport an illegal alien MS-13 gangbanger back into the United States. The political setup was delicious, to say the least.

President Trump and his team maintained that the deportation was justified, emphasizing the administration's commitment to national security and immigration enforcement. He criticized Democratic efforts to portray Garcia as a victim, suggesting that such narratives undermine the rule of law and public safety.

Stephen Miller, the White House deputy chief of staff, reinforced the president's stance and went viral for his cable TV appearances ferociously defending the deportation.

"This was just one of those examples of an individual that is an MS-13 gang member, multiple charges and encounters with the individuals here, trafficking in his background, was found with other MS-13 gang members—very dangerous person, and what the liberal left and fake news are doing to turn him into a media darling is sickening.

"I think this illegal alien is exactly where he belongs—home in El Salvador. He was in our country illegally, he is from El Salvador, was born in El Salvador, and, oh, the media forgot to mention: he is a MS-13 gang member. The media would love for you to believe that this is a media darling, that he is just a Maryland father. Osama Bin Laden was also a father, and yet, he was not a good guy, and they actually are both terrorists," Miller said.

The episode set up an interesting clash with the courts. And in April, the US Supreme Court issued a unanimous order in *Noem v. Abrego Garcia*, addressing the issue. The Court acknowledged that Garcia had been subject to a withholding order that prohibited his removal, rendering his deportation to El Salvador (but not to another country) illegal.

In its directive, the Court stated that the government must "facilitate" Abrego Garcia's return from El Salvador. However, the Court did not mandate that the administration "effectuate" his return, instead remanding the case to the district court to clarify the extent of the government's obligations.

This distinction led to differing interpretations, with the administration asserting limited responsibility in securing Garcia's return, while critics argue that the ruling implies a more proactive role is required to uphold judicial authority and due process.

As the legal case played out, it was apparent that Trump was winning the optics battle. Here's a president trying to deport illegal aliens and his political opposition—using activist judges—trying to stop him.

As for Garcia, as the weeks wore on, more evidence emerged that he was, in fact, not the sort of person that should be roaming the streets of the United States of America. On April 16, in fact, evidence emerged that he had "kicked, shoved, slapped, verbally abused her, detained her against her will and threatened to kill" his wife in the United States.

By then, the media had mostly moved on—but the damage was done. A suspected MS-13 gang member who never should have been here in the first place had been turned into a symbol of judicial over-reach and liberal victim politics. Trump's efforts to protect American communities were once again hamstrung by a legal system weaponized against him. The message from the Left was clear: even known crimi-nals in the country illegally are entitled to endless process, endless delay, and endless benefit of the doubt—while the president of the United States is treated like the criminal for trying to remove them.

On April 30, his 101st day in office, President Trump made it clear that this fight was only beginning. During a cabinet meeting that day, the topic of activist judges—who use national injunctions to block deportations—came up. The president didn't mince words. He said he was considering every legal option available to ensure these judges couldn't keep standing in the way of national security.

"One way that's been used by three highly respected presidents," he said. "We hope we don't have to go that route, but there is one way that's been used very successfully by three presidents."

He was talking about the suspension of habeas corpus—a wartime measure most famously invoked by Abraham Lincoln. Trump didn't say he'd do it. But he made it clear the possibility was on the table. It was a signal to the courts: if you stand in the way of this country's right to defend its borders, don't expect the executive branch to roll over.

The same message came through in an exchange with Secretary of State Marco Rubio. A reporter, running interference for the media narrative, tried to corner him with a loaded question about returning deported MS-13 gang member Abrego Garcia:

"Have you been in touch with El Salvador about returning Abrego Garcia? Has a formal request from this administration been made?"

Rubio fired back—calm, sharp, and uncompromising.

"Well, I would never tell you that. And you know who else I'll never tell? A judge—because the conduct of our foreign policy belongs to the president of the United States and the executive branch, not some judge. We will conduct foreign policy appropriately if we need to, but I'll never discuss it. And no one will ever make us discuss it—because that's how foreign policy works."

Total shutdown, and one of dozens of examples of Rubio's value to the president.

The message couldn't have been clearer. If you're coming here to build something great—come on in, as long as you follow our laws. If you're coming here to destroy, manipulate, or undermine American law, expect a door slammed in your face.

In the end, the message wasn't complicated. If you want to come to America to work hard, follow our laws, and contribute to the success of this country, we want you here. But if you're coming to spread violence, exploit our system, or wage ideological war against the West, you're not getting in. And if activist judges think they can stand in the way of that mission, they're in for a fight.

Already, we're seeing how hard they're trying. The Supreme Court blocked Trump's use of the Alien Enemies Act to expel dangerous Venezuelan nationals linked to terrorist groups, insisting they be given more notice, more process, more time. Even after evidence showed these men had violent gang ties—including to Tren de Aragua, a designated terror organization—the courts sided with delays.

And yet, President Trump has said—clearly—that he will follow the law. That he will abide by what the Supreme Court decides, even when he disagrees. I said exactly that when I went on *Real Time with Bill Maher* the night this issue was making headlines. Maher tried to corner me with quotes about due process, saying Trump just wants to throw people into "torture chambers." But I pushed back. "These gang members are not coming here to be productive Americans," I said. "They are coming here to rape, pillage, murder, steal, and wreak havoc on communities. The president was elected to fix it." And he's doing exactly that—within the bounds of the law.

Then, on June 27, the Supreme Court delivered a major blow

to the use of nationwide injunctions. In a 6–3 decision, the justices ruled that district courts may no longer block presidential policies across the entire country unless part of a certified class action. The ruling effectively ended the long-standing practice of lower courts issuing sweeping injunctions to halt federal actions nationwide. For the Trump administration, this was a turning point—removing one of the judiciary's most potent weapons for obstructing executive authority and clearing the way for broader enforcement of key immigration and regulatory policies, including parts of the president's order revoking birthright citizenship.

Taken together, the two rulings sent a powerful message: the administration would not be boxed in by activist judges or procedural hurdles. They were using the law—and winning.

As for Abrego Garcia, the Trump Administration eventually brought him back to the United States to face federal charges in Tennessee that he was part of a broad conspiracy to smuggle illegal aliens across the United States. Even after they did it, a federal magistrate judge outrageously tried to free Abrego Garcia, arguing that he wasn't a flight risk or a danger to his community. As of this writing, his fate remains unclear.

Trump's critics love to talk about the way he does things. The tone. The pace. The "wrecking ball nature," as Maher called it. But the American people are less worried about decorum and more worried about survival. They know who's really being protected by these legal maneuvers—and it's not them. Trump is making the case that American citizenship should mean something again. That due process should protect Americans first. And that defending our borders shouldn't be considered controversial.

He's said he'll follow the courts. But that doesn't mean he won't fight. And that's exactly why he's back in the White House.

CHAPTER EIGHT

Transitioning Back to Common Sense

"Under the Trump administration, we will defend the proud tradition of female athletes, and we will not allow men to beat up, injure, and cheat our women and our girls. From now on, women's sports will be only for women."

—PRESIDENT DONALD J. TRUMP, FEBRUARY 5, 2025, "KEEPING MEN OUT OF WOMEN'S SPORTS" EXECUTIVE ORDER SIGNING CEREMONY

In the immediate aftermath of the 2024 election, many commentators suggested that the Democratic Party was going to give up most of its most insane positions. The woke agenda, having led to the most embarrassing defeat in the history of American politics, would fade into the background. Much like the Left's draconian lockdown policies and the embarrassing race-related rituals that surrounded the George Floyd protests (more on that in the next chapter), the Left's insane stance on "gender-affirming care" for kids would be consigned to the ash heap of American political history.

The *Independent* said that "Democrats want to see the party push to the political middle in the wake of election losses."[1] A story in *Politico* revealed that "Some Democrats, reeling from Republican attacks tying their party to transgender rights issues, are privately furious at their leaders and explicitly warning they need a better strategy going into 2026."[2]

Things did not pan out this way.

Less than two months after President Trump took office and signed his executive order entitled "Keeping Men Out of Women's Sports," a bill to codify this came up for a vote in the Senate. This bill, titled the Protection of Women and Girls in Sports Act of 2025, sought to amend Title IX to prohibit school athletic programs from allowing individuals whose biological sex at birth was male to participate in programs designated for women or girls.

As I mentioned in the first chapter of this book, this is the ultimate 80–20 issue (maybe even 90–10!). Politically speaking, it's a slam dunk. The American people do not want men declaring that they're girls and then stepping onto the basketball or volleyball court, the soccer field, or into the boxing ring with biological women.

"It's so ridiculous, but here we are," the president said just before signing the executive order on February 5. "It's about time. Under the Trump administration, we will defend the proud tradition of female athletes, and we will not allow men to beat up, injure, and cheat our women and our girls."[3]

This event was remarkable, in that it produced one of the most iconic photos of Trump's first hundred days—the president surrounded by dozens of female athletes from around the country. Brave and courageous women like Riley Gaines, the former University of Kentucky swimmer who was unfairly forced to share a spot on the podium at an NCAA event after tying with Lia Thomas, the biological male from the University of Pennsylvania.

The overwhelming evidence of the trans-dangers faced by female athletes is punctuated by alarming victim accounts. In his speech to Congress on March 4, President Trump invited Payton McNabb, three years after she was knocked unconscious by a vicious spike from a biological male playing on a girls' volleyball team.

"When her girls' volleyball match was invaded by a male, he smashed the ball so hard in Payton's face, causing traumatic brain injury, partially paralyzing her right side, and ending her athletic career," Trump relayed the horrifying story. "Payton is here tonight in the gallery. And, Payton, from now on, schools will kick the men off the girls' team or they will lose all federal funding."[4]

"It's demeaning for women, and it's very bad for our country," Trump continued. "We're not going to put up with it any longer."

As Republican members of Congress stood to cheer for McNabb, Democrats sat and stared straight ahead, stone-faced.

"They really showed their hands," McNabb told *The New York Post*. "They can't get over it—80% of the country agrees on this and they're willing to die on this hill. It was really disappointing seeing none of them take a stand for women, because some of them have daughters, and if they don't they know at least one woman in their lives and voted against them."[5]

McNabb told the newspaper she still suffers cognitive issues and persistent headaches.

"The Democratic party has failed women," she said.

For Trump, the contrast on this issue "is only a small fraction of the commonsense revolution that is now, because of us, sweeping the entire world," he told Congress. "Common sense has become a common theme, and we will never go back. Never. Never going to let that happen."

Indeed, it is just common sense! For years now, the American people have been polite about those on the Left who claim that a boy can magically become a girl just by verbally "identifying" as one, or vice versa. But in my experience, there is only so much lunacy voters are willing to take before they say *enough*.

Faced with this, the American people finally saw that the Democrats, who had long positioned themselves as the party of average, everyday working people who tend to value common sense, had gone too far around the bend to save—at least for now.

One *New York Times*/Ipsos poll showed that 67 percent of Democratic voters believed transgender athletes should not be allowed to compete in women's sports.[6] Another poll, this one from the Manhattan Institute, a conservative think tank, found that 39 percent of Democrats opposed gender transition procedures for minors—compared to just 37 percent who supported them.[7] These were not fringe positions. They were mainstream views, shared by millions of people who had once felt at home in the Democratic Party. And even for those who didn't care as much about men competing in women's sports, discussion about the issue was impossible to ignore during the campaign cycle.

In part, this was because President Trump's team, who largely took their cues on issues from the man at the top of the ticket, was so adept at figuring out what would resonate with reachable voters the most. Just a few weeks before election day, they dropped one of the most effective ad campaigns I've ever seen. In one, Kamala Harris is shown speaking a few years earlier, telling an audience that taxpayer money should be spent on "gender-affirming care" for prisoners who identify as trans. Another ends with a phrase that would dominate online discussions for the next few weeks: "Kamala's agenda is they/them, not you," an ad that was memorable because it featured well-known progressive radio host Charlamagne tha God slamming Harris.

"No, I don't want my taxpayer dollars going to that!" an exasperated Charlamagne says on his show. Devastating stuff, as he was channeling the emotion that a vast majority of Americans felt when hearing Harris describe her ridiculous position. As one of the most authentic communicators in media today, Charlamagne knew just how badly the issue was hurting Harris and the Democratic Party—and he had the courage to say it.

As Chris LaCivita, President Trump's senior campaign strategist and the architect behind much of the ad strategy, told me, "We really didn't have a coordinated strategy to start—when releasing the ads aimed at the Left normalizing trans ideology. We found it curious that despite it being a central theme—almost a defining aspect of their party—they never talked about it. Of course, we knew why—it was deeply unpopular with the vast majority of voters."[8]

LaCivita pointed to the Harris video as a turning point: "The video, of Kamala Harris talking about trans care for prisoners—paid for by taxpayers, by a man dressed as a woman—demonstrated to voters that Kamala Harris's focus was not on the issues they cared about—economic ones. And while they didn't want to discuss their radical support for a kooky ideology, we were more than happy to."[9]

The campaign, LaCivita explained, rolled out three iterations of the ad. "The first in three generated a discussion point within the campaign—how much would we run behind it in the battleground states?" Internal debate followed. Chief pollster Tony Fabrizio urged balance—50 percent economic, 50 percent cultural messaging. But once the Harris ad aired, it was a breakout hit. "The ad, produced by Patrick McCarthy, was instant national news," LaCivita said. "It hit on a topic the Harris campaign was desperately trying to avoid."[10]

The follow-up was even more strategic: "We took the clip of Charlamagne lambasting the Harris campaign and worked it into ad #2—then targeted men only, almost exclusively running it on live sports: college and pro football." The third iteration was aimed squarely at suburban women and focused on men competing in women's sports.

If anything should have let Democrats know they had a serious problem on their hands, it was the way voters showed up in droves to reject the trans agenda. When the Protection of Women and Girls in Sports Act came up for a vote, the results shook out along party lines. Not a single Democrat in the House or Senate was willing to distance himself, herself, themselves, or xim/bug/zir-self from this insane set of ideas.

By the way, these are actual gender pronouns, according to the transgender activists who have tremendous sway in the Democratic Party. "Not a joke!" as Joe Biden used to say.

Before we move on to the electoral implications, it's worth asking why.

How is it that in the year 2025, the party that once demanded we all "trust the science" has fallen victim to such a cult-like, anti-scientific ideology?

(THOUGHT) CRIME AND PUNISHMENT

For a long time, Congressman Seth Moulton was a traditional Democrat. Working from Massachusetts, the political home of Mitt Romney and Elizabeth Warren, he stuck mostly to the party line. He spoke out often against Trump during his first term, said all the right things during the George Floyd riots, and echoed all the requisite talking points on diversity, equity, and inclusion.

In November of 2024, just a few days after President Trump was reelected for a second time, something changed.

During an interview with *The New York Times*, Representative Moulton raised a few non-offensive, almost off-handed points about why he believed Democrats lost the election. In that interview—which, it bears mentioning, wasn't some in-depth profile of Moulton, but rather a scattershot collection of quotes from high-profile Democrats about the election—the congressman said, "Democrats spend way too much time trying not to offend anyone rather than being brutally honest about the challenges many Americans face. I have two little girls, I don't want them getting run over on a playing field by a male or formerly male athlete, but as a Democrat I'm supposed to be afraid to say that."[11]

On its face, this seemed self-evident. But just in case it wasn't, left-wing activists moved quickly, as if trying to prove Moulton's point. He was denounced on X by the few radical lefties who hadn't yet fled to the safe space of BlueSky. From there, news of his "cancellation" reached Tufts University. According to leaked Slack messages, the head of the university's political science department contacted Moulton's office with a warning. A person on the call "said he consulted with his colleagues and doesn't want our office to contact Tufts about internships, and they won't facilitate internship opportunities for students with us."[12]

Over the next few days, Moulton was forced to clarify that he wasn't trying to be offensive. But he showed a remarkable level of backbone by refusing to retract his comments—which, after all, were about why Democrats lost the election. And on the former point, he was exactly right. Fathers of daughters who played sports *did* feel uncomfortable (and that was the mild end of the spectrum) about their girls having to compete against men. And they *did* feel uncomfortable speaking about it publicly, especially if they were Democrats. In part, they were worried they'd get the Seth Moulton treatment—enraged radical progressives hammering them for holding rather commonsense views.

It's no surprise that when the Democratic National Committee held its elections for leadership positions, nobody like Seth Moulton was even considered. Instead, they spent a good chunk of time debating the "gender balance" of the leadership team. Speaking from the podium, one officer said, "We have an amazing group of new officers. So far, as you know, our three at-large vice-chair positions are used to ensure gender balance among seven offices . . . Our rules specify that when we have a non-binary candidate or officer, the non-binary individual is counted as neither male nor female, and the remaining six officers must be gender balanced with the results of the previous four elections. Our elected officers are currently two male and two female. In order to be gender balanced . . . we must elect one male, one female, and one person of any gender."[13]

It's beyond parody but absolutely emblematic of how the Democratic Party has played into Trump's hands on the issue. One party is for common sense, while the other is mired in uncommon nonsense.

Of course, Seth Moulton was far from the only left-leaning person to find out what happens when you put one toe out of line. Unlike the modern Republican Party, which tolerates viewpoint diversity because of Trump's elastic coalition more than ever, the Democrats demand absolute conformity. If you express so much as a single shred of doubt about their many insane positions, you're cast out. Consider that if you want to be a Democrat in the year 2025, you must believe that the war in Ukraine should go on forever, bankrolled by the United States the entire time. You have to swear allegiance to diversity, equity, and inclusion programs, despite mounting evidence of their damage to the country. And you have to believe that MS-13 gang members living in the US illegally must be protected at all costs. If you don't believe these things, prepare to get canceled.

The truth is the Democratic Party is in a crisis of illiberalism, intolerant of any view that falls outside of accepted, anti–Western Civilization dogma. Left-wing students regularly ask for "trigger warnings" on content that might offend them. Liberal interest groups demand that classic works of literature from authors such as Ian Fleming and Roald Dahl be censored to reflect today's snowflake sensitivities. And many contemporary cancelations revolve around the trans issue. In 2020, the writer Abigail Shrier published a book titled *Irreversible Damage: The Transgender Craze Seducing Our Daughters.* In it, she carefully examined the evidence for and against so-called gender-affirming care for kids. As you might expect, she found that many young people—especially girls with autism—were being falsely led to believe that they were born in the wrong body and that medical intervention could make them their true selves. Her evidence was iron-clad, and the reasoning was sharp.

In response, the Left staged boycotts. They attempted to get the book pulled from shelves, and many retailers, including Target, agreed to pull it. The association of American booksellers labeled the book "violent" and refused to stock it. Amazingly, a lawyer at the American Civil Liberties Union, or ACLU, pushed for the book to be pulped forever, writing, "Stopping the circulation of this book and these ideas is 100% a hill I will die on." If nothing else, this incident proved just how far the Left had drifted on issues of free speech and censorship. To them, any evidence that taking confused kids and pumping them full of untested cross-sex hormones was akin to Nazi propaganda. It needed to be snuffed out of existence; otherwise, people might find it and begin to question the wisdom of the transgender cult.

Slowly, stories began to emerge. Activists like Chloe Cole, who transitioned as a teenager and later regretted the decision, spoke out to highlight the dangers of the trend proliferating on platforms like Reddit and Instagram. In congressional testimony in 2023, Cole said, "I used to believe that I was born in the wrong body. And the adults in my life, whom I trusted, affirmed my belief, and this caused me lifelong, irreversible harm." She went on to say, "My childhood was ruined . . ."[14] Cole faced immediate backlash from left-wing activists. She wound up endorsing Trump in 2024.

Given the mounting evidence against the cause of trans activists, it was no wonder they felt compelled to resort to extreme measures. Every day, new stories emerged of medical "experts" persuading children to undergo irreversible chemical and surgical mutilation. Parents recounted heartbreaking meetings with gender specialists who warned that their children would almost certainly commit suicide if they weren't allowed to transition.

One such parent was Elon Musk. His child, born Xavier, transitioned and now goes by Vivian Jenna Wilson. She has since severed ties with her father. In an interview, Musk explained how the process unfolded. "I was essentially tricked into signing documents for one of my older boys, Xavier," he said. "This is before I had any understanding of what was going on. COVID was going on, so there was a lot of confusion, and I was told Xavier might commit suicide if he doesn't."[15] The experience was devastating. "I lost my son, essentially," Musk said. "They call it 'deadnaming' but this was someone I raised and loved. Killed by the woke mind virus." Later in the same interview, he says that after the experience, he "vowed to destroy the woke mind virus."

The next time Democrats wonder how they managed to lose this tech titan—whom they claimed as one of their own just a few short years ago—they should listen to this interview in full. It shows the real consequences that deranged left-wing policies can have on families. And you can be sure that for every Elon Musk in the world who was willing to speak out on this issue, there are countless other parents who are afraid to speak out against the trans issue. They have jobs they might lose and friends who'd ostracize them for going against the prevailing left-wing orthodoxy.

With the election of President Trump, though, it seems that the tide is turning. If nothing else, parents are beginning to come out of the shadows and say things they never would have said while the Biden administration was in power. Trump's victory and subsequent governing actions have created a permission structure for people to speak out and restore common sense to this conversation.

Of course, anyone who thinks the Left is about to moderate on this issue (even *slightly*) is in for a rude awakening.

TWISTING THE EVIDENCE

Covering the insane political climate of the past few years, I often find myself digesting strange combinations of words. *Gender-affirming care for minors* is one such phrase. Another is "Maryland Man," which is how Democrats and the media described an MS-13 gangbanger who'd been living illegally in the United States for fourteen years.

Still, I'm not sure I was ever quite as surprised as I was on the afternoon of March 5, 2025, when I looked down at my notes on the set of *The Arena with Kasie Hunt* on CNN and saw the phrase "transgender mice."

Like more than 36 million other Americans, I watched President Trump's address to a joint session of Congress the previous evening. I had raised my eyebrows right along with them when, in the section of the speech about government waste, he said:

> Just listen to some of the appalling waste we have already identified. $22 billion from HHS to provide free housing and cars for illegal aliens. $45 million for diversity, equity, and inclusion scholarships in Burma. $40 million to improve the social and economic inclusion of sedentary migrants. Nobody knows what that is. $8 million to promote LGBTQI+ in the African nation of Lesotho, which nobody has ever heard of. $60 million for indigenous peoples and Afro Colombian empowerment in Central America—$60 million. *$8 million for making mice transgender.* This is real.[16]

President Trump sometimes uses hyperbole to illustrate a point. At first, I wondered if this might be happening with the trans mice. Could this really be true?

I feared this might be the case when articles about how the claim was false began popping up on the internet. Al Franken, the former senator from Minnesota, tried to explain it away in a post on X:

@alfranken: Just got off the phone with my friend, Norm Orn-stein, who explained to me the difference between transgen-der and transgenic. You see, Trump got a big laugh from the Republicans last night when he said the federal government "spent $8 million to make mice transgender." No, they didn't. They were actually transgenic mice (injected with DNA from another species). That said, I don't think transgenic mice should be allowed to swim competitively against regular mice. Imagine if they were injected with fish DNA![17]

This post, with all its smug superiority, went viral on X. Then it went even more viral on BlueSky. Before long, there were several articles that cited it to "debunk" the claim that the Biden administration had funded studies involving transgender mice. One of them was published by CNN.

It took only a few hours before we found out, once again, that the Trump team had been right all along. On March 5, just before I was set to go on air to discuss the fallout from President Trump's address, the White House press shop released a statement that would have stunned the public coming from any other administration. In clear, direct language, it said:

"Last night, President Donald J. Trump highlighted many of the egregious examples of waste, fraud, and abuse funded by American taxpayers, including $8 million spent by the Biden Administration 'for making mice transgender.'"[18]

Predictably, fact-checkers immediately raised doubts about the claim. But President Trump was right. Under the Biden administra-tion, the National Institutes of Health had awarded millions of dollars in taxpayer-funded grants for experiments involving transgender treat-ments on mice.

Soon after, CNN revised its fact check to reflect the truth. Their updated article now states: "An earlier version of this item incorrectly characterized as false Trump's claim about federal money being spent for 'making mice transgender.' The article has been updated with context about the spending, which was for research studies on the potential human health impacts of treatments used in gender-affirming care."[19]

As usual, the facts had caught up.

This was quintessential Trump. Rather than giving away the entire game during his speech, he phrased the line about trans mice in a way that was guaranteed to make liberals lose their minds. Trump is a master at deliberately triggering his opposition into furthering their credibility crisis.

In the weeks that followed, we learned from Elon Musk and his team at DOGE that the waste ran even deeper. According to *The Washington Times*, the Biden administration had also spent at least $64 million through the National Institutes of Health (NIH) to manipulate animals' sex organs and sexual preferences—supposedly in the name of benefiting the transgender community. This included nearly $10 million to Oregon Health and Science University to see if gay rams could be "converted" to prefer ewes through prenatal testosterone infusions and $11.2 million to Tulane University to implant testosterone-releasing capsules in female mice to study vascular health in transgender patients. Even more absurdly, NIH funneled $1.1 million into a DEI grant to overdose "trans rats" on a sex party drug.

You might wonder why "Scranton" Joe Biden, a man who often proclaimed his commonsense, middle-American roots, would fund such nonsense. One answer is that he had no idea it was going on, which seems true, in light of what we know now about his cognitive decline. But that leaves us with another, far more troubling question: *Who was in charge? And why did they want to spend so much money on transgender mice studies?*

When you look at the state of transgender science, the answer is pretty clear. Left-wing activists have been telling us for years that "gender-affirming care" is a science-backed, evidence-based course of action for people experiencing gender dysphoria. But they have a problem, which is that none of the science adds up. Every time someone conducts a literature review or a rigorous review of the science, "gender-affirming care" looks worse and worse.

In 2024, a well-respected doctor in the United Kingdom named Hilary Cass conducted the first-ever serious review of the evidence for "gender-affirming care" in kids. Among other things, she found that the evidence for medical interventions such as puberty blockers and cross-sex hormones is "remarkably weak," with "poor quality" data and "gaps in evidence" that make it impossible to draw solid conclusions about their long-term safety and efficacy. Cass stated bluntly, "We have no good evidence on the long-term outcomes of interventions to manage gender-related distress."[20]

Her report also warned that many of the studies activists cite in support of puberty blockers have flawed methodology, based on small sample sizes, short follow-up periods, and lacking in proper control groups.

But at least she was able to publish her findings. Here in the United States, that doesn't always happen. Consider that Dr. Johanna Olson-Kennedy, who conducted a similar study, refused to publish her research for fear that the data could be "weaponized" by critics of transgender ideology. Olson-Kennedy led a $9.7 million taxpayer-funded study, titled "The Impact of Early Medical Treatment in Transgender Youth," which tracked the effects of puberty blockers and cross-sex hormones on children over two years. Yet despite the massive public investment, the results have remained unpublished.

Clearly, something is wrong with our standards of evidence here. When it comes to kids, the Left is willing to completely overlook the usual scientific method, even prescribing untested off-label drugs to be used as puberty blockers so that kids won't develop properly. According to the US Food and Drug Administration (FDA), these drugs—gonadotropin-releasing hormone (GnRH) agonists—are only approved for treating prostate cancer and central precocious puberty, yet they are increasingly prescribed for gender dysphoria without long-term safety data. In fact, a study found that from 2013 to 2016, the proportion of children receiving puberty blockers for off-label indications more than doubled, from 12 percent to 29 percent.

In other words, the left-wing gender activists in the Biden administration were desperate. They'd been telling us that gender-affirming care was backed up by science, but they were lying. It's no wonder they were flailing for data to support this insane idea. That's how they ended up pumping mice full of hormones and, in one study funded by the Agriculture Department, looking at "menstrual cycles in 'transgender men.'" When the science doesn't tell them what they want to hear, they keep spending your money to find a different answer. And as honest reporters such as Abigail Shrier have shown, it's the kids who suffer.

Fortunately, the fever seems to be breaking on this issue. In March 2025, Gavin Newsom—a man whose presidential aspirations are so clear that you can practically see them from space—interviewed Charlie Kirk on his podcast and admitted that allowing men to compete in women's sports was "deeply unfair."[21] This was considered such a big story in liberal circles that *The New York Times* sent a breaking news alert about it. Things had certainly come a long way since the Biden administration had earmarked money for, among other things, a program that would "educate transgender and queer farmers on food justice and equity" in San Francisco to the tune of a few hundred thousand dollars. (This is a program, by the way, that President Trump's secretary of agriculture, Brooke Rollins, canceled in late March 2025, another commonsense rebuke of the previous administration's insanity.)

Still, the people who set up such ludicrous programs didn't just disappear when Kamala Harris lost the election. Many are firmly rooted in the federal bureaucracy, in media, and in the Democratic Party and its affiliated think tanks. They will not be giving up on the trans agenda anytime soon.

AN EASY ONE

One of the first major events of President Trump's second term was a meeting of a bipartisan group of governors at the White House on February 22, and not all of them were pleased with the man who'd just taken office.

This was especially true of Janet Mills, the governor of Maine.

A few days earlier, Governor Mills declared that she would not comply with President Trump's new executive order banning men from playing women's sports, clinging to debunked and discredited left-wing orthodoxy.

A few minutes into his remarks to the governors, Trump mentioned his executive order and said, "Is Maine here? The governor of Maine?"

"Yeah," Mills said. "I'm here."

"Are you not going to comply with it?" Trump asked.

"I'm complying with the state and federal laws," Mills fired back.

"Well, we are the federal law. You better do it. You better do it, because you're not going to get any federal funding at all if you don't. And by the way, your population, even though it's somewhat liberal (although I did very well there), your population doesn't want men playing in women's sports, so you better comply. Because otherwise you're not getting any federal funding."

"I'll see you in court," Mills said.

"Good. I'll see you in court. I look forward to that. That should be a real easy one."[22]

After ten years of Donald Trump dominating American political discourse, it's easy to overlook just how revolutionary this approach to politics is. But we shouldn't. In all of American history, there has never been a president who knows how to force an issue—and to do it in full view of the public—better than our forty-fifth and forty-seventh president. Rather than allowing this issue to be fought out through letters, newspaper op-eds, and stump speeches, Trump directly confronted those who defied his commonsense agenda. This kind of confrontation makes headlines, and it shows the American people you won't abandon them or your promises.

It also serves as yet another example of how much the second Trump administration relishes the fight, in actual court and in the court of public opinion. So it came as no surprise when, immediately following that dust-up at the White House, the administration launched an investigation into whether Maine had violated Title IX, the law that prohibits sex-based discrimination in school programs. They also referred the case to the Department of Justice for enforcement action, initiated proceedings to terminate Maine's federal K–12 education funding, and filed a federal lawsuit arguing that the state's policy discriminated against female athletes.

Forcing this issue into a courtroom is the ultimate chess move. President Trump has noticed that Democrats, for whatever reason, have willingly strapped this deeply unpopular issue to their backs. Now he's going to push them into the deep waters of the American legal system and let them sink while all of America watches. Some, I'm sure, will untie the ropes and come to their senses on this matter. But if history is any indication, most will not. Regardless of how the courts rule, Trump has drawn a beautiful, bright line on a clear political winner.

Still, it's hard to imagine even the most deranged Democrats stepping up to defend the actions of the judge who intervened in the case of male prisoners who, after being transferred back to male prisons on President Trump's orders, were "unable to access bras and women's underwear." On March 19, these lunatics were granted a preliminary injunction to keep them housed in women's prisons, where they will be free to roam among biological women at will.

And this wasn't the only case involving the trans agenda that is now moving through the court system. Another involved President Trump's executive order banning transgender troops from serving in the military. And in this case, as Fox News pointed out shortly after the decision came down, the judge has a long history of "left-wing activism and Democratic donations," having given more than $38,000 to campaign groups since 2008.

These judges are standing in the way of common sense in this country. And unlike Democratic politicians, they have immense power to stop President Trump's agenda in its tracks. As Stephen Miller, the White House deputy chief of staff, put it, the district judge who intervened in the trans prisoner case has effectively "appointed [himself] as the head of the Bureau of Prisons to nullify election results." As I review the beginning of President Trump's second term, it becomes clearer that it will stand out in history as the moment the executive branch finally took on activist judges who flex their power for political purposes. The trans issue is just one of the many that will be decided in courtrooms rather than the Oval Office.

The fight is critical: Can the president be the president if he's constantly sharing power with over six hundred individual district court judges? In his first term, Trump fought "the resistance" in the form of liberal politicians who investigated and impeached him into oblivion.

This time around, though, the resistance to Trump mostly comes from the courts, where supposedly impartial federal district court judges are clearly trying to usurp the president's authority and prevent him from governing for as long as possible.

In late June, the Supreme Court issued a landmark 6–3 ruling that significantly limits the power of federal judges to block presidential actions nationwide—a decision that emerged from challenges to President Trump's executive order ending birthright citizenship. While at the time of this writing it remains to be seen how the Court will rule on the administration's interpretation of the Fourteenth Amendment, the biggest takeaway is that President Trump scored a major victory for the will of the American people. Judges can no longer issue injunctions that prevent a presidential policy from being enforced across the entire country.

"Federal courts do not exercise general oversight of the Executive Branch; they resolve cases and controversies consistent with the authority Congress has given them," Justice Amy Coney Barrett wrote for the majority opinion. "When a court concludes that the Executive Branch has acted unlawfully, the answer is not for the court to exceed its power, too."

CHAPTER NINE

DEI Dies

"My administration has taken action to abolish all discriminatory diversity, equity, and inclusion nonsense— and these are policies that were absolute nonsense— throughout the government and the private sector."

—PRESIDENT DONALD J. TRUMP'S REMARKS TO
WORLD ECONOMIC FORUM, JANUARY 24, 2025

Democrats and Republicans don't agree on much. As someone whose job it is to argue with my political opponents on television, I know that better than just about anyone.

But there are places where we do come together. Or at least we used to. There was a time, for instance, not so long ago, when everyone agreed that racism was bad. If you picked a random person off the street and asked whether it was okay for someone to discriminate against someone else based on the color of his or her skin, that person would probably say "no." It wouldn't matter whether that person was a Republican or a Democrat.

These days, though, things are different. Republicans, in my experience, are still pretty much guaranteed to say no. Democrats, on the other hand, are more apt to pause, think for a moment, and then say something along the lines of "Well . . . what do you mean by *discriminate*? And what color is the skin of the person doing the discriminating? For that matter, what color is the skin of the person being discriminated against? And by the way, your use of 'his or her' is not gender inclusive. *Do better.*"

I'm not sure when this happened.

It might have been at the tail end of the Obama administration, when we first began hearing Democrats replace "equality" with "equity," which means something entirely different. But certainly the concept of "equity" became state religion for Democrats during the infamous "Summer of Love" in 2020, when cities across America burned during the George Floyd riots. "Antiracism" studies followed and demands for people to become "allies" began shortly thereafter. What I *do* know is that around this time, I began to hear Democrats saying things that would have sounded insane to most people just a few years earlier. *People of color cannot be racist* was one. Another was *The United States is addicted to white supremacy.*[1] (This last one comes from the X account of Katherine Maher, who is, for now at least, still the president of the taxpayer-funded National Public Radio.)

Liberals of this stripe delighted in pointing out their own racism. They posted pictures of themselves reading the latest "antiracist" textbooks, talking about them as if they were religious texts. When *The Atlantic* magazine published the antiracist writer Ta-Nehisi Coates's "The Case for Reparations," white liberals devoured it. Or at least claimed to. (The aforementioned Katherine Maher even tweeted that she stayed home from work to read it, despite later saying in congressional testimony that she did not remember reading it at all while incorrectly identifying it as a book.) One of the most famous prophets of this strange era was Ibram X. Kendi, a man whose bestseller *How to Be an Antiracist* contains the line "The only answer to past discrimination is present discrimination."[2]

In other words, it was time to discriminate against white people (as well as Asian people, if that helped) in order to make up for the sins of the past. In the opinion of the Democratic Party, this should be done at all levels of government.

The official party platform of 2024 reflected this. It called for home-buyer programs and student loan cancellation programs that would "disproportionately benefit people of color." It called for the expansion of race-based affirmative action programs, and the appointment of officials whose top priority would be "equity" in hiring, procurement, and enforcement. Under the Biden administration, this philosophy quickly became practice.[3] His first executive order directed every federal agency to conduct assessments of how they were meeting diversity, equity, and inclusion goals.

The message was clear: equality under the law was no longer the goal. Equity—meaning unequal treatment to achieve politically preferred outcomes—was. And for government agencies, their purpose was no longer to fight wars or help farmers grow crops, but instead to operationalize the "equity" agenda of the progressive left.

The policy extended to the White House itself, much to the later chagrin of Democrats everywhere. On the campaign trail, Joe Biden had strongly indicated that he would choose his vice president based on two qualifications: race and gender. After promising he would pick a woman, the far left fringes of his party pressured him to pick a woman of color. That had left him exactly one viable option. And that option was an unskilled politician who, when she ran for president herself in 2020, failed to win a single vote. Kamala Harris even once implied that Biden was racist himself during one of the Democratic primary debates!

The same thing happened when it came to the Supreme Court. During the campaign, Biden promised voters that he would nominate the first African American woman to the court, and he said it before he'd considered any candidates. That narrowed his options considerably, and it led to the nomination of Justice Ketanji Brown Jackson. When Biden announced he would choose a Supreme Court justice based on race and gender—instead of on that person's educational achievements and legal experience—he effectively minimized Jackson's qualifications, which were not insubstantial.

For the entirety of the Biden-Harris years, DEI was the official policy of the United States government. It was also, rather troublingly, the official policy of most Fortune 500 companies.

This hadn't started with Joe Biden. In some sense, it stretches back to the Civil Rights Act of 1964, which—while necessary and noble in its time—created a legal framework that allowed the federal government to punish companies for failing to meet statistical hiring targets. Over the years, those targets quietly morphed into quotas, and the threat of federal investigation became an ever-present pressure. But things kicked into high gear in a very public way during the George Floyd uprising of 2020, when it was a regular occurrence for major companies such as Nike and Target to post somber black squares on social media, issue lengthy corporate "anti-racism" manifestos, and direct employees to attend mandatory (and humiliating) diversity training.

Videos circulated online of white employees kneeling in boardrooms as part of guided "privilege" workshops. At the same time, companies like Walmart, American Express, and Lockheed Martin rolled out employee trainings that divided staff by race and taught that concepts like "rugged individualism," "perfectionism," and "objectivity" were relics of white supremacy culture. Walmart required staff to acknowledge that the United States operates as a "white supremacy system" and labeled white workers as having "internalized racial superiority" and "white supremacy thinking," while identifying qualities like individualism and objectivity as hallmarks of white supremacist culture. Lockheed Martin sent white male executives to workshops aimed at dismantling their "white male privilege," urging them to reexamine traits like a "can-do attitude" and "hard work" as culturally conditioned rather than universal truths.

By the time the 2024 election season really ramped up, Americans were fed up. Even to some Democrats, retaliatory racism didn't seem to make sense (even though they weren't allowed to speak those thoughts out loud, lest they be canceled in their workplace and social circles). It might have sounded nice in the summer of 2020 to say that we needed "present discrimination to remedy past discrimination." But in practice, things got very ugly (and very confusing) very quickly. In a case that came before the Supreme Court, the American people saw just how strange it was that many of our nation's top universities openly, and sometimes secretly, discriminated against white and Asian applicants so they could fill diversity quotas. That 2023 case, *Students for Fair Admissions v. Harvard*, overturned the Court's 2003 decision in *Grutter v. Bollinger*, which had upheld the limited use of race in admissions decisions.

In truth, this kind of discrimination has never been popular among the American people. It was an "80–20 issue" long before the phrase "80–20 issue" came into common parlance. Once, musing about how long affirmative action programs would be necessary, Supreme Court Justice Sandra Day O'Connor wrote in 2003's *Grutter* decision: "*We expect that 25 years from now, the use of racial preferences will no longer be necessary to further the interest approved today.*"[4] That prediction turned out to be almost exactly right.

Public opinion was similarly clear on this point. According to a 2023 Pew Research Center survey, 50 percent of Americans—including majorities of white, Black, Hispanic, and Asian respondents—said race or ethnicity should *not* be a factor in college admissions. Just 33 percent said it should.[5] The Court's decision in *Students for Fair Admissions* reflected that public sentiment—and signaled that the days of race-based decision-making, at least in name, were coming to a close.

Which, in early January 2025, is exactly what happened.

ROOT AND BRANCH

The twenty-first century has seen its share of stunning political developments. President Trump's second election is probably the most stunning so far, though by the time this book is published, maybe something will have taken its place. When it comes to pure policy, though, most political scientists agree that the most seismic shift in American life this century was the implementation of Obamacare in 2010. This completely revolutionized the American healthcare system, as well as the American government more generally. It dramatically expanded the federal government's role in health care, created new entitlements, imposed mandates on individuals and businesses, and sparked a decade-long debate about the limits of executive power and the reach of federal bureaucracy.

However, Obamacare's streak is now over. It ended on January 21, 2025, when President Trump signed an executive order titled "Ending Illegal Discrimination and Restoring Merit-Based Opportunity." In the plain, forceful language for which this administration had already become famous, the order reversed decades of federal policy that had normalized racial and sex-based preferences under the guise of "diversity, equity, and inclusion." It terminated affirmative action mandates for federal contractors, revoked multiple executive orders from the Clinton and Obama years, and launched a sweeping campaign to roll back DEI programs across both the public and private sectors.

Importantly, President Trump stressed in the order that DEI programs destroy national unity:

> Illegal DEI and DEIA policies not only violate the text and spirit of our long-standing Federal civil-rights laws, they also undermine our national unity, as they deny, discredit, and undermine the traditional American values of hard work, excellence, and individual achievement in favor of an unlawful, corrosive, and pernicious identity-based spoils system. Hardworking Americans who deserve a shot at the American Dream should not be stigmatized, demeaned, or shut out of opportunities because of their race or sex.[6]

If you watched the news during the first months of President Trump's second term, you might not have thought that the DEI order was the most consequential. You might not even think it was the most significant thing he signed that *day*, which also included executive orders on immigration, fossil fuels, and government transparency. But according to the journalist Christopher Caldwell, the repeal of DEI policies was indeed the most consequential policy decision of the twenty-first century. This wasn't because it marked a major shift in the attitudes of most Americans toward policies such as affirmative action. Those had been roughly the same for many years. It was because President Trump's executive order had dismantled the tangled web of DEI policies in nearly every major institution that had been gumming up the gears of government and corporate America alike.

As Caldwell wrote in a piece for Bari Weiss's *The Free Press*, most Americans don't quite understand how much their lives are touched by DEI policies. But they are. This is because DEI is not just a bunch of slogans and vague initiatives. It is a system of law that has grown so big that we can barely see it anymore. And it does not, as most people understand it, come from the Civil Rights Act of 1964. As Caldwell points out:

"Affirmative action is mentioned in the Civil Rights Act of 1964. But the program as we now understand it was launched a year later with Lyndon Johnson's Executive Order 11246. The president ordered companies and institutions doing business with the government to have activist nondiscrimination policies—and empowered officials (now consolidated in the Office of Federal Contract Compliance Programs) to enforce them . . . Executive orders don't require a democratic vote. They just lay down the rules for the executive branch, of which the president is the boss. They have the force of law within all the federal agencies, which buy and sell enormous amounts of goods and services. According to the Labor Department, Executive Order 11246 covered 20 percent of the American workforce, potentially giving the president personal leverage over the economy."[7]

For years, companies have responded to that leverage by enacting the kind of diversity policies that they believed the federal government wanted to see. So, "whenever a 'global chief diversity officer,' like Ken Barrett of GM, intoned 'diversity is our strength,' he was doing more than philosophizing. He was keeping billions of dollars of shareholder value safe from the sanctions and penalties laid out in Chapter 60 of the Code of Federal Regulations." In other words, Corporate America didn't arrive at these policies through deliberation or market testing. They were strong-armed into it by the regulatory state. For a long time, this didn't seem like a major threat. These policies were relatively mild—annoying, maybe, but manageable. You hired a few consultants. You threw in some vague HR language about "inclusion." And the lawyers signed off. Life went on.

But something changed around 2020. That was the year the regulatory scaffolding—slowly built up over decades—suddenly became infused with ideological energy. The slogans that had floated around the margins for years—"diversity is our strength," "equity over equality," "silence is violence"—were now coming straight from the top. The death of George Floyd, and the nationwide riots that followed, created a moral panic so intense that every institution, from the Ivy League to Goldman Sachs, scrambled to prove its righteousness.

That panic coincided with the rise of ESG investing—environmental, social, and governance metrics—that pushed these ideas even further into the bloodstream of corporate America. According to a report in *The New York Post*, some of the biggest players in global finance began rating companies based not on how well they served their customers or shareholders, but on how faithfully they met progressive social benchmarks.

More specifically, those asset managers outsourced the job of grading companies to activist groups like the Human Rights Campaign (HRC), which assigns what's known as a CEI, or Corporate Equality Index. The HRC, funded in part by George Soros's Open Society Foundations and run by former Obama aide Kelley Robinson, became one of the most influential institutions in American corporate life—without anyone really noticing.

As the *Post* reported: "The main categories [of the CEI score] are: 'Workforce Protections,' 'Inclusive Benefits,' 'Supporting an Inclusive

Culture,' and 'Corporate Social Responsibility and Responsible Citizenship.'" [8] A company can lose CEI points if it doesn't fulfill HRC's demand for "integration of intersectionality in professional development, skills-based or other training" or if it doesn't use a "supplier diversity program with demonstrated effort to include certified LGBTQ+ suppliers."[9]

In practice, this meant that if your company didn't host mandatory DEI training, post rainbow logos during Pride Month, or partner with LGBTQ+ vendors—even if those vendors were more expensive or less qualified—you would be docked points. And if you were docked enough, you became a target. That could mean pressure from activists, bad press, a shareholder revolt—or all three.

So what began as a bureaucratic nudge in the 1960s had, by the 2020s, become something much more coercive. Not just a system of legal compliance, but a system of ideological enforcement. Not just about representation, but about reeducation. And as this system matured, it reached every corner of American life—hiring, education, healthcare, even aviation. In some cases, it became so all-encompassing that safety itself was treated as secondary to the mandates of DEI.

Part of the underpinnings of Western Civilization are merit, excellence, hard work, creativity, effort, and individualism. The DEI regime, and those most committed to it, were a wrecking crew against the West, which they regard as inherently evil.

This moment was a gut check for our society. And by the time Donald Trump began drawing huge crowds for his 2024 campaign, the American people realized just how strange it was to hire people based on immutable characteristics such as race and gender. Even liberals who supported DEI in theory began to notice that something was seriously off with the way it had been implemented, and that there might be negative consequences to doing things this way.

The seeds of President Trump's executive order in 2025 were planted during his campaign, when voters of disparate backgrounds decided to back him because of the oppressive DEI regime that was sure to flourish even more under a Kamala Harris presidency.

THE DANGERS OF DEI

In the aftermath of the tragic fires in Los Angeles in January 2025, many people searched for answers. Some focused on the concrete causes of the fire, such as the failure of the state to have adequate water reserves. Others said that this was no time for politics. There were some people, however, who found themselves troubled by a series of videos that had been posted by the news outlet *Now This* in the years before the fire occurred.

I was one of them.

In one of these videos, a female firefighter addresses the need for greater diversity in the department. She says, "People ask me, 'Oh is she strong enough to do this,' and 'Oh, can she carry my husband out of a fire?' To which my response is usually, he got himself in the wrong place if I have to carry him out of a fire."[10]

The first time I saw it, I had to rewind and watch it again, just to make sure it was real.

Although I have never been a firefighter, I have always assumed that one of the most important things about the job is . . . well, *carrying people out of fires*. I'm aware that real firefighters probably don't do this as often as the ones on television, but I'm told by people who know what they're talking about that it is, indeed, a big part of the job. And yet this female firefighter—who, upon further inspection, turned out to be the LA Fire Department's chief of diversity and inclusion, a position that earned her just over $300,000 per year—insists that asking her to rescue a male victim is some kind of imposition.

I think most ordinary Americans would agree that firefighters—as well as airline pilots, bankers, and just about everyone else who works for a living—should get their jobs based on merit, not skin color, gender, or other characteristics over which they have no control. This sounds so basic to most people that it hardly needs saying. In school, we learned about the Civil Rights Movement and all the brave people who struggled for equality. According to Martin Luther King Jr., the most famous moral voice of that movement, people should be judged not "by the color of their skin, but by the content of their character."

It's a quote so often repeated that it risks becoming cliché—but that doesn't make it any less true. King wasn't calling for reverse discrimination or bureaucratic bean-counting. He was demanding something far more profound: equal treatment under the law. As he said in his 1963 "I have a dream" speech at the Lincoln Memorial, Black Americans had come to Washington "to cash a check," a promissory note guaranteed by the Constitution and the Declaration of Independence—a check for the same rights, the same dignity, the same opportunity afforded to every American. Not more, not less. Just the same. Equal.[11]

Somewhere along the way, that basic promise got twisted. Instead of a government that guarantees equal opportunity, we got a government that enforces equal outcomes—unless, of course, you happen to be the wrong race or sex. Instead of eliminating discrimination, DEI programs institutionalize it, treating people as representatives of a category rather than as individuals with unique talents, ambitions, and ideas. When you do this kind of thing at a bakery, for instance, the results might be negligible. A little icing dripping down the side isn't a big deal, right?

But when you start doing it in companies that can kill people, things get very scary . . . very quickly.

For a period of time at Boeing, for instance—the company that designs machines that carry thousands of people per day through the sky at high speeds, all of which rely on precision engineering to stay up— DEI initiatives came to rule. In the aftermath of a midair door panel blowout on an Alaska Airlines flight in early 2024, Elon Musk ripped the company, asking, "Do you want to fly in an airplane where they prioritized DEI hiring over your safety? That is actually happening."

He wasn't the only one sounding the alarm. A company whistle-blower told *City Journal* that Boeing had tied executive incentive compensation to inclusion goals, and that its internal target for 2022 was to ensure at least 90 percent of interview slates for manager and executive roles were "diverse." By the following year, the company raised the bar even further—mandating at least 92.5 percent of interview slates be diverse, with no indication that candidate quality or engineering experience was a factor.[12]

The horrific plane crash that occurred during the first weeks of Trump's second presidency at Reagan National Airport forced this issue back into the public domain. During a press conference at the White House, President Trump suggested, rather bluntly, that DEI hiring practices may have been at fault. Although it was too soon to know whether that was true in this specific instance, it was undeniable that under the Biden administration, the Federal Aviation Administration had racial quotas in place for hiring. According to a 2023 report in *The Washington Times*, the FAA had been using so-called biographical questionnaires to "supplement" aptitude tests—tests that had previously ensured that air traffic controller candidates actually knew what they were doing. The change wasn't about safety. It was about diversity. The goal was to increase "underrepresented" hires, even if it meant passing over highly qualified candidates who had graduated from collegiate aviation programs or scored well on objective assessments.[13]

The issue wasn't new. It dated back to the Obama-Biden years, when in 2014 the FAA abandoned its long-standing knowledge-based hiring pipeline—built on Collegiate Training Initiative programs and technical aptitude tests—and replaced it with a biographical "personality" questionnaire designed to boost demographic targets. As a result, applicants who had passed the rigorous skill-based exams were often screened out in favor of candidates who scored better on the new diversity-focused assessment. In some cases, highly qualified candidates—including racial minorities—were effectively penalized by the questionnaire, while lesser-qualified candidates benefited. The policy was so controversial that it led to a class-action lawsuit filed by about 1,000 applicants who alleged they were unfairly excluded under the new system.[14]

But the most high-profile example of DEI gone wrong came in 2023, when President Biden nominated Phil Washington to serve as FAA administrator. Washington was the CEO of the Denver International Airport but had no actual aviation experience. He was a logistics executive, not a pilot, not a controller, not a regulator. And when he was asked basic technical questions at his Senate confirmation hearing—like what causes an airplane stall?—he couldn't answer. He literally didn't know. Senator Ted Budd of North Carolina had to explain it to him.

This wasn't a trick question. It was Aviation 101. And Washington's failure to answer it wasn't just embarrassing—it was disqualifying. His nomination was withdrawn, quietly, but it was a flashing red warning light: DEI was no longer just a side project. It was deciding key federal appointments and shaping life-and-death decisions.

When the January plane crash happened, Americans had every right to ask whether DEI had played a role. President Trump did. And instead of treating it like a scandal, he treated it like a serious governing priority. Within a week, he directed the Department of Transportation to audit all FAA hiring practices, with specific instructions to eliminate any remaining DEI criteria. No more biographical questionnaires. No more racial quotas. No more social justice games.

When President Trump had the courage to raise these issues, he was, of course, savaged by Democrats and the mainstream press. But they were fair questions to ask given how pervasive DEI hiring policies were in the federal bureaucracy, especially in agencies where competence is of the utmost importance.

The bottom line is that people want to be safe. They want to know that when they put their lives in the hands of other people, which they do every time they get on an airplane, that those people were selected for their positions based on merit alone.

Once again, this is a simple issue that the Left manages to make extremely complicated. As Elon Musk once said, when you lower the standards, people are put at risk.

DRIVING THE POINT HOME

The executive order that President Trump signed on his first day in office was just the beginning of addressing this issue. In the months since, the White House has also taken aggressive steps to root out DEI ideology from every corner of the federal government—starting with the Department of Defense.

One of the first priorities was cleaning up the military's education system. Under the Biden administration, military academies were flooded with race-obsessed literature and ideology. At West Point, cadets were assigned books like *Critical Race Theory: An Introduction* and exposed to materials describing "whiteness" as structural privilege and framing Black Americans as living in "modern-day slavery in the USA." Course slides instructed cadets to consider how critical race theory applies to concepts like affirmative action, desegregation, and integration, and introduced related theories like queer theory and feminist theory as part of a social sciences curriculum. Meanwhile, the Air Force Academy trained cadets on "inclusive language," advising future officers to avoid words like "mom" and "dad" in official contexts to foster a more inclusive environment.[15] When Trump took office, all of this nonsense stopped. President Trump directed the Pentagon to purge these reading lists and curriculums, and to remove racially divisive content from professional military education. DEI officers were reassigned or fired altogether, and senior commanders were told, in no uncertain terms, to focus on readiness, not "identity."[16]

And the effect was immediate. In just a few months, it was announced that the Army had "surpassed its recruiting target for this fiscal year, exceeding a goal that was already significantly higher than it had been in the past."[17] Enlisted service members had grown tired of being told that the biggest threat to national security was "unconscious bias." They joined to fight and win wars—not sit through a PowerPoint about privilege. The Trump administration made it clear that our military should be a fighting force, not a sociology seminar. During an interview for this book, Treasury Secretary Scott Bessent said, "The highest compliment I can give President Trump is that my son wants to go to a service academy or do ROTC in college, and I would be so happy if the president were the commander in chief while he's in the service."[18]

The administration also focused on federal hiring. President Trump's Office of Personnel Management issued new guidance instructing federal agencies to abandon race- and gender-based quotas in hiring and promotion. Job postings that previously included "preferred demographics" were taken down. Positions created solely to advance DEI goals were eliminated altogether. The result has been a restoration of the basic idea that the best person should get the job. That used to be common sense. Under the Biden administration, it was controversial.

But the ripple effects didn't stop in Washington. Corporate America—long held hostage by ESG pressure and DEI shakedowns—started following suit. When the government stopped enforcing "diversity benchmarks" for federal contractors, many companies took the hint. Quietly, they began unwinding their own internal DEI bureaucracies. JP Morgan dropped racial targets for internal promotions. A major consulting firm scrapped its diversity review panel entirely. Several top law firms pulled back from using race-based fellowship programs, which had already come under legal scrutiny.

In corporate America, President Trump's election gave CEOs cover to do the right thing. The show was over and the performative BS could come to an end.

Some companies have been slower to react, still clinging to the same old talking points. But the smartest ones have realized that aligning with merit, not identity, is not only good policy, it's good business. There's a reason public trust in institutions cratered under the DEI regime. People want excellence. They want fairness. And they want to know that the person building their bridge, managing their retirement, or flying their plane is there because they're the best—not because they checked the right box.

Despite the continuing screeds heard on cable news, this is one of the most underreported but important successes of the Trump administration's second term. And it's only just beginning. DEI wasn't just a policy failure. It was a moral failure. It told Americans that their race mattered more than their effort. That their gender mattered more than their talent. That the way they looked was more important than the things they could do.

President Trump didn't just stop that message, he reversed it. He reminded Americans that we're not a nation of tribes. We're a nation of individuals. And if you're willing to work hard and play by the rules, there should be a place for you at the table, no matter what you look like or where you come from.

That's the country most people want to live in. And now, finally, we're getting back to it.

CHAPTER TEN

Trade War II

"Foreign leaders have stolen our jobs, foreign cheaters have ransacked our factories, and foreign scavengers have torn apart our once-beautiful American Dream. But it's not going to happen anymore."

—PRESIDENT DONALD J. TRUMP

On the afternoon of June 24, 2025, I traveled to the Treasury Department headquarters in Washington, DC (right next to the White House) for an interview with Scott Bessent, the former hedge fund manager who had served as the seventy-ninth United States secretary of the treasury. In a city full of career bureaucrats and political lifers, Bessent stood out—not just because he wasn't one of them, but because he was far better at what they all claimed to do: understand how the American economy actually works.

On paper, he was an unconventional pick. For decades, Bessent had been one of the most brilliant minds in high finance, building his reputation as the chief investment officer for George Soros's hedge fund, Soros Fund Management. There, he helped to engineer the famous short of the British pound on "Black Wednesday" in 1992—one of the most profitable and audacious trades in modern financial history. He later founded his own highly successful fund, Key Square Group, managing billions and delivering outsize returns. And he'd spent much of his life as a Democrat, moving comfortably in elite financial and political circles.

But like so many Americans, Bessent's faith in the old establishment had collapsed over the past decade. Watching what Democrats had done to the economy under Joe Biden—exploding deficits, punishing regulations, and rising inflation—he came to believe that Donald Trump was the only leader with the vision and courage to reverse course and actually put American workers at the center of national economic policy.

"I always wanted to serve my country," he told me that afternoon, speaking with the calm confidence of a man who understands the full machinery of the economy and knows how to fix it. "I went out on the campaign trail because I was alarmed about what was going on with the budget and the deficit . . . [I was worried] that we were going to become like Europe."

By the time Trump launched his second campaign, Bessent was one of his most trusted economic minds. He'd seen firsthand how Trump's policies had worked the first time. "The Democrats created the perfect economic storm," he said. "They went out and borrowed a huge amount of money. So they created a demand shock. Then, with all the regulation, they created supply constraints. In President Trump's first term, he created a demand shock in the private sector, through the tax bill. And the deregulation met the demand shock with supply."

The plan for the second term was to do the same thing: unleash the private sector and clear the bureaucratic wreckage left behind by the Biden years. Later, Bessent would help successfully shepherd through Congress what the president called the "big beautiful bill"—a sweeping tax and deregulation package aimed at rebuilding American industry.

The literal centerpiece of Trump's domestic agenda—the issues on which he ran and won the national election the previous November—was Bessent's baby.

And he delivered, working with Republican senators and congressmen until the last minute to get the bill to the president's desk by the Fourth of July.

But there was another critical piece of the puzzle: tariffs.

Tariffs have always been part of the American economic tradition. They predate the income tax by more than a century, first used by the federal government in the late eighteenth century to raise revenue and protect domestic industry. No one understood their purpose better than the man who designed the nation's financial system.

"Alexander Hamilton was the original tariff man," Bessent said. "And he used tariffs to raise money for the treasury because that's all there was; there wasn't an income tax. Two, to protect US industry. And President Trump has added a third leg to the stool. He uses them to negotiate."

Despite what you might have heard, this wasn't exactly an uncommon practice. For instance, on April 1, 2025, Senator Lindsey Graham introduced a sanctions bill proposing a 500 percent tariff on any country buying Russian oil—aimed squarely at China. The measure drew wide bipartisan support in the Senate. To Bessent, the contrast was telling.

"So," he said, "on behalf of the Ukrainian people, 80 US senators are willing to put 500 percent tariffs on China to keep them from buying Russian oil. But they get queasy when we put 30 percent tariffs on China to stop them from destroying US jobs and sending in the precursor chemicals for fentanyl."

That was the heart of the Trump-Bessent strategy: use every tool available—tax cuts, deregulation, and yes, tariffs—not as blunt instruments of economic punishment, but as strategic levers to restore American power.

In Bessent's telling, the so-called experts who dismissed tariffs as outdated or counterproductive had always misunderstood them. Tariffs were not just taxes on trade. They were pressure points, levers of negotiation, and, above all, a declaration of sovereignty. For decades, American presidents of both parties had ceded ground to foreign competitors and called it "free trade." Trump, Bessent said, was the first president in his lifetime to reject that orthodoxy and call the whole rigged system what it was: a raw deal for the American working class.

As we spoke that day in June, aides ran in and out of Bessent's office. The next day, the Treasury Department would announce that three major Mexico-based financial institutions—CIBanco, Intercam, and Vector—had been formally identified as primary money-laundering concerns for facilitating cartel operations and the flow of fentanyl precursor chemicals into the United States.* It was a historic move, the first use of new authorities under the Fentanyl Sanctions Act and the FEND Off Fentanyl Act, cutting off the cartels' financial lifelines by barring the institutions from accessing the US financial system. "Financial facilitators like CIBanco, Intercam, and Vector are enabling the poisoning of countless Americans," Bessent said in the announcement, which was being finalized as we spoke, "making them vital cogs in the fentanyl supply chain. Today's actions affirm Treasury's commitment to using all tools at our disposal to counter the threat posed by criminal and terrorist organizations trafficking fentanyl and other narcotics."

This was emblematic of the Trump 2.0 strategy: identifying the weak points in America's economic and security architecture and striking them directly, using tools no other administration had dared to use. It was creative, aggressive, and unapologetic—showing the world that the United States was finally willing to defend its interests without hesitation. On yet another front, America had replaced a weak president with a strong one. And the results were obvious.

---

* All three financial institutions—CIBanco, Intercam, and Vector Casa de Bolsa—denied any wrongdoing following the Treasury Department's designation. As of the initial announcement, sanctions were postponed until September 2025, allowing time for the firms to respond and potentially negotiate with US authorities.

At one point during our conversation, I noticed that Secretary Bessent had a portrait of President Abraham Lincoln behind his desk. I asked if our sixteenth president was his favorite, other than Donald Trump, of course. He said no. It was Teddy Roosevelt. "I always say President Trump is a lot like Roosevelt," Bessent told me. "Have you ever read descriptions of what it was like for someone to walk in a room and meet Teddy Roosevelt?" I had. "Teddy Roosevelt would overwhelm people. And the president can overwhelm people. I always say, if there'd been Ritalin, there would have been no Teddy Roosevelt. He stayed up all night tending butterflies. If Trump had taken Ritalin, there wouldn't have been Donald Trump."

Roosevelt's biographer Edmund Morris once wrote that America's twenty-sixth president was so explosively energetic that people "just felt innervated by being close to him." After spending decades chronicling Roosevelt's life in his celebrated multivolume biography, Morris admitted he needed to take a break after each book just to calm down, so overwhelming was Roosevelt's personality—even on the page. Having written just this one book about President Trump's astonishing first few months back in office, I have to say: I understand the feeling.

Secretary Bessent went on to tell me that under his predecessor, Janet Yellen, the office looked like the Berkeley faculty lounge: no furniture, no curtains. He enjoyed the redecorating process, and he picked out all the art himself. But for all the time he spent here, most of the action was in the Oval Office—the place members of the Trump 2.0 cabinet call "the nerve center." Speaking about the president's dynamic, off-the-cuff management style, Bessent said that meetings can often cover five or six topics at once. Having witnessed one back in February, I can attest to the truth of this.

"My job is to give the president options and outcomes," Secretary Bessent said. And he doesn't just mean on the economy. More than ever, Bessent has been dealing with matters of national security—something that makes sense, given how often the White House uses economic means to fight big national security battles.

It's a bold strategy. But if the president pulls it off, his name will go down in the history books beside George Washington, Abraham Lincoln, and Teddy Roosevelt. Before wrapping up, I asked Bessent what he wished more Americans understood about the economy. He thought for a moment before giving me a simple, yet chilling, answer.

"The status quo was about to break," he said of America's economic condition. "And it's getting fixed before we hit a crisis."

This is how they averted that economic disaster—by throwing out the old playbook and shocking the system back to life.

AVERTING DISASTER

In what amounted to the biggest reordering of the global economy in modern history, CNN reported one of President Trump's most consequential decisions this way on April 2:

"Using national emergency powers, Trump announced 10 percent tariffs on all imports into the United States, and even higher tariffs on goods from about sixty countries or trading blocs that have a high trade deficit with the US."[1]

Bam. That was the big one. There probably isn't an issue on which Trump has been more consistent than tariffs, talking about them for the last forty plus years in public life. It is perhaps his most closely held belief—that the United States has been ripped off by other countries for decades, that previous US presidents have allowed and even encouraged this imbalance, and that only tariffs can reset the global trade order and rebalance the scales in favor of the United States.

Interestingly, my first meeting with Trump in the Oval Office came just a few days after he had begun to roll out bits and pieces of his new tariff policies. On February 1, it was tariffs on Mexico, Canada, and China—10 percent on Chinese imports and 25 percent on our neighbors to the north and south. Then, on February 3, he paused this decision for thirty days but only for Canada and Mexico.

On February 4, the new Chinese tariffs went into effect and our biggest global adversary retaliated by slapping 15 percent tariffs on coal and liquefied natural gas, and 10 percent on crude oil, agricultural machinery, and large-engine cars.

On February 10, a few hours after I met with Trump, he announced steel and aluminum tariffs that were set to begin March 12, effectively giving all steel imports a 25 percent tariff and raising his 2018 aluminum tariffs to 25 percent (it was 10 percent, previously).

From there, other tariffs were announced, including on February 13, a plan for reciprocal tariffs to match what other countries charge the United States "for purposes of fairness." He indicated at the time that even allies would not be spared. This foreshadowed what was to come on April 2, which Trump billed as Liberation Day.

Appearing on CNN that afternoon at the very moment the president strode into the Rose Garden to make his global reciprocal tariff policy official, I commented that I was struck by the number of hard hats I saw in the crowd. The optics of the announcement were clear: this was for the working men and women of the United States, who have been left behind by years of bad trade deals and globalization.

"For decades, our country has been looted, pillaged, and plundered by nations near and far, both friend and foe alike," Trump said from the podium to a cheering crowd. "American steelworkers, auto workers, farmers, and skilled craftsmen—we have a lot of them here with us today—they really suffered gravely. They watched in anguish as foreign leaders have stolen our jobs, foreign cheaters have ransacked our factories, and foreign scavengers have torn apart our once beautiful American dream."[2]

There is probably no other issue on which Trump adheres less to modern Republican Party orthodoxy than his belief in the power of tariffs. From President Reagan through both Bush presidencies, the party had been run by men who believed that tariffs are taxes and that higher taxes are generally bad for the economy (although it should be noted that my old boss, Bush 43, did impose tariffs on the steel industry in a bid to court steelworkers in swing states; he left them in place for eighteen months).

And until Trump in 2016, there were no Republican candidates running on a tariff strategy. In fact, there is no shortage of video of GOP senators and candidates slamming tariffs as a terrible idea.

In his first term, Trump did levy some tariffs—especially on China—but didn't go all in on a global strategy. Still, there was much hand wringing at the time about what Trump was doing to China. Nobody thought Trump would actually do it, and no American political leader dared touch China; instead, the opposite was true. The political consensus was that China, which is a terrible business partner for many reasons, must be hugged ever tighter instead of kicked in the you know what.

That all changed on April 2.

"Our country and its taxpayers have been ripped off for more than fifty years, but it is not going to happen anymore. It's not going to happen. In a few moments, I will sign a historic executive order instituting reciprocal tariffs on countries throughout the world. Reciprocal. That means they do it to us and we do it to them. Very simple. Can't get any simpler than that," Trump said.[3]

What Trump was announcing was perhaps the biggest attempt at a political DNA transplant in modern American history. He took a political party that had been openly hostile to tariffs for decades and in one fell swoop implanted a new, pro-tariff operating system.

"April 2, 2025, will forever be remembered as the day American industry was reborn, the day America's destiny was reclaimed, and the day that we began to make America wealthy again," Trump said.

While this all may have sounded strange coming from a Republican, Trump was not the first modern presidential candidate to assert that tariffs were the only way to level the global playing field.

In 1992, running as an independent for president, Texas billionaire Ross Perot captivated the nation with his well-funded if quixotic bid for the White House. A key feature of his campaign was slamming the North American Free Trade Agreement (NAFTA)—he would talk about "a giant sucking sound" that Americans would hear as businesses closed shop in the States and moved to Mexico.

Perot's platform on tariffs was simple: "Where tariff barriers exist, the rates should be roughly equivalent. Where the rates are not equivalent, we should push for it."

I bring up Perot because I have often thought of his runs in 1992 and 1996 as templates for what Trump successfully pulled off in 2016. A colorful, independent-minded wealthy businessman who presented as a Republican on many issues but was not afraid to buck the conservatives on a big-ticket idea like tariffs.

Though he captured the Republican Party in 2016 and is one of the strongest party bosses in the history of the GOP, I've often thought of Trump as our first truly independent president. He isn't hemmed in by party edicts or apparatchiks, and he doesn't compromise his own views simply because the party has always done things or thought of policy a certain way.

BEAUTIFUL TARIFFS

At first, the sentence came with no qualifier.

"*Tariff*," President Trump used to say, "is the most beautiful word in the dictionary." He said it during campaign speeches and roundtable events with business leaders. He said it during interviews about what he would do to fix the economy after he took back the White House. Then, one evening late in the campaign, he said it to an audience that included many evangelical Christians. The line got some lighthearted pushback, and by the time he finally took office, President Trump had "tariff" ranked as the fourth most beautiful word in the English language. The top three, he said, were "God," "love," and "religion."[4]

The guy certainly knows how to adjust his message. He also knows how to get everyone onboard with ideas that would have sounded insane to most Republicans just a few years ago. When I was working for President George W. Bush, we certainly loved God and religion. Tariffs, on the other hand, we weren't so sure about. No one was. In the opinion of most economists and politicians, high tariffs were a relic of another age. In fact, President Trump's inspiration for loving tariffs is drawn from a predecessor, William McKinley. As a member of the House of Representatives in 1890, the then Ohio congressman fought to enact what amounted to nearly 50 percent tariffs for many imported products, which caused sharp price increases for average Americans (in fairness to McKinley, some products like sugar, molasses, tea, and coffee saw tariffs eliminated under the law). The tariffs helped American manufacturers but were unpopular with working-class people who paid higher prices.

"President McKinley made our country very rich through tariffs and through talent. He was a natural businessman," Trump has said. The president believes that the United States was at its wealthiest "from 1870 to 1913. That's when we were a tariff country. And then they went to an income tax concept."[5]

For McKinley's Republican Party, there was some instant political backlash to the 1890 tariff law. Republicans took a bath in that November's midterm as Democrats won huge majorities, and McKinley himself was defeated for reelection (a loss that was also aided by some good old-fashioned Democratic gerrymandering on top of the national mood).

But all was not lost for McKinley. He was elected governor of Ohio in 1891 and again in 1893, and then president of the United States in 1896. His presidential election ushered in a political realignment, with Republicans mostly controlling national politics until 1932.

Combing through years of public statements and in conversations with President Trump, it is obvious that his belief in tariffs is unshakable.

While the Republican Party of McKinley's era was protectionist and pro-tariff, that position had long since been abandoned as the GOP became the party of lower taxes and free trade. Before Trump, the ideological godfather of the Republican Party was President Ronald Reagan, who railed against protectionism and believed the Smoot-Hawley Tariff of 1930 caused the Great Depression. In fact, in a radio address in 1988, Reagan said he voted for Democrat Franklin D. Roosevelt in 1932 because he "opposed protectionism and called for the repeal of that disastrous tariff."[6]

But on this issue, Trump was willing to defy modern Republican orthodoxy. In his first term, he imposed some tariffs on China and in certain industries (notably steel, aluminum, and washing machines) but was obviously held back to some degree by advisors and a party that wasn't yet ready for the full Trump tariff worldview.

By 2025, even though opposition to tariffs lingered in the hearts of many Republicans like Senator Rand Paul of Kentucky, who fought Trump publicly on the issue, most elected Republicans had no appetite to fight Trump on the matter.

"[This] is what is required, in my mind, to start the process of repairing and restoring the American economy," House Speaker Mike Johnson said about halfway through the president's first one hundred days, amid a domestic stock market dip that had erased all the gains made since Trump's reelection. "I believe the strategy is going to work . . . I think you got to give it time . . . Give the president a chance to have his policies play out," Johnson said.

And in time, the stock market did recover. By July 4, the S&P 500 and Nasdaq Composite had broken all-time record highs, and the Dow Jones Industrial Average was back over 44-thousand. By summer, April's panic over the tariffs had given way to cautious optimism over Trump's strategy and in the resilience of the US economy.

The day I first met Trump in the Oval Office I recall him discussing tariffs as a way to deal with several of the international issues at hand. "Tariff the hell out of them," Trump said. And when we discussed the Reagan painting he had just hung on the wall, he said, "Boy, was he terrible on trade."

The tariff issue, politically, is one of the most fascinating policy debates of the Trump era. While old-guard Republican pooh-bahs continue to hate the idea, Trump believes the use of tariffs to stimulate manufacturing growth in the United States matches the desires of his new populist, working-class, blue-collar coalition.

And there's evidence that he's right. CNBC reported on March 10 that "The head of the United Auto Workers has become an unexpected ally for President Donald Trump's plans for North American tariffs . . . Shawn Fain, who was boisterous about his disdain for Trump during the president's campaign, is openly voicing approval of the tariffs, which include 25% levies on automobiles and supporting parts. 'Tariffs are an attempt to stop the bleeding from the hemorrhaging of jobs in America for the last 33 years,' Fain said Sunday on ABC News's *This Week*, referring to the implementation of the North American Free Trade Agreement in 1992. 'Tariffs aren't the end solution, but they are a huge factor in creating, fixing the problem.'"[7]

The fear was that tariffs were blunt instruments. They could do serious damage if wielded incorrectly. They are, in so many words, government-imposed duties on imported goods, designed to protect domestic industries by increasing the cost of foreign products. By altering price incentives, tariffs can influence trade balances, shift supply chains, and serve as leverage in economic negotiations. However, they also risk triggering retaliatory measures, raising consumer prices, and distorting market efficiencies. I say "risk" because, for a while, it was mostly theoretical. No one was quite sure what would happen if we went back to an economic era in which tariffs were used as a common weapon in trade wars.

Then came President Trump, who sees tariffs as more than just a protectionist measure. He sees them, as did Perot, as a matter of fairness—leveling the playing field.

During his first term, he worked with advisors such as Peter Navarro and Larry Kudlow to rebalance our trade deals and craft aggressive economic policies. This was the fulfillment of a promise Donald Trump had made to the United States years ago, long before he'd ever voiced presidential aspirations. Right now, you can look up old videos of Trump speaking with the likes of Larry King and David Letterman on late-night television. (He was, you'll find, beloved by the media industry right up until the moment he won the White House in 2016.) In all these videos, no matter what else comes up, the future president discusses our imbalanced trade relationships. Speaking with Larry King in 1987, he said, "If the United States were a corporation, it would be bankrupt. It's losing $200 billion a year. For years now, it's been losing that. I believe it's very important that we have free trade, but we don't have free trade right now because if you want to go to Japan or you want to go to Saudi Arabia or various other countries, it's virtually impossible for an American to do business in these countries."[8]

Many years later, during a political speech he gave in 2011, President Trump outlined a plan for taxing China, as well as other countries he believed were "ripping us off." Speaking to the crowd in a toned-down version of the freewheeling, off-the-cuff style for which he'd later become famous, he said, "It's so easy. I'd drop a twenty-five percent tax on China. But it's really the messenger that's important." (Here, Trump slips into an impersonation of a meek, terrified man, all shaky voiced and nervous.) "I could have someone say, '*Uh, we're going to tax you twenty-five percent . . .*' Or, you could have a different guy, and I could say . . . "—back to the normal voice, one finger raised in a tough posture—"Listen you mother-fuckers, we're going to tax you twenty-five percent."[9]

And the crowd went nuts, as they would so many thousands of times over the next few decades.

During his first term, Trump levied tariffs on China, addressing long-standing issues such as intellectual property theft and trade imbalances. This bold move led to the "Phase One" trade deal, compelling China to commit to purchasing more American goods, thereby strengthening American industries and safeguarding jobs.

He also imposed tariffs on Japan, aiming to rectify trade disparities and support domestic producers. Recognizing the importance of the US market, Japan engaged in negotiations, resulting in agreements that opened their markets to more American agricultural products. This not only benefited American farmers but also reinforced fair trade principles, ensuring a more balanced economic relationship between the two nations.

Joe Biden, who ran for office promising to undo every single thing his predecessor had done, left some of Trump's tariffs in place. In some cases, he even *increased* them. In September 2024, the Biden administration quietly moved to finalize tariff hikes on key Chinese imports, including electric vehicles, solar cells, batteries, critical minerals, steel, and aluminum. The new tariff rate on Chinese-made electric vehicles shot up to 100 percent, while tariffs on solar cells doubled to 50 percent.

The Biden administration also raised tariffs to 25 percent on a range of other strategically important imports, from ship-to-shore cranes to face masks—a clear continuation, and even escalation, of the trade policies set by Donald Trump. They also introduced new limits on foreign goods entering the US tariff-free under the "de minimis" rule, which had allowed shipments valued at $800 or less to avoid tariffs. The vast majority of these exempted shipments had been coming from China, effectively allowing Chinese companies to sidestep Trump-era tariffs. By tightening the rule, the Biden administration further restricted Chinese imports, reinforcing the protectionist approach it once criticized. It's no wonder that when the Biden administration announced these rules, they usually did it through one of the administration's trade representatives rather than a big ceremony at the White House.

By the time President Trump got up in front of the crowd at the Capitol One Arena and called "tariff" the fourth-most beautiful word in the English language, though, there was serious speculation about whether he'd really kick things into the high gear he'd promised on the campaign trail. After all, we had warnings from several economists, even deeply conservative ones who supported Trump, that tariffs could lead to a great deal of pain for American consumers, who would, they said, ultimately pay the higher prices that resulted from import taxes.

Part of the Trump plan is to stimulate new investment in the United States (you pay no tariffs if you make your product here!) and some early indications are positive. Even media outlets that aren't exactly keen to hand President Trump wins have been forced to print headlines announcing that companies such as Apple, Mercedes-Benz, Eli Lily, and others have decided to build facilities in the United States.

On June 26, GE Appliances announced it would invest $490 million in its existing Kentucky plant, creating 800 new jobs. The company's CEO, Kevin Nolan, said the reshoring effort "aligns with the current economic and policy environment."[10]

And in a more precise point, GE Appliances executive Lee Lagomarcino told CBS News: "This was the right time to strike on the business opportunity given the environment with tariffs."[11]

Trump's strategy has made fools of many Democrats who said nothing when Biden kept or raised tariffs, but outright predicted calamity when Trump made his tariff announcements. Kentucky Governor Andy Beshear, an ambitious Democrat exploring a 2028 presidential run, told MSNBC that Trump's tariffs "are going to make life that much more difficult."[12] He then called the tariffs "the Trump tax on the American people."

But like a rooster taking credit for the sunrise, Beshear personally announced GE's job creation news while conveniently omitting Trump's role in it. If it hadn't been for Trump's tariffs, the GE news would not have happened when it did.[13]

Of course, there has been other coverage that isn't nearly as kind. The left-wing media's reporting on President Trump's economic policies has followed what's known in political circles as "The Erickson Rule." Named for my friend who invented it, the brilliant radio talk-show host and political commentator Erick Erickson, the rule states as follows: *The press focuses on policy beneficiaries when Democrats are in charge and policy victims when Republicans are in charge.*[14]

Once you have this rule in your head, you'll begin finding examples everywhere. Take a look at the front page of *The New York Times* or *The Washington Post* from any day during Joe Biden's presidency, for instance, and you're apt to see at least two stories on each profiling the people who benefited from his economic policies. My hat goes off to the journalists who wrote those stories, by the way, because their subjects couldn't have been easy to find. I can't imagine having my assignment in the morning be: "*Go find someone who's happy that a gallon of milk now costs $75.*" But somehow these people always managed to pull it off. *Area woman grateful purse now weighs less thanks to Biden economic policies.*

Take a look at these same websites now, though, and you're more likely to find stories about all the people President Trump is supposedly harming. Again, the journalists involved will search high and low until they find suitable victims, even if they have to check under the rug and in the drawers before anyone turns up. Take the following article from *The Washington Post*, posted by Erick Erickson himself on X:

"He bet his life savings on paper straws. Trump may destroy his business."

The president says paper straws "don't work," setting off a wave of turmoil for small manufacturers around the country.

The paper straw, Guy Spinelli was sure, would be the way of the future.

After 50 years toiling in the country's paper mills, the 75-year-old plunked his life savings into creating a "24 hours strong" straw that he manufactures in Woodstock, Illinois, and sells to more than 1,000 restaurants, bars, coffee shops, and casinos.

But now, two years in, Spinelli says the party is over. President Donald Trump's executive order last month calling to "end the use of paper straws" dealt a swift, decisive blow to his business, Boss Straw. Orders have stalled, even though the action only stopped purchases of paper straws by the federal government. Instead of selling $800,000 worth of straws this year, Spinelli fears it'll be one-tenth of that.[15]

Of course, even with the normal negative media coverage, it must be acknowledged that tariffs might lead to negative consequences for Americans, at least for a little while (something Trump himself has acknowledged). The prices of many household goods might go up. So might the prices of homes, cars, and consumer electronics. President Trump has said that he's willing to take that pain if it means convincing enough companies to return to the United States to make things at home. For Trump, the first hundred days was a launch pad for a long-term structural change in the American economy. And by summer, there was strong statistical evidence that it was paying off for American citizens. By early July, the Bureau of Labor Statistics showed that native-born American workers had gained two million jobs since Trump had taken office, whereas foreign born workers had lost 543,000 jobs.[16]

As of this writing, he has some allies. In a recent piece for *Breitbart*, the outlet's economics editor John Carney explained that President Trump's approach to tariffs might not be as strange as the media has led you to believe. The core insight of "optimum tariff theory," as he calls it, is:

"When a country is big enough, it can influence world prices. The United States is not a small, open economy. We are the world's largest buyer. When we buy less of something, the world notices. Prices move.

"Now imagine we put a tariff on imports. That's just a tax at the border. It raises the domestic price of a foreign good. As a result, we buy less of it. But if we're a major share of global demand for that product—steel, semiconductors, autos, solar panels, whatever—the global price starts to fall. The country selling it can't easily find other buyers. Supply outstrips demand. So, prices drop.

"In this case, the tariff doesn't just make the product more expensive at home. It pushes down its world price, so we end up paying less for it than we would without the tariff. We give up some volume of trade, yes—but what we do trade, we trade on better terms. This is what economists call a terms-of-trade gain."[17]

As of this writing, the United States government is in the midst of historic negotiations with many nations, all of which are set to reshape the global marketplace in a serious way. We don't know what's going to happen in the future. A trade deal with the United Kingdom was announced in May, and even the beginnings of a deal with China was announced as well.

But I do know that Donald Trump was put on this Earth to make deals, and he had set in motion a situation where he needed to make a bunch of them in the months ahead.

LIBERATION DAY

During the first months of President Trump's administration, after a few minor moves on tariff policy, the aides I had been speaking with in the White House began telling me to wait for April 2.

That was the date, they assured, me, that everything was going to change.

By late March, I had begun hearing that this date would be called "Liberation Day," and that it would include the announcement of tariffs not just on China, Mexico, and Canada, but *every single one* of the countries the United States had been trading with for years. There was speculation about the exact rates in the media. Some said the tariffs could reach 100 percent on some countries; others suspected that each rate would be unique.

In the end, I decided to hold off. If I had learned anything about covering the Trump administration during its first mile-a-minute months, it was that things could change at the drop of a hat.

And they did.

On April 2, 2025 (a date Trump selected so people wouldn't think it was some kind of April Fool's joke), President Trump strode onto a stage in the Rose Garden with a chart. By this point, his affinity for charts was well known around the building. If he was going to go out and explain something to the American people, he wanted to have something he could point to, and he wanted to make sure everything he was pointing to was something everyone in the country could understand.

This hadn't been easy. After arduous calculations, the result was a flat 10 percent baseline tariff applied to virtually all imported goods, with additional country-specific rates layered on top for major trading partners. For example, China's total tariff exposure reached 145 percent after combining the new measures with existing Trump-era duties. Mexico and Vietnam saw additional rates of 35 to 46 percent, depending on the category of goods. The administration's formula also included nontariff barriers that effectively blocked or at least discouraged US imports. The idea was simple: match them, country by country, with the same kind of economic pressure they had been applying to us for decades.

The press melted down, pointing out (correctly) that this was unlike anything that an American president had ever attempted. On CNN, I was assailed by hosts and colleagues daily: Hadn't Trump campaigned on lower prices? Isn't this just chaos with no real plan? What about the stock market? Isn't Trump sacrificing our relationships with traditional allies?

My points to them were the same ones I had been making for months. President Trump had promised to enact tariffs on the campaign trail, and now he was doing that. It wasn't as if he had talked like Milton Friedman on the campaign trail and then suddenly turned into the tariff guy on Inauguration Day. And he wasn't going in without a plan. Whether that plan was to bring countries to the table or to stick with some of the tariffs to try to reap the economic benefits, clearly there was something going on here. And it would take time to play out.

As it turned out, the selection of an economic team had been enormously important to President Trump during the transition. For weeks, newspapers and political newsletters were crammed with stories about whom the president might select as his treasury secretary. For a while, it appeared certain that it would be Howard Lutnick; then, almost out of nowhere, came Scott Bessent, whose comments to me opened this chapter.

In an interview with Tucker Carlson that ran shortly after President Trump announced his Liberation Day agenda, Secretary Bessent spoke at length about those lessons. Turning to tariffs, he said:

> I think we have to try this. And I have a high confidence ratio it's going to work . . . The good news is, we have President Trump's previous term, when everyone said none of this was going to work: "Oh, the China tariffs are going to do this. They're going to cause inflation." They didn't. "This is going to hurt working-class Americans." Well, guess what? Working-class Americans—hourly workers—did better than supervisory workers. The bottom 50% of households—their net worth increased faster than the top 10% of households. I'm not happy with what's going on in the market today, but the distribution of equities across households? The top 10% of Americans own 88% of equities. Eighty-eight percent of the stock market. The next 40% owns 12%. The bottom 50% has debt. They have

credit card bills. They rent their homes. They have auto loans. And we've got to give them some relief."[18]

Much like President Trump himself, Scott Bessent did not need the headaches that come with accepting a high-level position in public service. He had plenty of money and prestige already. I'm sure that the positions he took—which, inevitably, caused some volatility in markets—did not make him many friends among his former colleagues on Wall Street. But he recognized that the media's fixation on Wall Street did not adequately reflect the concerns of working people. In the words of Larry Kudlow, who spoke to Fox News during the worst of the stock market chaos, "the elevated role of Scott Bessent . . . is very reassuring to markets. He's a market favorite . . . He's a brilliant market strategist. I think the Bessent factor is real."

Democrats, as it turned out, used to think the same thing. As soon as President Trump's tariffs were announced, videos surfaced on X of Chuck Schumer, Bernie Sanders, and many others extolling the virtues of tariff policy in Congress. As Elizabeth Warren put it recently, tariffs are "an important tool in our economic toolbox."[19] During his 2008 campaign, Barack Obama gave a speech in which he endorsed an America First foreign policy. After describing the devastation that occurred when NAFTA shipped jobs overseas, Obama said, "That's what happens when the American worker doesn't have a voice at the negotiating table, when leaders change their positions on trade with the politics of the moment, and that's why we need a president who will listen to Main Street, not just Wall Street; a president who will stand with workers not just when it's easy, but when it's hard."[20] Back then, of course, Democrats claimed to be the party of hardworking Americans, painting Republicans as the party of Wall Street. This, clearly, is no longer the case. During those first tense days, President Trump rebuffed the Wall Street constituency many times in favor of holding strong on tariffs.

As an aside, this is yet another example of the worst part of Trump Derangement Syndrome. As Trump rolled out his tariff policies,

Democrats were falling all over themselves to leap in front of television cameras to extol the virtues of free trade and lower taxes! For decades the Democratic Party had advocated for higher corporate tax rates and aggressive tariffs. But when Trump does it—they immediately abandon their old views and reflexively oppose it. I quipped on CNN that Trump should embrace this new spirit of free markets and lower taxes by calling for a zeroing out of the capital gains tax and a slashing of the corporate income tax rate to see if any Democrats would take him up on it.

Democratic criticism of the tariff policy seems ridiculous, given their previous statements and positions. Once again, Trump proved that Democrats stand for nothing other than: if Trump is for it, I'm against it.

In the days following April 2, countries clamored for Trump's attention to renegotiate their trade arrangements with the US. President Trump's book *The Art of the Deal* once again climbed the bestseller lists, presumably as leaders of foreign countries wondered how to go about negotiating new trade agreements with the United States. As an olive branch, President Trump announced a ninety-day pause on tariffs just a few days after Liberation Day, signaling that at least some of the new rates might not be in place by the time this book comes out (China was not included in the pause, and in fact was hit with additional tariffs beyond what was announced on April 2). A White House aide told CNN that President Trump "loves this shit," referring to the hectic nature of the world economic environment. The trade war, according to the same aide, "is like air for him."

The time for cutting deals, it seems, has finally come.

According to Stephen Miller, the most important policy advisor in the Trump White House, the fight will be long, but the United States will emerge victorious. Speaking to Fox News in mid-April, he said, "History will record that the actions President Trump has taken in recent days were the beginning of saving the West from complete economic domination by another power."

News anchors at my home network went out into the field to ask working-class Americans what they thought of the tariffs. I'm sure the answers they got were not what they had been expecting.

"Well," said one man in a green hat, "I feel like for years, we've been getting ripped off. And I want to make it fair, zero-zero. Trump was up front about it. We're gonna hurt some now." Another woman said, "Aren't the other countries starting to come around? I really believe that." When the anchor asked, "So you have faith in President Trump?" the woman didn't hesitate before answering.

"Yes," she said. "I do."

As I waded through the crowd at Trump's rally in Michigan on April 29, I asked several of his supporters about the tariffs. Were they worried? Not a single one said yes. And every one of them told me they trusted Trump to do the right thing and cut the right deals.

CONSERVATIVE COLLISIONS

Sometimes I like to imagine what it might be like to get in a time machine and go back to the early 2000s, when I was still working in the Bush White House. I wonder what kind of reaction I would have gotten if I walked into the Eisenhower Executive Office Building and told people that: (a) Donald Trump, the billionaire real estate developer, had just become president for the second time, and (b) his economic policy largely revolved around the kind of protectionist tariffs that were last used by President William McKinley in the late 1800s.

Probably startled disbelief followed by a forced trip to the White House medical unit.

Of all the things I could have told them—for instance, that one of the guys who founded PayPal now regularly shot rockets into space and worked in a semi-official capacity with President Trump to slash government costs—the tariffs might have surprised them the most. By the early 2000s, when I really got into professional Republican politics, you tended to encounter the word "tariff" in history books more than position papers.

At the time, we were all about free markets. We believed that if trade barriers were removed, capital and labor would naturally flow to their most efficient uses, resulting in higher productivity, lower costs, and more innovation. We believed that cheaper imports would leave American consumers with more disposable income, which they would then spend in other sectors of the economy, creating new jobs to replace the ones that disappeared. And we believed that America, as the world's dominant economy, had little to fear from competition—our workers were the most productive, our businesses the most innovative, and our entrepreneurs the most resilient. And we believed that the free flow of goods around the world would carry with them the free flow of American values.

For the most part, this worked. It certainly raised the gross domestic product (GDP) of this country and made many consumer goods more affordable than they'd been before. Anyone who doesn't believe it need only look at the prices of televisions, computers, and clothing in the early 2000s and compare them to the prices of those same items today. According to a study in the National Bureau of Economic Research, inflation-adjusted prices for electronics fell by over 80 percent between 1995 and 2015, thanks in large part to global supply chains and foreign manufacturing. Meanwhile, industries like agriculture and tech, where the US had a comparative advantage, saw export growth that created enormous wealth.

But the effects of free trade haven't always been positive. For some people, they've been disastrous.

You don't have to spend much time in places like Ohio or Pennsylvania to see it. The boarded-up factories, the gutted small towns, the people who used to work on assembly lines and now cobble together a living in retail or gig work—if they can find work at all. We told them that free trade would lift all boats. And for a while it seemed to.

But what we failed to see—or perhaps refused to see—was that the benefits weren't distributed evenly. It turns out, the rising tide lifted some boats into the stratosphere while others were left taking on water. Whole industries, particularly in manufacturing, were hollowed out as companies chased cheaper labor overseas. Between 2000 and 2010, the US lost more than 5 million manufacturing jobs, many of them disappearing after China entered the World Trade Organization in 2001. It wasn't just that jobs left, it was that nothing replaced them. The people who had spent decades working those jobs, who thought they had a stable middle-class life, suddenly found themselves stranded. In theory, free trade was supposed to create new jobs to replace the ones that disappeared. In practice, that didn't always happen. A factory worker in Dayton, Ohio, couldn't just pack up and move to Silicon Valley to start coding software. A guy who'd spent twenty years making car parts in Michigan couldn't suddenly transition into finance in Manhattan. And so, when Trump came along in 2016 and said "The system is rigged, and I'm going to bring those jobs back," a lot of people felt heard and seen for the first time in a very long time.

In 2019, American journalist Batya Ungar-Sargon traveled around the country for a few months and spoke with some of the people who'd been hit hard by unchecked globalization and other policies pushed by elites in both parties. She spoke with truck drivers, textile workers, and factory foremen who'd been laid off or had their hours cut when manufacturing jobs began being shipped overseas in the early 2010s. Some of the stories are heart-wrenching. Most of the people she interviewed for her book *Second Class: How the Elites Betrayed America's Working Men and Women* hadn't had a voice in national politics for some time—at least not until Donald Trump, who put them at the center of his worldview, his rhetoric, and, ultimately, the coalition that delivered him the White House.

Among other things, Ungar-Sargon's book argued that even while corporate profits, labor productivity, and our nation's GDP skyrocketed between 1965 and 2020, working-class wages stagnated, barely moving more than a few percentage points in more than sixty years. According to Ungar-Sargon, "a number of factors played a role. Before 1970, the biggest sector of the U.S. economy was manufacturing; a quarter of our nation's wealth was once generated there, where workers got great health care, excellent wages, and a pension. Fast forward to 2022 and the biggest share of the U.S. economy—one-fifth of it—is in finance, real estate, and insurance, parts of the economy that make money off Wall Street speculation rather than production and which cut the American worker out of the picture. Manufacturing, meanwhile, makes up just 11 percent of today's economy."[21]

My childhood is marked by a few core memories, none more vivid than my father and stepmother living through the undulations of being American factory workers in the 1980s and 1990s. I remember my father losing his job when the local textile plant closed in Dawson Springs, Kentucky. I remember his wife (my stepmother) being hired by the Goodyear Tire and Rubber plant in nearby Madisonville, Kentucky. I remember her being laid off and recalled over and over. During her layoffs, she cleaned houses and worked overnights at a gas station. I remember that plant closing and then both of them being hired by Goodyear in faraway Union City, Tennessee, where they drove 107 miles each way to get to work every night.

I remember the economic anxiety of living in a household where your parents were under constant threat of being laid off. I remember those layoffs lasting what seemed like excruciating lengths. I remember my dad taking a job at the garbage dump (the "convenience center," we called it).

And I remember sitting around the kitchen table with them during those long stretches being acutely aware of the stress and strain of raising kids in a world that seemed to chew up and spit out regular, working-class folks like Jeff and Sherry Jennings.

Incidentally, my dad was a huge Bill Clinton guy. The biggest I knew. He was a Democrat, like his father before him. Morton Jennings was a New Dealer and my dad believed in unions and the Clintons.

Later, he would become the first guy to tell me that Donald Trump would be the next president. And he's probably more emblematic of the shift in Republican Party constituencies than any man I know—working-class union guys pushed away by a Democratic Party that catered to elites, effetes, and forgot about the working men and women of middle America.

Donald Trump, on the other hand, had not forgotten. And when it came time to select his team for a second term, he turned to advisors who also hadn't forgotten. Rather than allowing Wall Street to dictate the policy moves, these people kept working men and women in mind. They realized that *something* needed to change, and they believed that tariffs were the best instrument to change things. The situation we were in under Joe Biden was a ticking time bomb. The government had run up debt without any plan to pay it back. As Scott Bessent put it during the early months of the administration, a crisis was possible, but it would almost certainly avert a much worse crisis down the line. Traditional conservatives, many of whom I like and respect, would respond that manufacturing isn't going to come back to the United States, and we probably wouldn't want those kind of jobs anyway. They'd respond that we'd rather have a high-tech, service-based economy where we lead the world in software, biotechnology, and financial services. They'd argue that economic progress means moving up the value chain, focusing on intellectual property rather than industrial production, and ensuring that Americans work in high-paying, high-skill jobs instead of standing on factory floors. They'd point out that, despite all the nostalgia for manufacturing, the sector is more automated than ever, meaning that even if companies did return production to the US, the number of jobs created would be a fraction of what they were in the past.

But these people have been in charge for a long time. They controlled the Republican Party for a long time, and some people were dissatisfied with that. Now, President Trump has brought a new contingent of American voters under the GOP tent, and he has not abandoned them just because he's a lame duck president with no more elections to win. If nothing else, the tariff fight is proof of President Trump's ability to bring together disparate factions of the new Republican Party. The GOP is perhaps the most ideologically diverse party in the history of the United States. Because Trump is something of an independent and even nonideological on many matters, he attracts a wide range of supporters who wouldn't normally be grouped together.

Of course, tariffs remain a divisive issue. But with large investments flooding in, the Trump White House will continue to have a story to tell—one of an administration that is bringing jobs back instead of outsourcing them around the world. In fact, the White House was touting in April a chart showing more announced investments since the beginning of Trump's second term than were made during all four years of Biden's administration.

Since the Obama years, there's been a pervasive and corrosive view on the American left—adopted by the media—that the United States is not exceptional. That we are just another country, like any other. In Trump's opinion, this worldview has allowed the United States to be taken advantage of in many ways, but especially on trade. He doesn't understand why we have to kowtow to Botswana, Canada, or China, especially when that means leaving American workers behind.

If Trump has proven anything, it is that he believes the United States is exceptional. That we do stand alone, and for good reason. And that we ought to throw our weight around if it means advantaging the American people.

More than any president in my lifetime, Trump has expanded the definition of "Republican" so that it includes people who would have never thought of themselves as GOP'ers until Trump came along and invited them in. With that kind of coalition, amazing things can happen.

THE TRUMP EFFECT

As I write and finish this book in the summer of 2025, I must acknowledge that the end result of Trump's tariff policy won't be known for quite some time. What the president is proposing will take time to work, both economically and politically. The question as I finish this manuscript endures: How much leash will the American people give President Trump to see this tariff policy through? Trump himself has acknowledged that some short-term pain will come from the decision in the form of higher prices and stock market undulations.

But the picture is also coming into sharper focus.

Just one hundred days into his second term, President Trump has presided over one of the most staggering investment booms in American history. Trillions in US-based investments have been announced since his return to the White House—investments that are projected to create hundreds of thousands of jobs and reshape the American economic landscape for years to come. Companies are building, expanding, and hiring in every corner of the country: IBM is investing $150 billion in US-based operations; Thermo Fisher is pouring $2 billion into manufacturing and innovation; Merck is constructing a $1 billion biologics plant in Delaware. And that's just the beginning.

"Roughly forty years ago, President Trump wrote the international bestseller *The Art of the Deal*," Doug Burgum told me. "This term, he is delivering the sequel in real time as he negotiates historic America First deals with countries from around the world."[22]

Apple and NVIDIA have each announced $500 billion investments in American technology and infrastructure. Johnson & Johnson is investing $55 billion in R&D and manufacturing. Roche, Novartis, Hyundai, Amgen, GE Aerospace, and dozens more have committed billions to new domestic projects. Foreign governments, too, are getting in on the action: Japan has pledged $1 trillion in US investment, Saudi Arabia $600 billion, and the United Arab Emirates a jaw-dropping $1.4 trillion.

The world is watching this resurgence with renewed respect—and a healthy dose of self-interest. In the new Trump economy, you can either partner with America and benefit from her strength, or you can get left behind. Tariffs may bring short-term uncertainty, but the long-term signal is clear: the United States is once again the most attractive place on Earth to build, invest, and grow.

And it's not just economic leverage that's changing. What the president is doing—through trade policy, tax incentives, and his relentless focus on reshoring American industry—is remaking the geopolitical order itself. Countries that once treated economic relationships with the US as transactional are now reconsidering the value of long-term alignment. What began with tariffs and America First rhetoric is maturing into a durable realignment in which global capital increasingly flows toward strength, stability, and fairness.

On May 8, 2025, President Trump and British prime minister Keir Starmer announced the details of a new US-UK trade agreement. Speaking from the Oval Office, Trump explained the broader purpose behind his tough-on-tariffs strategy: "Every country throughout the last forty, fifty years has literally ripped off the United States—on trade, on military, on protection, on everything else. We are now making fair deals . . . This [deal] just went very smoothly. A lot of common sense, as I like to say."

The agreement included a mutual reduction in key tariffs—particularly in autos, energy, and agricultural goods—and marked a shift away from decades of lopsided arrangements that had favored foreign competitors at the expense of American workers. But it wasn't just about economic terms. It was symbolic of a deeper shift: the world was no longer negotiating with a United States that could be bullied into bad deals.

But as this book goes to print in the summer of 2025, the American economy has seen none of the catastrophic consequences that Democrats and media pundits assured us were coming. If anything, the opposite has happened. In June 2025, in fact, a top Wall Street economist who'd virulently opposed President Trump's tariffs admitted that he might have been right all along. Writing in an analysis posted to a blog run by his firm, Apollo Capital Management, Torsten Sløk wrote that President Trump "may have outsmarted all of us" on tariffs. In July, the S&P 500 index reached a new high, and consumer confidence remained strong.

What will the world look like come November 2026, when the American people get their next chance at the ballot box? Only time—and Trump's own dealmaking with other countries who wish to align with the United States against China—will tell.

CHAPTER ELEVEN

Unleashing American Energy

One of the happiest returns of the Trump era is the death of political pablum. Trump's victory in 2016 was the beginning of a war on the mindless pablum and political language that had come to define our politics and bore people to tears. And since Trump has given all politicians in both parties a true lesson in communications, you need to stop reading the scripts that say nothing and just speak authentically. The era of scripted puppets is over; the people who succeed in this business will be the ones who speak their own minds, authentically, and not someone else's. Again, common sense—speak to the people in a way they can understand. One of the reason's Trump has been so successful is that he has given millions of people who thought they had no voice a leader who speaks for them in way that they themselves would speak if anyone ever bothered to listen.

Nowhere is this clearer than his commonsense reality check on energy. Under Barack Obama and Joe Biden, US energy policy focused on how *not* to produce reliable, affordable energy rather than encouraging adequate electricity to meet the needs of consumers and the American economy. They launched a War on Coal and regarded high energy rates as an acceptable tactic to discourage consumption, increasing costs to industry, energy bills, health, and prosperity.

And they did it all while covering these anti–working-class policies in indecipherable pablum designed to confuse and paper over the truth: that the policy sucks.

Democrats are backed by what Texas-based energy journalist Robert Bryce describes as the "anti-industry industry," which spends billions of dollars to throttle coal, natural gas, and nuclear energy in favor of renewables. "If the climate aristocracy succeeds in doing so, the results will be staggering increases in energy costs and dangerous decreases in the reliability and resilience of our electric grid," Bryce warns.

In short, Obama and Biden pushed regulations to rush a transition away from the most reliable energy sources, resulting in increased energy costs and dire blackout warnings.

Doug Burgum, President Trump's interior secretary and chairman of the National Energy Dominance Council, later summed it up this way: "The Biden-Harris Climate Extremist ideology put America in danger. Their planned 'transition' defied physics, economics, and common sense. This long-term liberal desire to make us dependent on unreliable, unaffordable energy sources while declaring war on reliable, affordable baseload would have caused irreversible social and economic damage had Biden or Harris been given four more years to continue imposing it on our country."

At home in Kentucky, Tony Campbell, a reasonable and respected leader of a member-owned electric co-op, spent the last four years pleading with the federal government not to screw up a good thing. Campbell, the president and CEO of East Kentucky Power Cooperative, wrote President Joe Biden eight blunt yet respectful letters, imploring him to reconsider regulations that are deteriorating the reliability of America's power grid and jacking up electric rates.

"I have expressed growing alarm at the deteriorating reliability of America's power grid due to government policies driving the rapid closure of reliable, resilient power plants that have served our nation well for decades," Campbell wrote to Biden in August 2024. "As the undeniable impacts of these policies come into sharper focus, and as the nation's economy gains momentum, it is clear U.S. economic growth will be unsustainable. Energy policies are constraining the nation's energy supply, while other policies are driving up electricity demand by incentivizing the shift to electric vehicles and forcing a transition in heating from fossil fuels to electricity."

Except for one form letter response, the Biden administration ignored Campbell's pleas.

But seventy-nine days into the second presidency of Donald Trump, Campbell's voice was finally heard, and he was invited to appear alongside Trump as the president signed a series of executive orders reflecting energy reality. Trump asked Campbell to explain the issue.

"Affordable and reliable electricity is the cornerstone of our economy, especially American manufacturing," Campbell said from a White House lectern, Trump standing at his side and a group of West Virginia coal miners beaming behind them. "However, too many government leaders have pushed policies that have made our electric grid significantly less reliable and our energy too expensive. That begins to change NOW."

The crowd stood and cheered. Trump applauded, too.

For years, we had been told by the Biden administration that the president of the United States could do very little to affect energy prices. Speaking from a stage in Washington, DC, President Biden had once said, "There's a lot going on right now. But the idea we're going to be able to click a switch, bring down the cost of gasoline, is not likely in the near term."

It's not clear whether Biden believed this at the time he said it. Given all that we've learned about his state of mind during his term, it's not even clear he knew *what* he was saying at the time he said it. What is clear to us now, after just over one hundred days of President Trump's second term, is that the American president does indeed have control over the price of gasoline, the price of oil, and the general trajectory of the American energy industry. It is possible, in other words, to "click a switch." And that's exactly what President Trump and his team have done.

Here's how.

CLICKING THE SWITCH

Like so much else in the second Trump term, the first successes can be traced back to the very first day. Just hours after giving his second inaugural, President Trump "clicked the switch" that Biden told us didn't exist, and it took him about as much time as turning on the lights in the White House residence.

And he didn't do it alone. To bring American energy up to speed, he relied on yet another person who'd attempted to run against him in the primaries: the former governor of North Dakota, Doug Burgum.

I first met Doug Burgum in May 2024, five months after he had suspended his longshot bid for the Republican presidential nomination.

Burgum was elected governor of North Dakota the same night Trump was elected president in 2016, having never before sought public office. Both men ran outsider campaigns to upend insider types in their primaries and general elections.

When Burgum, after a short-lived presidential bid, endorsed Trump on January 14, 2024, just ahead of the Iowa caucuses, it began a remarkable partnership. At rallies and in the courtroom, Burgum, emerging as one of the campaign's most reliable surrogates, projected an unwavering confidence in Trump, even as the mass media breathlessly conjectured on his demise. The North Dakota governor conveyed an earnestness and a deeply held belief that the country must be saved from another Biden term.

"Working with President Trump as a governor was like having a beautiful breeze at your back," Burgum said at a huge Trump rally in New Jersey. He added that the "Biden regulatory regime is like having a gale force wind in your face because the Biden bureaucrats are treating our constitutional republic like a dictatorship."

Despite the regulatory headwinds, under Burgum's leadership North Dakota thrived, ranking second in energy production per capita and sporting a low unemployment rate.

"You won't find anybody better than this gentleman in terms of his knowledge . . . he probably knows more about energy than anybody I know," Trump said of his Jersey Shore stage mate. "So get ready for something, okay, just get ready. But Doug Burgum has been incredible."

I arrived early for my breakfast date in late May with the former software executive (in 2001 Burgum sold his company to Microsoft for $1.1 billion, then managed Microsoft Business Solutions).

When Burgum strode into the restaurant where we'd agreed to meet in Washington, DC, I had a Trump thought. "This guy is straight out of central casting." He checked every box to be part of Trump's future administration, a middle-America governor who cares more about the intersection of energy policy and national security than political self-aggrandizement, and a commonsense passion for taming federal bureaucracy.

Burgum returned the compliments as we settled into breakfast. Following my intermittent fasting protocols that morning, I stuck to black coffee while he wolfed down a full platter.

When talking to Burgum about his record, you can feel a passion for innovation and a true understanding of what the federal government can do to help—and hurt—individual states, especially when it comes to energy policy.

And that's exactly the role the casting director in chief had in mind for Burgum. Not only naming him interior secretary, but also chairman of the newly created National Energy Dominance Council, responsible for formulating recommendations and presenting action items to President Trump.

Four days before the official creation of the council, I interviewed Burgum while guest-hosting a radio show on SiriusXM, asking him about energy as the foundation of American prosperity and national security.

"It's just a fact," Burgum replied. "It's an economic fact that energy is a component of everything. Everything we eat, everything we drive, everything we heat our homes. The food we eat, the clothes we wear, there's an energy component. If we get the cost of energy down because we have abundance in energy, not scarcity, we have abundance that lowers inflation, that drives affordability, that drives prosperity across every industry. Energy security is also national security."

Underscoring how seriously President Trump prioritizes reliable and affordable energy, the council is a powerhouse. Members include the secretaries of state, treasury, defense, agriculture, commerce, transportation, the administrator of the Environmental Protection Agency (EPA), and the attorney general. The vice-chair is Energy Secretary Chris Wright.

"The creation of this council under the leadership of Secretary Wright and Secretary Burgum is a strong step toward securing our energy future, and ensuring we have the resources necessary to meet the demands that AI will place on our grid," said House Energy and Commerce chairman Brett Guthrie, a close friend and fellow Kentuckian. "President Trump is continuing to fulfill his promise to the American people to return our nation to energy dominance."

"Energy security is national security," Guthrie said. "By utilizing our domestic energy resources to create baseload power, we can lower prices, secure our grid, and provide the energy needed to grow manufacturing, heat our homes, and fill our gas tanks."

This is exactly what President Trump did on his first day. He declared a national emergency with regard to energy, which allowed agencies across the federal government to bypass standard permitting delays, fast-track critical infrastructure projects, and reclassify domestic fuels like coal and natural gas as strategic assets. The reason was clear. During his second inaugural, the president had said we would "drill, baby, drill." Energy companies would be permitted to harness the amazing fuel that Joe Biden had made it all but illegal (or at least impractical) to take out of the ground. It was yet another commonsense move in a long string of them. During President Trump's first term, the United States had become a net energy exporter for the first time in nearly seventy years, a milestone we hadn't reached since 1952. We had so much oil and liquid natural gas, in other words, that we could afford to meet our own needs and sell the excess on the global market.

According to Secretary Burgum, liquefied natural gas, or LNG, was a perfect example of that turnaround. "Joe Biden halted new export permits in an attempt to kill this vital industry," he said. "This was a brutal blow to American workers, capital investment, and fighting inflation. Biden took this selfish and destructive action to appease the Climate Extremist wing of his party. President Trump immediately reversed this insane Biden-era policy."

Under Trump's new energy strategy, America is not just meeting domestic needs, we're helping our allies, too. "We now live in a world where our allies are free to buy LNG from America," Burgum explained. "And we're working tirelessly to strike historic deals for new LNG infrastructure in Alaska. One of the first trips I took was with Energy Secretary Chris Wright to a new facility that President Trump greenlit in Louisiana. We stood right next to a ship that was getting ready to bring LNG to Germany. One shipment alone was enough to power 100,000 German households for a year!"

Summing it up, Burgum said it plainly: "President Trump is governing with a simple philosophy: when we sell energy to our friends and allies, it means they don't have to buy it from our adversaries. President Trump's agenda makes our economy stronger and the world safer, whereas Biden-Harris's war on American energy made our country poorer and the world far more dangerous by enriching countries like Russia, Iran, and Venezuela. That's a stark contrast in leadership and vision."

Along with Lee Zeldin, who was confirmed as President Trump's head of the Environmental Protection Agency, Wright and Burgum formed what I call the "Energy Triad." Over the course of the first hundred days, these three men have made more progress on moving America forward on energy than the Biden administration could have made in a hundred years. They have completely changed the way the government of the United States views its role in this space. The problem, they recognize, is not that we aren't doing enough to protect the climate, it's that we have been doing the *wrong* things at the behest of far-left interest groups for too long.

For years, Democrats have told us that the United States needs to switch to cleaner, more reliable sources of energy. But the options they've put forward, primarily solar and wind power, are not cleaner than fossil fuels in the long run, and they are not reliable. During an interview I conducted with Doug Burgum shortly after he became President Trump's secretary of the interior, he gave the basic, commonsense reason for this, saying, "The last time I checked, Scott, the sun doesn't shine twenty-four hours a day, and the wind—at least in North Dakota, where we produce a lot of electricity—doesn't blow twenty-four/seven/three-sixty-five."

This might sound obvious. It might even sound overly simplistic. But it's true. Recent studies have shown that compared to fossil fuels, solar and wind power are simply not up to the job of powering a modern society, and they probably never will be. According to a 2025 Reuters analysis of European energy markets, Germany—a country long held up by the Left as a model for where the United States should go—saw clean energy output from wind and hydro drop significantly in early 2025, forcing a 13 percent increase in fossil fuel generation to stabilize the grid and meet demand, underscoring the unreliability of solar and wind power to provide constant, dependable energy.[1] At almost every given point, solar and wind needed to be backed up by "some reliable source of energy," namely fossil fuels. Otherwise, the country would have suffered rolling blackouts and brownouts.

What the Left doesn't tell you about these "renewable" sources of energy is that they require huge amounts of materials to work. For solar power, according to the writer Alex Epstein, an advocate for fossil fuels, "such materials can include highly purified silicon, phosphorous, boron, and compounds like titanium dioxide, cadmium telluride, and copper indium gallium selenide. For wind, they can include high-performance compounds (like those used in the aircraft industry) for turbine blades and the rare-earth mineral neodymium for lightweight, high-performance magnets, as well as the steel and concrete necessary to build thousands or tens of thousands of structures as tall as skyscrapers."

Or we could just drill for the fuel right under our feet. At least when it comes to drilling, we know the process because we've been doing it for years. And it makes us a great deal of money, especially when we harvest so much that we're able to sell it to other countries to make a profit. This, as we've seen, is exactly what President Trump was able to do during his first term. In those years, American energy production helped reduce the national trade deficit by over $300 billion in 2019 alone. The oil and gas industry supported nearly 100,000 jobs across at least thirty-one states, and the benefits rippled across the economy. Then Joe Biden, who could have continued these policies even after the COVID-19 pandemic briefly wrecked our economy, decided to undo them all, sending us into freefall.

In addition to what Trump did via executive action, Congress added to it with key energy deregulation in the president's signature "big beautiful bill," which "ends long-standing federal support for solar and wind power, while creating a friendly environment for oil, gas, and coal production," according to CNBC's summary.[2] Trump signed the bill into law on July 4.

The law opens federal lands and waters to oil and gas drilling, after the Biden administration had restricted it. The law also cuts the royalties that energy producers pay the federal government for oil and gas pumped on federal lands, which should encourage more output.

"This bill will be the most transformational legislation that we've seen in decades in terms of access to both federal lands and federal waters," Mike Sommers, president of the American Petroleum Institute, told CNBC.

The bill also opened up at least 4 million acres of federal land for mining. For many Trump supporters, Trump's commonsense agenda on reliable fossil fuels is not only good for the existing economy, but for the economy to come.

"Common sense in U.S. energy policy has been all too uncommon in recent years, so it's a breath of fresh air to have been in the room and heard President Trump talk about using more of America's most abundant energy source. This is particularly true given that the U.S. has run down its electricity reserve margins at the same time that power needs are rising due to data centers and AI. As President Trump brings manufacturing back to the United States, the country requires affordable and reliable—and this too points to the need for a sensible energy mix not driven by politics," Jim Grech, president and chief executive officer of Peabody coal company, told me.

"While the media suggests that the world is turning away from coal, in fact the world used more coal last year than any year in history. America can learn from the mistakes of Europe in creating their own energy shortages and driving industry away by turning from reliable generation to more expensive weather-dependent energy. Meanwhile, countries like China and India are rapidly increasing coal use to fuel major economic growth," Grech said.

Everyone in the energy business knows that we need cheap, reliable, and efficient energy now more than ever.

And we need a *lot* of it.

THE AI ARMS RACE: A NEW MANHATTAN PROJECT

When most people use AI, they don't think much about what they're doing. They simply put a question into ChatGPT, look at the answer that comes in—usually in a fraction of a second—and then move on with their day. Sometimes that answer is right, and sometimes it's wrong. But the speed at which it comes in is amazing.

It's amazing, according to energy experts at the Department of Energy, because out in places like eastern Washington and West Texas, massive data centers—some the size of football stadiums—are running high-performance processors around the clock, drawing enormous amounts of electricity to power the computations that allow the interface on your computer to deliver answers almost instantly. These facilities are packed with AI-specific chips capable of handling trillions of operations per second. But without the right energy supply—constant, stable, and high-volume—they can't function.

And more are being built every second. According to recent estimates, hundreds of thousands of square feet of data centers will come online by 2030, allowing the United States to remain the world's leader in Artificial Intelligence technology. And those data centers are going to take a lot of energy. Asked about this in March, Secretary Chris Wright said, "Not only *can* we meet that demand, we *must* meet that demand. I liken it to the Manhattan Project, where we had to make an atomic bomb before Nazi Germany. China is going all out on AI. . . . It has massive national security implications. We need to stay ahead in the AI arms race."

Over the years, I've heard many presidents compare things to the Manhattan Project. And it makes sense. Invoking the scientists who worked at Los Alamos, New Mexico, to make sure we created an atomic weapon before Adolf Hitler did makes anything sound vital and urgent. In this case, though, the comparison is more than apt. Just a few weeks into President Trump's second term, news that China had developed an app known as DeepSeek hit the wires, causing market tumult and panic among Silicon Valley engineers. The panic stemmed from the fact that engineers in China seemed to have made remarkable progress on an AI program in a frighteningly short amount of time: only about twenty months. By comparison, it took American engineers several years to develop and scale models like ChatGPT to that level of performance. If things kept up at this speed, China would stand a real chance of overtaking the United States in global AI leadership.

Somehow, China had managed to achieve this despite export controls and sanctions intended to prevent them from accessing high-end chips and other AI-critical technologies. It appeared that this was yet another example of China's go-to move on the world stage. The Communist Party would blatantly steal intellectual property that had come from the United States and Europe, find a way to produce it cheaply, and attempt to overwhelm the West by force. They did this largely by employing people at low wages, something that is not possible in the United States, and by willingly flouting the laws around intellectual property theft. But it had worked for them many times before, such as with solar panel manufacturing and 5G telecom infrastructure.

This, in part, was what Secretary Wright was responding to during his interview in March 2025. Continuing, he said, "America is an energy powerhouse. We're the biggest producer of oil and natural gas in the world by far. Can we grow that? The biggest challenge is going to be building the electrical grid and the electrical infrastructure. Not oil and gas production, but electricity production. We went backward on that for four years. Electricity prices went up massively during the Biden administration without any meaningful growth in production capacity. We need to go the other direction now. We need to expand production, stop the rise in prices, and ultimately bring electricity prices back down. It's a challenge, but the Trump administration is up for the challenge."

Considering how much electricity is required to power even our current AI systems, it's no wonder Secretary Wright was speaking with such urgency. Experts estimate that data centers consumed approximately 460 terawatt-hours (TWh) of electricity globally in 2022, accounting for about 1 to 2 percent of the world's total electricity usage. By 2026, this consumption is projected to double, potentially reaching levels comparable to the entire electricity consumption of countries like Sweden or Germany. For comparison, Sweden's total electricity consumption was around 130 TWh in recent years.

Luckily, it seems that the Energy Triad is up to the challenge. During my interview with Secretary Burgum, he made a point of telling me about the work he'd been doing on the electrical grid. He said, "[The Biden administration] was under the impression that we were going to go through some kind of energy transition, that you could transition from dependable sources to ones that were unreliable and intermittent. People were upset when I was saying that wind and solar were unreliable . . . You still need your thermal baseload, the dispatchable 24/7–365 sources of electricity, and then you can add a little intermittent, unreliable, expensive stuff on top of it. But if you try to have your whole grid be run by that? [In March 2025], when we had that cold spell in America, there were 239 million Americans under cold-weather warnings. If you looked at the dashboards of our regional grid operators, every one of them was operating so close to failure and then the prices on the margin were spiking through the roof . . . This is a time when every AI developer in the country needs more electricity . . . The ability [for China] to launch a cyberattack against our electrical grid is one of the weak points of our country. If our electrical grid were to go down, think about that. What that would mean to industry. It would mean that our data centers wouldn't be working. It would mean we don't have the ability to protect ourselves from a national defense standpoint because software and AI and IT is going to be an increasing component of every aspect of what we do in defense."

To prepare for this, Secretary Burgum has engaged in discussions with some of the most cutting-edge companies in the country. Just before our interview occurred, for instance, Chevron announced that it would get into the electricity business, using the tools it had developed over decades in the oil and gas industry to strengthen our electrical grids. The administration also moved to cut regulations, remove red tape, and clear the way for real reforms to go through. In early April, Secretary Burgum announced that the government would soon make land available for drilling in the newly coined Gulf of America.

Speaking on Fox, he said, "A lease sale is an announcement that allows private sector companies to be able to come in and bid on certain geology in a certain geography, to be able to do future development. When they bid on that lease, they pay the federal government money, and then when they develop those minerals, they pay a royalty. All of that goes toward reducing our debt and reducing our deficit. This is great for the American public. It's great for business. And it's great because right now we've got fifteen percent of U.S. oil production that comes from the Gulf of America. The Biden administration was trying to shut that down."

In other words: China is not going to slow down, and we're not either.

"And we have a man here that I don't know, but he's defending me all the time on CNN. Scott Jennings, where is Scott? Where are you, Scott? Come here, Scott. This guy, really, I've watched him for years. I don't know him, but he likes Trump. Come here, Scott. Oh, CNN. This is the end of Scott."

—DONALD J. TRUMP, APRIL 29, 2025

I pitched President Trump on this book in early February, just as he was in the opening throes of changing America and restoring common sense across a broad swath of American government and culture.

When I asked him if he'd cooperate and participate, he asked me a simple question:

"How do you know it's going to go well?" he said, as he leaned back in his chair and crossed his arms.

And I answered him that, a couple of weeks in, it was already going well and I had no reason to believe anything would change. And I thought he deserved a robust defense of his actions because I knew he would be roundly criticized by all the usual suspects no matter what he did or what the results were. This man could cure cancer and Democrats would be lamenting the loss of revenue at area funeral parlors.

Just as I do on CNN night after night, I wanted to give half the country a voice in debating the merits of the Trump 2.0 agenda and help explain why Republicans were more than happy with the governing results of their 2024 votes.

Sitting in the basement of the West Wing on April 29, President Trump's hundredth day in office, I mulled over the conversation we had several weeks earlier. Had it gone well? Was I right in predicting that Republicans would be thrilled with an activist president who smashed the Democrats, the media, the bureaucracy, and anything else that got in his way?

I considered all that I'd observed and learned while sitting on a comfy basement couch (your phone doesn't work down there, so you are just alone with your thoughts and whoever talks to you along the way) that sunny day. And while I waited, I watched young presidential aides breeze in and out of the hallway leading to the White House Mess, a small dining area for the president's senior staff run by the US Navy. I had eaten countless meals there as a staffer for George W. Bush (probably a few too many if you've seen pictures of me from back then) and recalled fondly the energy I derived from that perk when I was a young man in a hurry.

On this day, the president's staff looked chipper. Happy. They were in a hurry to meet lunch companions and to pick up containers to head back to their offices. Even though their boss, Donald Trump, had been a whirling dervish since the minute he took the Oath of Office on January 20, the staff I saw looked no worse for the wear.

They were clearly happy to be there, energized by what they were doing, and tackling another day in one of the most special places you can ever work.

I was sworn in as special assistant to the president by Andy Card, the White House chief of staff. He gave me some advice I never forgot.

"The minute you walk in here and don't feel a sense of awe, that's the day you should resign," Card told me. "Never take it for granted. Do you know how many people would kill to be in your shoes?"

Every day I walked through the doors of the White House as a Bush 43 staffer, I thought about that advice. And I was thinking about it on that beautiful April day, not to navel gaze but rather to wonder if the staff I saw running around the West Wing truly understood the immense difference they were making.

It's hard, sometimes, to recognize the enormity of a situation when you are in the middle of it. But after a few years, you start to look back and think—damn, that was a big deal. I certainly feel that way about my previous White House and political service, and I believe President Trump and his team will ultimately feel the same.

Their days are filled with meetings, calls, trips to the Oval Office, flights on Air Force One, and the grind and churn of what it means to serve a president and the American people in the highest stakes place on earth. They may not fully realize just yet how consequential they were. But one day they will.

Throughout the process of writing this book, I gained a further appreciation for just how consequential the Trump presidencies have been in American life and culture. I spent actual time with the president, coming to learn who he was as a person rather than just someone I cover and analyze on television. I watched him interact with people up close, and I found new appreciation for his leadership style.

On that hundredth day, around one p.m., I walked out of the West Wing basement and across West Executive Avenue (the parking lot that runs between the White House and the Eisenhower Executive Office Building) to board a very nice staff van for the trip out to Andrews Air Force Base. The president had invited me to travel with him to Michigan for a stop at Selfridge Air National Guard Base and then a rally commemorating his hundredth day in office.

The van was full. It takes several people to staff the president when he leaves the White House grounds. I spent most of my time on the drive out chatting with Karoline Leavitt, the president's press secretary;

Matt Brasseaux, the White House political director; and Michael Whatley, the chairman of the Republican National Committee.

We talked through the issues of the day and some political situations that were of mutual interest. A few folks on the van, Brasseaux included, were making their first ever trip on Air Force One.

I hadn't been on the plane myself since 2007, when I made my last trip with President Bush before leaving public service and heading home to Kentucky, where I have lived ever since. I always got goose bumps when boarding the president's plane back then, and I started to get them again when we pulled onto the tarmac at Andrews Air Force Base for the trip.

Despite President Trump's correct opinion that the current Air Force One is old and needs to be retired in favor of a new model, you cannot help but swell your chest when it comes into view and you see the words "United States of America" emblazoned on the side.

When people see that plane and see those words, it evokes powerful emotions. Pride, if you are an American. Fear, if you are our enemy. And respect if you are another world leader who wishes he commanded the kind of military, economy, and society that the American president does.

Hopping off the van, we all snapped a few pictures and then walked up the steps to board. President Trump wasn't there yet; he would be coming a few minutes later aboard Marine One, the presidential helicopter that carries him from the South Lawn of the White House to Andrews Air Force Base.

One cool thing about riding on Air Force One is that you have an assigned seat and there's a name placard in front of where you are supposed to be. Looking around the staff cabin, we couldn't find mine. And then someone from up front said, "Mr. Jennings is in here."

I walked into the president's conference room, where he conducts meetings in the air with the cabinet and other high-ranking officials. And there my name placard was at the end of the table. Down the sides were a few others: Pete Hegseth, secretary of defense; the aforementioned Michael Whatley; Dr. Mehmet Oz, the newly appointed administrator of the Centers for Medicare & Medicaid Services; Sergio Gor, the president's top personnel advisor; and James Blair, the White House deputy chief of staff and key political advisor from the 2024 campaign.

There was also a placard for Michael Waltz, who that day was replaced as the president's national security advisor. He was supposed to be on the trip but had found out that morning that the president was making a change and would instead nominate him to be ambassador to the United Nations.

Hegseth, Oz, Whatley, and I watched the television in the conference room, which was showing President Trump on the South Lawn of the White House making a few comments to the press before coming to us. He expressed optimism about upcoming trade deals and then walked to the chopper.

Upon arrival at Andrews, the president boarded, and we swiftly took off for Michigan.

The plane ride to Michigan was the first time I'd ever met Pete Hegseth. I had defended him on the air during his confirmation battles and again during the kerfuffle over his use of the messaging app Signal. But we had never actually met and he was appreciative of the effort.

During the ride, and before the president joined us, Hegseth and I had a substantive conversation about a number of topics: military recruitment, troop morale, the injection of left-wing social causes into military culture, the Signal story, the president's management of his national security team, what the "warfighter ethos" means to Hegseth, the Panama Canal, the southern border, the anti-American axis of Iran, China, and Russia, and which countries Hegseth considers our most and least prepared allies.

I found Hegseth to be affable and knowledgeable, far beyond the caricature painted of him in the mainstream press.

"The warfighter ethos is a real thing," Hegseth told me. "The Department of Defense was swamped by a wet blanket of liberal ideology. We got rid of all the months and the social stuff. Ultimately, we engaged in a liberation exercise of the uniform class," he said.

And in the early days of Trump 2.0, the commander in chief and his defense secretary had results to show for the change in attitude.

"Enrollment in the military is at a record. That's testament to what's happening in terms of the spirit of our country," Trump said. And he's right—recruitment in 2025 was exploding. In March, the Pentagon told Congress that the Army had already signed up 73 percent of the year's annual goal of 61,000 recruits, and that was before an expected summer surge.

Hegseth also talked to me about the overall command structure of the military, and said it was "top heavy." He described a plan to rebalance the ranks and put more resources into rank-and-file and mid-level leadership positions. A few weeks later, his full plan would begin to leak out, with news outlets reporting that "20% of the 44 authorized top active duty general and admiral jobs would be eliminated, along with 10% of the more than 800 one-, two- and three-star positions," according to numbers compiled by the Associated Press (as of this writing, the final orders had not come down).

Hegseth was extremely well versed on the situation in Panama. He described his recent trip there and the necessity of the United States fortifying itself against Chinese influence in the region. He called his meetings with the Panamanian government "significant progress" and touted his wins from the trip: agreements to enhance security cooperation between the US and Panama, including increased military training and information sharing; a "framework agreement" to allow US warships and auxiliary ships to transit the canal with priority; and plans for reestablishing and enhancing joint US-Panama military training centers and security force cooperation.

Hegseth was more than eager to discuss the US strategic shift of focus and resources to the Indo-Pacific theater. I asked him what a hallmark of his leadership would be when he leaves the job, and he said plainly that recalibrating the US military around this strategic goal would certainly be one of them.

I asked him which countries, in light of this strategic focus, were our most prepared allies, militarily. He considered the question and finally offered: Australia, the Philippines, and Great Britain.

Before long, President Trump joined us in the conference room.

We exchanged some conversation about the interview he had done that morning with Terry Moran of ABC News, who interviewed the president in the Oval Office for a prime-time special to air later that evening.

I could tell the president was a little miffed with the way Moran had handled himself. But his fears about how it might turn out on the air were unfounded; Trump owned the space and Moran looked overmatched in the process when the interview finally aired later that night. We all watched it in the cabin on the way home from Michigan and agreed that Trump had acquitted himself quite well despite hostile (and in some cases nonfactual) questions.

"They're giving you the big break of a lifetime," Trump told Moran during the interview. "I picked you because, frankly, I never heard of you, but that's OK . . . I picked you, Terry, but you're not being very nice."

Trump's streak of dominating mainstream media was intact. Incidentally, Moran would later lose his job at ABC when he went on a late-night social media tirade against Trump advisor Stephen Miller, revealing just how partisan the supposed journalist was.

Watching Trump conduct a conversation with multiple, disparate people is like watching six Olympic-level Ping-Pong matches at once. He's towel snapping a reporter; he sees a graphic on the TV screen about a surge in manufacturing jobs and launches into trade policy; he looks at me and says "this guy defends me against some very dishonest people, and he does it in a way where he doesn't get fired . . . it's a real skill"; he pivots to recent rallies by Alexandria Ocasio-Cortez and denigrates the crowd sizes compared to his; and finally, he takes down recent media polls that have oversampled Democrats and, once again, failed to capture the true nature of his support.

Dr. Oz moved up next to the president to show him some charts on the upcoming debate over Medicaid and how to position the party's messaging. The phone rang—it was Newt Gingrich, who wanted to discuss the same thing. That topic would dominate the national conversation in the coming weeks as Trump's Republican allies in Congress worked to pass his "one big beautiful bill."

After the Medicaid discussion, he turned to me and I hand him a glossy cover of this book. He approves. A few weeks earlier I had asked his aides what photo the president thought best embodied the attitude of the Trump 2.0 era. The one on the cover is what came back.

After some more discussion of the news of the day, Air Force One, speeding toward Michigan, began to descend. The president popped up and heads to his office as we prepared for landing.

Our first stop: Selfridge Air National Guard Base in Macomb County. We hopped off the plane and jump in the motorcade for a short trip to a hangar, where the president announced twenty-one new F-15EX fighter aircraft to be based there.

"For generations, the men and women of Selfridge have always been here, and they've always been for us. Whether you're a Republican or a Democrat, they've always been for us. They've been for America. And under the Trump administration, we're going to be there for you," Trump said to the cheering troops. He was flanked by two jets; one carried the decal "45" on its nose and the other "47." A cool touch from the local command. A nod to their commander in chief.

The announcement effectively saved the base, which used to warehouse an A-10 Thunderbolt II squadron set for retirement in 2026. Without a clear mission, the base faced possible closure, which would have been a major economic blow to the region.

Even Michigan governor Gretchen Whitmer, a Democrat who days earlier tried to hide her face with a binder while meeting President Trump in the Oval Office, showed up to praise the announcement. Trump had saved about $30 million in wages from disappearing.

Trump was in a great mood as he bounded into that military rally. His speech was well received, and he even called up Hegseth for a turn at the mic. The joint appearance was effectively a vote of confidence in his secretary of defense after a tumultuous few weeks in the press. Hegseth delivered a short, rousing address.

At the first event's conclusion, the traveling party hustled out of the hangar and jogged around the corner of the building to clamber back into our staff van. It was a few hundred feet and the number one rule of presidential motorcades is (unless you are the president): it will definitely leave without you.

But we made it in time and the procession zoomed away to the next stop: Macomb Community College, where an athletic arena filled with Trump supporters awaited our arrival. We jumped out for the main event: the president's first campaign-style rally since he won back in November.

The energy in the room was palpable. I waded through the crowd and talked to Trump supporters who had come from near and far. I asked them all if they were happy with the first hundred days, and what issues were on their minds.

To a person, all were more than fine with the results. Immigration came up over and over again as the biggest accomplishment. And although a few expressed nervousness about the tariffs, all said roughly the same thing: we trust the president to make the right deals for our country. One guy told me that "everyone talks about standing up to China. Only Trump had the balls to do it."

The arena was decked out in unsubtle imagery. Huge signs hung behind the podium: "The Golden Age," read one of them. "Investing in America" and "Jobs! Jobs! Jobs!" screamed another.

The final two: "100 Days of Greatness" and "Buy American Hire American." The trouble with subtlety is that not everyone gets it. Donald Trump, of course, has never suffered from being subtle.

As the crowd listened to the familiar hits of the Trump campaign era, the signal came that the president was coming out—"Proud to Be an American" by Lee Greenwood. When he appeared on the stage the crowd roared and began chanting "USA USA USA."

Perhaps the greatest showman in the history of the presidency basked and finally stepped behind the podium adorned with the presidential seal.

The ringmaster had arrived.

"Thank you very much! Hello Michigan. Hello. We love you Michigan. We love you. We just had the biggest victory in Michigan. They said, 'Sir, it's going to be hard.' Well, we won it twice. We actually won it three times if you want to really know. But I'm thrilled to be back in this beautiful state. I love this state," Trump said.

In a ninety-minute address, Trump touted his accomplishments: immigration, economic, law and order. He was primed and in selling mode, offering a vigorous defense of what had been the most head-spinning open to a presidential administration since FDR.

As he ticked through the issues and expertly "weaved" his way through topic after topic, he returned to the theme of his Inaugural Address and summed up the new branding of the Republican Party and the political realignment we've undergone since 2016.

"What the world has witnessed in the past 14 weeks is a revolution of common sense. That's all it is really. You're conservative, you're liberal, whatever the hell. You know what it's all about? It's about common sense when you think about it, we're for common sense."

Standing on the press riser at the back of the event space, that line hit me like a ton of bricks. Trump's "revolution of common sense" line in January had inspired me to write this book in the first place, and we were back where we started—the most transformative political figure of my lifetime hammering home the branding that has come to reshape and redefine a Republican Party I'd been in and around my entire adult life.

During the president's remarks, I was stationed in front of CNN's cameras for several hits with Jake Tapper, the network's star political anchor who was anchoring back in Washington, DC. While my fellow commentators Van Jones and Alyssa Farah Griffin were in studio and in full attack mode against Trump, I was in the room and feeling the energy of a movement that showed no signs of slowing down.

"Well, I disagree with Van that nobody voted for this. I just talked to several dozen people here who are more than happy with what's happened over the last 100 days. I was asking people, what's your proudest moment for the 100 days? A lot of people said the border, they're extremely happy with immigration, but a lot of people told me the tariffs. They said they were waiting for someone to come along and rebalance the scales because they believed the United States has been taken advantage of, and only Trump had the guts to come along and try to rebalance the scale. So, I'm not sure it's as unpopular, at least among his base, as maybe Van and Alyssa want you to believe," I said.

I always try to be measured in my CNN appearances. I stick to the facts and reject hyperbole if I can help it. But during the early weeks of Trump's second term, I was astonished at the hyperbolic nature of the statements made by his biggest detractors around the notion that Trump's base was regretting their votes. The assertion was absolutely ludicrous, yet I listened to a parade of pundits and anti-Trump media types parrot the same talking points over and over. The defeated liberal establishment wasn't offering analysis, but rather self-therapy.

On May 16, CNN's data reporter Harry Enten aired a report that laid out the truth—Trump was getting more popular, not less. Enten laid out the facts—Trump's numbers had shot up in the first two weeks of May, and he was in far better public opinion shape versus the same time during his first term.

"He is considerably higher than he has traditionally been," Enten said, noting that voters were responding to favorable economic indicators. "Sometimes Donald Trump has some pretty good political instincts," Enten concluded.

Another polling feature of the early Trump 2.0 era—optimism. National poll after poll showed that higher numbers of the American people thought the country was on "the right track" than had believed that in years. Amidst the media noise that always surrounds Trump, you can hear the signal if you listen for it—huge swaths of the American people trusted Trump to break the Carter-like malaise that gripped the country during the Biden years.

Back in the rally hall, Trump was rolling.

"We're here tonight in the heartland of our nation to celebrate the most successful first 100 days of any administration in the history of our country, and that's according to many, many people. This is the best, they say, 100-day start of any president in history, and everyone is saying it. We've just gotten started. You haven't even seen anything yet."

After I finished my CNN on-air duties, I jumped down some

makeshift stairs (which were really video equipment trunks) like Super Mario navigating an obstacle and headed to the front of the arena, where some of the president's senior staff were watching off to the side of the stage behind some bicycle rack barriers.

I found White House deputy chief of staff Stephen Miller, arms folded, watching intently the man that turned him into a rockstar among the MAGA faithful. Miller was one of the first and most loyal Trump supporters and the mastermind of so many of Trump's executive actions and subsequent public explanations. We chatted about immigration, the economy, tax cuts, and other issues as we both watched Trump command the crowd.

And then the end of the speech was near. And the president, feeling good, started calling folks up one by one. Miller was called to the stage, as he had been many times before, and offered a full-throated endorsement of Trump's leadership.

"Who's enjoying 100 golden days of America? President Trump has achieved the most secure border in American history. He's fighting violent crime. He's fighting the drug cartels. He's cutting your taxes. He's cutting wasteful spending. He's draining the swamp. He's standing up to the radical left. He's standing up to the communists, and he's making America stronger than it has ever been. President Trump will never stop fighting for you, your children, and your family. And President Trump will make sure that in this country, not illegal aliens, not criminals, not gangbangers, but American citizens come first, last, and always. Thank you, and thank you President Trump for being the greatest president in American history," Miller boomed to roars of approval.

I didn't know Miller at all before meeting him at a dinner during the presidential inaugural in January. But we struck up a text and phone relationship during the opening weeks of Trump 2.0 that impressed me greatly. When I needed to understand the technical or legal rationale behind a policy decision or executive order, Miller was always ripe for a discussion. He's a clear communicator who knows how to formulate sharp arguments and predict the attacks of Trump's detractors.

After he finished his remarks, I figured we were headed for the exits soon enough. But I was wrong. I was about to go from observer to participant in the greatest political show on earth.

"And we have a man here that I don't know, but he's defending me all the time on CNN. And he defends me really well, but he can't go too far. Because if he goes too far, he'll get fired. I said, 'You're amazing, you can take it right to the edge.' And he really does a good job. He's not allowed to go any further. He would be off if he really went totally crazy, which he'd like to do, but I think he's terrific. Scott Jennings, where is Scott? Where are you, Scott? Come here, Scott. This guy, really, I've watched him for years. I don't know him, but he likes Trump. Come here, Scott. Oh, CNN. This is the end of Scott. Who cares? Don't worry. We'll take care of you, Scott. Scott Jennings, really great."

If you spend any time with President Trump, you will learn—the man is funny. He's a professional towel snapper. He's like Don Rickles, Rodney Dangerfield, and Dave Chappelle rolled into one. I was bemused at the introduction, and had to admit—it was funny as hell.

On this night, the president was in rare form. He had been in a good mood all day, despite his worries about the ABC News interview, which he had actually aced. He was bouncy. Energetic. Optimistic. He didn't seem like a man with the weight of the world on his shoulders, which all presidents carry.

He seemed like he was having the time of his life, and he had an infectious way of sharing it with everyone around him. This was a man who was fully confident in what he was doing and could care less about the "haters and the losers," as he might say.

While being called up was unexpected, I didn't want to disappoint him or the crowd. So I jogged down the makeshift path toward the stage, bounded up the stairs, and accepted an invitation from the president to address the crowd.

Keep it short and make it funny, I thought.

"Thank you, thank you, Michigan! We were flying in here today and I said, 'Look at these farms. I got to get a farm in Michigan.' Because when you own as many libs as I do, you got to have a place to put them all. Thank you all very much!"

The MAGA faithful loved it. The president beamed. I pumped the president's hand and hopped off the stage knowing I had a great story to finish this book you are reading.

I walked to the backstage area where the president's staff had gathered, preparing to leave. And when he finished a few minutes later we all headed for the motorcade and the short trip back to the air base where we had first landed.

Toward the end of the flight home, and after we watched the president's ABC News interview, the president invited me up to his private office in the front of the plane. I sat down in a chair across from him to discuss what was on his mind. Tonight, it was the ABC interview and tariffs. And more than a few notes from the TV producer-in-chief about the finer points of cable news and the personalities therein.

As we wrapped up our conversation, the president asked me: "Do you want my hat?"

I said, "Mr. President, I do. But not for me. Would you mind if I gave it to my dad? He's the first person who ever told me you were going to be the next president of the United States."

"Of course, what's his name?" he asked.

"Jeff Jennings," I said. "He's like a lot of blue-collar guys where I come from. Grew up Democrats and are now the biggest Trump supporters in the world."

"Sounds like a smart guy," Trump said as he signed the hat "To Jeff. You are great. Signed, Donald J. Trump.

An underappreciated Trump trait: he's extremely gracious. He literally gave me the hat off his head.

I took the hat from the president and made my way back to the conference room to collect my stuff. By this time, Air Force One was landing back at Andrews Air Force Base in Maryland.

Back down the stairs, back in the van, and back to the White House complex, the traveling party traded old campaign stories and observations as we wrapped up a whirlwind day.

RNC chairman Michael Whatley and I exited the motorcade and walked together out of the exit at 17th Street and State Place, in the shadow of the Eisenhower Executive Office Building where I worked in President Bush 43's second term.

On the street, we encountered a group of tourists who were taking pictures of the EEOB.

"Hey, you're the guy from the rally!" one of them said.

Laughing, I said, "Probably the most famous 30 seconds of my life."

"We love what you do on CNN. Keep fighting!" he said, as the group moved on down the sidewalk. I looked up at the EEOB corner balcony overhanging 17th Street, the one I had stood on countless times during my Bush years because it jutted off the back of my office.

It was like looking into ancient history. For the Republican Party and for the entire country.

And all because of one man: Donald J. Trump.

ACKNOWLEDGMENTS

First, my deepest thanks to President Donald J. Trump, who graciously allowed me to spend time with him and gain a sense of his approach to governing and decision-making.

I'm also grateful to the White House team: Taylor Budowich, Karoline Leavitt, Steven Cheung, Katie Miller, Chris LaCivita, and Harrison Fields. Thank you to Secretary of State Marco Rubio, Secretary of Defense Pete Hegseth, Secretary of the Interior Doug Burgum, and Secretary of the Treasury Scott Bessent, and EPA administrator Lee Zeldin for taking the time to be interviewed, and to Elon Musk for his perspective.

Special thanks to Mauro DiPreta and Allie Johnston at HarperCollins; to Matt Latimer at Javelin; and to Joe Arnold and Sean McGowan.

My partners at RunSwitch, who have been incredible friends and colleagues: Kaylee Price, Steve Bryant, and Gary Gerdemann.

To my family, friends, colleagues, partners, and those in my life who made this book and all my professional pursuits possible: from the bottom of my heart, thank you. This especially includes my spouse, Autumn, who ensures that our world in Prospect, Kentucky, keeps spinning while I perpetually bite off more than I can chew.

Chapter One: No Holds Barred

1. Christopher R. Browning, "The Suffocation of Democracy," *New York Review of Books*, October 25, 2018, https://www.nybooks.com/articles/2018/10/25/suffocation-of-democracy/.

2. Ashley Parker and Michael Scherer, "Biden Sees a New Threat: 'Ultra MAGA' Republicans," *Washington Post*, May 13, 2022, https://www.washingtonpost.com/politics/2022/05/13/biden-ultra-maga/.

3. Elie Honig, "Prosecutors Got Trump—But They Contorted the Law," *New York Magazine*, May 31, 2024, https://nymag.com/intelligencer/article/trump-was-convicted-but-prosecutors-contorted-the-law.html.

4. Ibid.

5. Jason Cohen (@JasonJournoDC), July 8, 2025, https://x.com/JasonJournoDC/status/1942696817906573496.

6. Monica Alba, "Mayorkas Defends Biden as 'Sharp, Intensely Probing, Detail-Oriented,'" NBC News, May 15, 2025, https://www.nbcnews.com/politics/white-house/mayorkas-defends-biden-sharp-intensely-probing-detail-oriented-rcna138192.

7. National Republican Congressional Committee (@NRCC), "DAN GOLDMAN: Biden is 'sharper than anyone I've spoken to,' X (formerly Twitter), May 28, 2024, https://x.com/NRCC/status/1795481504837226953.

8. Western Lensman (@WesternLensman), "2024 Chuck Schumer: Biden is in command, mental acuity is great, any suggestion otherwise is right-wing propaganda," X (formerly Twitter), April 25, 2025, https://x.com/WesternLensman/status/1922429951284019338.

9. "Biden's Mental Acuity: A Closer Look," YouTube video, 7:11, April 25, 2024, https://www.youtube.com/watch?v=H7MdUGOPjkI.

10. "Donald Trump's Victory Speech in Full: Transcript," *Newsweek*, November 6, 2024, https://www.newsweek.com/donald-trump-victory-speech-full-transcript-1981234.

11. James Comer, *All the President's Money: Investigating the Secret Foreign Schemes That Made the Biden Family Rich* (New York: Broadside Books, 2025), 4.

12. *Newsweek*.

13. George W. Bush, "President George W. Bush on Compassionate Conservatism," *The Catalyst*, George W. Bush Presidential Center, Fall 2018, https://www.bushcenter.org/catalyst/opportunity-road/george-w-bush-on-compassionate-conservatism/.

14. "Trump Signs Executive Orders in the Oval Office," https://www.rev.com/transcripts/trump-signs-executive-orders-in-the-oval-office.

15. Jo Yurcaba, "Trump Promises to Ban Transgender Women from Sports if Re-Elected," NBC News, January 31, 2022, https://www.nbcnews.com/nbc-out/out-politics-and-policy/trump-promises-ban-transgender-women-sports-re-elected-rcna14248.

16. Ibid.

17. "Trump Denounces 'Transgender Craziness' at Virginia Rally," YouTube, November 3, 2024, https://www.youtube.com/shorts/Bbg3UM8KBvE?app=desktop&si=Tmi4bUxkD2raUXl2.

18. Ibid.

19. Interview with the author, May 2, 2025.

Chapter Two: DOGE: The Deep State Chainsaw Massacre

1. Interview with the author, April 30, 2025.

2. Russell Vought, "Trump's Budget Hawk Takes Over the DOGE Agenda. First Up: The Military," *Wall Street Journal*, May 11, 2025, https://www.wsj.com/politics/policy/doge-russ-vought-trump-elon-musk-0a1bbeb4.

3. "Musk to Attend Cabinet Meeting as He Bids Farewell to Washington," CNN, April 30, 2025, https://www.cnn.com/2025/04/30/politics/musk-cabinet-meeting-farewell.

4. Interview with the author, April 31, 2025.

5. "Elon Musk Speaks at CPAC," C-SPAN, February 20, 2025, https://www.c-span.org/clip/public-affairs-event/elon-musk-speaks-at-cpac/5154261.

6. Congressional Research Service, *Federal Workforce Statistics Sources: OPM and OMB*, updated March 25, 2021, https://sgp.fas.org/crs/misc/R43590.pdf.

7. Eric Katz, "See Where and How Biden Grew the Federal Workforce," *Government Executive*, January 3, 2025, https://www.govexec.com/workforce/2025/01/see-where-and-how-biden-grew-federal-workforce/401945/.

8. Eric Katz, "See Where and How Biden Grew the Federal Workforce," *Government Executive*, January 3, 2025, https://www.govexec.com/workforce/2025/01/see-where-and-how-biden-grew-federal-workforce/401945/.

9. Eric Katz, "See Where and How Biden Grew the Federal Workforce," *Government Executive*, January 3, 2025, https://www.govexec.com/workforce/2025/01/see-where-and-how-biden-grew-federal-workforce/401945/.

10. Rahm Emanuel, "Let's Make Sure This Crisis Doesn't Go to Waste," *Washington Post*, March 25, 2020, https://www.washingtonpost.com/opinions/2020/03/25/lets-make-sure-this-crisis-doesnt-go-waste/.

11. Eric Katz, "See Where and How Biden Grew the Federal Workforce," *Government Executive*, January 3, 2025, https://www.govexec.com/workforce/2025/01/see-where-and-how-biden-grew-federal-workforce/401945/.

12. William Proxmire, "Golden Fleece Awards, 1975–1987," Wisconsin Historical Society, https://content.wisconsinhistory.org/digital/collection/proxmire/id/252.

13. William Proxmire, "Golden Fleece Awards, 1975–1987," Wisconsin Historical Society, https://content.wisconsinhistory.org/digital/collection/proxmire/id/252.

14. Jonathan Swan, Theodore Schleifer, Maggie Haberman, Ryan Mac, and Kate Conger, "How Elon Musk Executed His Takeover of the Federal Bureaucracy," *New York Times*, February 28, 2025, https://www.nytimes.com/2025/02/28/us/politics/musk-federal-bureaucracy-takeover.html.

15. https://www.whitehouse.gov/remarks/2025/03/remarks-by-president-trump-in-joint-address-to-congress/.

16. The Festivus Report 2024, https://www.hsgac.senate.gov/wp-content/uploads/FESTIVUS-REPORT-2024.pdf.

17. Ibid.

18. Rapid Response 47, (@RapidResponse47), July 9, 2025, https://x.com/RapidResponse47/status/1942938126554407402.

19. Jim Geraghty, "Maxine Waters: Send Elon Musk 'Back from Wherever He Came From,'" *National Review*, March 6, 2025, https://www.nationalreview.com /corner/maxine-waters-send-elon-musk-back-from-wherever-he-came-from/.

Chapter Three: Empire Strikes Back

1. Interview with the author, May 2, 2025.
2. Adam Cancryn, Lauren Egan, Adam Wren, and Ally Mutnick, "Biden Shrinks from View Ahead of Trump's Return to Washington," *Politico*, December 9, 2024, https://www.politico.com/news/2024/12/09/biden-absent -washington-00192575.
3. Ibid.
4. Katie Hawkinson, "Trump trolls Jill Biden as he hawks new perfume: 'A fragrance your enemies can't resist,'" *The Independent* (UK), December 8, 2025, https://www.independent.co.uk/news/world/americas/us-politics/donald -trump-jill-biden-notre-dame-perfume-b2660952.html.
5. https://www.whitehouse.gov/remarks/2025/03/remarks-by-presi dent-trump-in-joint-address-to-congress/.
6. *Honestly*, podcast with Victor Davis Hansen.
7. Ibid.
8. Lazar Berman, "Netanyahu calls Trump 'greatest friend Israel has ever had,' hailing his actions in past 2 weeks," *Times of Israel*, February 5, 2025, https:// www.timesofisrael.com/liveblog_entry/netanyahu-calls-trump-greatest -friend-israel-has-ever-had-hailing-his-actions-in-past-2-weeks/.
9. David Reamer, "'Seward's Folly' is a myth. Spread the word," *Anchorage Daily News*, January 22, 2025, https://www.adn.com/alaska-life/2025/01/12/sew ards-folly-is-a-myth-please-tell-a-friend/.
10. Anthony Kleven, "Belt and Road: Colonialism with Chinese Characteristics," *The Interpreter*, Lowy Institute, August 30, 2018, https://www.lowyinstitute .org/the-interpreter/belt-road-colonialism-chinese-characteristics.
11. "How BlackRock's Larry Fink Won Over Donald Trump," *Wall Street Journal*, April 5, 2025, https://www.wsj.com/finance/investing/blackrock -larry-fink-donald-trump-panama-canal-963b600a.
12. Marianna Parraga and Brendan O'Boyle, "Could Panama throw a new wrench into BlackRock's ports deal?," Reuters, April 3, 2025,

https://www.reuters.com/business/could-panama-throw-new-wrench
-into-blackrocks-ports-deal-2025–04–03/.

13. David E. Sanger, "Visiting Greenland, Vance Finds the Weather and the
Reception Chilly," *New York Times*, March 28, 2025, https://www.nytimes
.com/2025/03/28/us/politics/greenland-jd-vance-usha.html.

14. April Roach, "JD Vance accuses Denmark of failing to keep Greenland secure
as he slams European allies," CNBC, March 29, 2025, https://www.cnbc
.com/2025/03/29/jd-vance-accuses-denmark-of-failing-to-keep-greenland
-secure.html.

15. Adriana Gomez Licon and Michelle L. Price, "Trump revels in Democratic
turmoil as he returns to campaign trail and teases VP pick," NBC6 Miami,
July 9, 2024, https://www.nbcmiami.com/news/local/trump-to-hold-rally-in
-doral-with-vp-deadline-nearing-amid-calls-for-biden-to-withdraw/3356504/.

16. Marco Rubio Speaks at RNC 2024 Night Two, July 16, 2024, https://www.rev
.com/transcripts/marco-rubio-speaks-at-rnc-2024-night-two.

17. Interview with the author, May 2, 2025.

18. Ibid.

19. Interview with the author, February 11, 2025.

20. Interview with the author, May 2, 2025.

21. The Vigilant Fox, April 13, 2025, https://x.com/vigilantfox/status/1911
428276007886901?s=42.

22. Interview with the author, May 2, 2025.

23. The Inaugural Address, January 20, 2025, https://www.whitehouse.gov
/remarks/2025/01/the-inaugural-address/.

Chapter Four: Briefing Room Battles

1. Josh Christenson, "Trump says he has an 'obligation to be open and available'
to press, insists he's not looking for retribution," November 18, 2024, *New York
Post*, https://nypost.com/2024/11/18/us-news/trump-says-he-has-an-obligation
-to-be-open-and-available-to-press-insists-hes-not-looking-for-retribution.

2. Amanda Barrett, "AP style guidance on Gulf of Mexico, Mount McKinley,"
Associated Press, January 23, 2025, https://www.ap.org/the-definitive-source
/announcements/ap-style-guidance-on-gulf-of-mexico-mount-mckinley/.

3. Jonathan S. Tobin, "The Associated Press' progressive bias is out of control,"

New York Post, October 22, 2020, https://nypost.com/2020/10/22/the-associated-press-progressive-bias-is-out-of-control/.

4. Becket Adams, "Who radicalized the Associated Press?" March 11, 2024, *The Hill*, https://thehill.com/opinion/campaign/4519187-who-radicalized-the-associated-press.

5. Associated Press, January 27, 2023, https://x.com/AP/status/1618886923828748288?lang=en.

6. APStylebook, May 3, 2023, https://x.com/APStylebook/status/1653798091403804672?lang=en.

7. Bonchie, May 13, 2025, https://x.com/bonchieredstate/status/1922380930280276323?s=42.

8. Hadas Gold, "The White House is now deciding who can cover the president, reversing decades of precedent," CNN, February 25, 2025, https://www.cnn.com/2025/02/25/media/white-house-correspondents-pool/index.html.

9. James Lynch, "NPR Admits Error on Refusing to Cover Hunter Biden Laptop Story," *National Review*, March 2025, accessed July 29, 2025, https://www.nationalreview.com/news/npr-ceo-admits-outlet-was-mistaken-in-refusing-to-cover-hunter-biden-laptop-story/.

10. U.S. Department of Justice press release, "Robert Hunter Biden Convicted on Three Felony Tax Offenses and Six Misdemeanor Tax Offenses," https://www.justice.gov/archives/sco-weiss/pr/robert-hunter-biden-convicted-three-felony-tax-offenses-and-six-misdemeanor-tax-offenses.

11. *The American Journalist Under Attack: Media, Trust and Democracy*, S.I. Newhouse School of Public Communications, Syracuse University, 2022, https://newhouse.syracuse.edu/news/survey-of-journalists-provides-insights-into-the-state-of-journalism-today/.

12. Ian Ward, "Meet the 8 MAGA Outlets Disrupting the White House Briefing Room," *Politico*, April 22, 2025, accessed July 29, 2025, https://www.politico.com/news/magazine/2025/04/22/trump-white-house-briefing-correspondents-natalie-winters-00290063.

13. Edward Luce, "Lunch with the FT: Henry Kissinger," *Financial Times*, July 20, 2018, quoted in Benjamin Fearnow, "Henry Kissinger Says Donald Trump Could Be Seen as 'One of Those Figures in

History . . .," *Newsweek*, July 20, 2018, https://www.newsweek.com
/henry-kissinger-donald-trump-figures-history-end-era-1034319.

14. Jeff Bezos, letter to *Washington Post* staff, February 26, 2025, quoted in Eli
Stokols, "Jeff Bezos Orders *Washington Post* Editorial Shift Toward 'Personal
Freedoms and Free Markets, '" *Politico*, February 26, 2025, https://www
.politico.com/news/2025/02/26/jeff-bezos-washington-post-opinion-022790.

15. Dan Kennedy, "For Five Years, Trump Outrage Has Fueled Media
Profits. So Now What?" WGBH News, January 27, 2021, https://www
.wgbh.org/news/commentary/2021-01-27/for-five-years-trump-outrage
-has-fueled-media-profits-so-now-what.

16. Chris Cillizza, post on X (formerly Twitter), February 25, 2025, https://x.com
/ChrisCillizza/status/1894557307700183338.

17. Peter Baker, post on X (formerly Twitter), February 25, 2025, https://x.com
/peterbakernyt/status/1894461539110850985.

18. Stephen Sorace, "White House Deputy Chief of Staff Rails Against Reporters
over MS-13, TdA Coverage," Fox News, May 1, 2025, https://www.foxnews
.com/politics/white-house-deputy-chief-staff-rails-against-reporters-over-ms
-13-tda-coverage.

Chapter Five: Bad Faith Actors

1. Brian Krassenstein, February 3, 2019, https://x.com/krassenstein/status/1092
195778817335296.

2. Daniel D'Addario, "Kamala Harris's Republican Appeal Is Growing. So
Why Is Democratic Support Collapsing?," *Rolling Stone*, April 3, 2024,
https://www.rollingstone.com/politics/politics-features/harris-repu
blican-appeal-democratic-support-collapse-1235156634/.

3. The Lincoln Project, July 22, 2024, https://x.com/ProjectLincoln/status
/1815408997517697138?lang=en.

4. Ryan Grim, "Lincoln Project Members Posed as White Supremacists at Glenn
Youngkin Rally," *The Intercept*, November 3, 2021, https://theintercept.com
/2021/11/03/lincoln-project-charlottesville-glenn-youngkin/.

5. James Kirchick, "The Real Lincoln Project Scandal," *Tablet Magazine*,
February 19, 2021, https://www.tabletmag.com/sections/news/articles/lin
coln-project-steve-schmidt-john-weaver.

6. "Mr. Maher Goes to Washington," YouTube, April 11, 2025, https://www
.youtube.com/watch?v=RxlopbcfXpQ.

7. Tim Walz, March 18, 2025, https://x.com/Tim_Walz/status/190219758
1586833643?lang=en.

8. startribune, March 19, 2025, https://www.threads.com/@startribune/post
/DHYmcZjuYht/im-not-a-vindictive-person-or-anything-but-i-take-great
-pleasure-in-the-fact-tha.

9. "Texas Democrat goes after Ted Cruz: 'This dude has to be knocked over
the head,'" Fox News, March 25, 2025, https://www.foxnews.com/video/637
0511647112.

Chapter Six: Fighting for Peace

1. Carol E. Lee, Courtney Kube, Kristen Welker, and Dan De Luce, "Biden Lost
Temper with Zelenskyy in June Phone Call over Ukraine Aid," NBC News,
October 31, 2022, https://www.nbcnews.com/politics/national-security/biden
-lost-temper-zelenskyy-phone-call-ukraine-aid-rcna54592.

2. Anusha Rathi and Christina Lu, "Trump-Zelensky Oval Office Meeting:
Full Text Transcript," *Foreign Policy*, February 28, 2025, https://foreignpolicy
.com/2025/02/28/trump-zelensky-meeting-transcript-full-text-video-oval
-office/.

3. Ibid.

4. Interview with the author, May 2, 2025.

5. Glenn Greenwald, March 4, 2025, https://x.com/ggreenwald/status/18969
25842443534427.

6. Peter Baker, "Obama Said to Resist Growing Pressure from All Sides to
Arm Ukraine," *New York Times*, March 10, 2025, https://www.nytimes
.com/2015/03/11/us/politics/obama-said-to-resist-growing-pressure-from-all
-sides-to-arm-ukraine.html.

7. Josh Rogin, "Trump administration approved lethal arms sales to Ukraine,"
Washington Post, December 20, 2017, https://www.washingtonpost.com
/news/josh-rogin/wp/2017/12/20/trump-administration-approves-lethal
-arms-sales-to-ukraine/.

8. "German delegation at U.N. appears to laugh at Trump," *Washington Post*,
September 25, 2018, https://www.washingtonpost.com/video/world/german

-delegation-at-un-appears-to-laugh-at-trump/2018/09/25/03ed3d1a-c0e4
–11e8–9f4f-a1b7af255aa5_video.html.

9. Erin Banco, Max Hunder, and Olena Harmash, "Trump Says Ukraine Willing to Negotiate, Russia 'Ready for Peace,'" Reuters, March 4, 2025, https://www .reuters.com/world/europe/trump-halts-all-us-military-aid-ukraine-white -house-official-says-2025–03–04/.

10. Thomas Sowell quotes, March 3, 2025, https://x.com/ThomasSowell /status/1896627608512852284.

11. Harry Enten, March 3, 2025, https://x.com/forecasterenten/status/18966 18726906376650?s=42.

12. Steven Hendrix and Mariana Alfano, "European leaders 'doubling down' on backing Zelensky after Trump blowup," *Washington Post*, March 3, 2025, https://www.washingtonpost.com/world/2025/03/02/zelensky-europe -leaders-meeting-ukraine/.

13. Cynical Publius, March 3, 2025, https://x.com/cynicalpublius/status/189658 3014273933506?s=43.

14. Barak Ravid, "U.S. and Ukraine sign minerals deal," *Axios*, April 30, 3035, https://www.axios.com/2025/04/30/ukraine-minerals-deal-signing.

Chapter Seven: Alien Enemies: The Immigration Fights

1. Christina Lu, "Vance Munich Speech: Read Full Transcript," *Foreign Policy*, February 18, 2025, https://foreignpolicy.com/2025/02/18/vance-speech -munich-full-text-read-transcript-europe/.

2. Ibid.

3. "Italy's Meloni Says 'We Hope to Make the West Great Again' in Trump Meeting," BBC News, April 17, 2025, https://www.bbc.com/news/live/cewgn4jnkd2t.

4. https://www.whitehouse.gov/remarks/2025/03/remarks-by-president -trump-in-joint-address-to-congress/.

5. U.S. House Committee on Homeland Security, "September 24 Startling Stats," October 2024, https://homeland.house.gov/wp-content/uploads/2024/10 /September-24-Startling-Stats.pdf.

6. "Migrant Arrests at US-Mexico Border in March Lowest Ever Recorded," Reuters, April 1, 2025, https://www.reuters.com/world/us/migrant -arrests-us-mexico-border-march-lowest-ever-recorded-2025–04–01/.

7. Avery Lotz and Stef Kight, "Border Crossings Plunge to Lowest Levels in Decades: New Data," *Axios*, March 4, 2025, https://www.axios.com /2025/03/04/illegal-border-crossings-february-decline-trump.

8. Camilo Montoya-Galvez, "Amid Trump Crackdown, Illegal Border Crossings Plunge to Levels Not Seen in Decades," CBS News, March 3, 2025, https:// www.cbsnews.com/news/illegal-crossings-plunge-to-levels-not-seen-in -decades-amid-trump-crackdown/.

9. Pangambam S, "FULL TRANSCRIPT: Trump's MAGA Rally At MSG, New York City," *Singju Post*, October 28, 2024, https://singjupost.com/full -transcript-trumps-maga-rally-at-msg-new-york-city/?singlepage=1.

Chapter Eight: Transitioning Back to Common Sense

1. Ariana Baio, "More Democrats want to see party push to the political middle in wake of election losses, poll finds," *The Independent* (UK), February 14, 2025, https://www.independent.co.uk/news/world/americas/us-politics/democrats -move-moderate-poll-b2698575.html.

2. Nicholas Wu, Daniella Diaz, and Kelly Garrity, "Dems torn over transgender issue: Centrists worry that party is 'reading the public wrong,'" *Politico*, November 13, 2024, https://www.politico.com/news/2024/11/13 /democrats-moderates-transgender-issues-strategy-00189123.

3. Will Steakin, Rachel Scott, and Julia Reinstein, "Trump signs executive order banning transgender athletes from women's sports, directing DOJ to enforce," ABC News, February 5, 2025, https://abcnews.go.com/Politics/trump-sign -executive-order-banning-transgender-athletes-womens/story?id=118468478.

4. https://www.whitehouse.gov/remarks/2025/03/remarks-by-president -trump-in-joint-address-to-congress/.

5. Chris Nessi, "Volleyball player hurt by trans opponent—and honored by Trump—calls out Democrats for 'failing women,'" *New York Post*, March 5, 2025, https://nypost.com/2025/03/05/us-news/volleyball-star-hurt-by-trans -opponent-say-dems-are-failing-women/.

6. "NYT Poll Finds Majority of Democrats Oppose Transgender Athletes in Women's Sports," *New York Post*, January 19, 2025, https://nypost .com/2025/01/19/us-news/nyt-poll-finds-majority-of-democrats-oppose -transgender-athletes-in-womens-sports/.

7. Jonathan Rauch, "America's New Consensus: How Rising Polarization Masks Bipartisan Agreement," *Manhattan Institute*, July 11, 2024, https://manhattan .institute/article/americas-new-consensus.

8. Interview with the author, May 9, 2025.

9. Ibid.

10. Ibid.

11. Reid J. Epstein, Lisa Lerer, and Nicholas Nehamas, "Devastated Democrats Play the Blame Game, and Stare at a Dark Future," *New York Times*, November 7, 2024, https://www.nytimes.com/2024/11/07/us/politics/democrats-kamala -harris.html.

12. Ryan King, "Tufts University backs off vow to cut off interns from Rep. Seth Moulton's office over trans athlete views," *New York Post*, November 12, 2024, https://nypost.com/2024/11/12/us-news/tufts -university-backs-off-vow-to-cut-off-interns-from-rep-seth-moul tons-office-over-trans-athlete-views/.

13. Emma Colton, "DNC lambasted for 'beyond parody' leadership vote that included singing, gender rules: 'Can't stop laughing,'" Fox News, February 2, 2025, https://www.foxnews.com/politics/dnc-lambasted-beyond -parody-leadership-vote-included-singing-gender-rules-cant-stop-laughing.

14. Josh Christenson, "Detransitioner tells Congress her 'childhood was ruined' by gender reassignment," *New York Post*, July 27, 2023, https://nypost.com /2023/07/27/detransitioner-tells-congress-her-childhood-was-ruined-by-gen der-reassignment/.

15. Collin Rugg, July 22, 2024, https://x.com/collinrugg/status/18154961703342 04202?s=10&t=STltr6z-fWRGtd8UEDupvw.

16. https://www.whitehouse.gov/remarks/2025/03/remarks-by-president -trump-in-joint-address-to-congress/.

17. Al Franken, March 5, 2025, https://x.com/alfranken/status/189741682 8994904438.

18. "Yes, Biden Spent Millions on Transgender Animal Experiments," White House, March 5, 2025, https://www.whitehouse.gov/articles/2025/03/yes -biden-spent-millions-on-transgender-animal-experiments/.

19. "Fact-checking Trump's address to Congress," CNN, March 5, 2025, https:// www.cnn.com/2025/03/04/politics/fact-check-trump-address-congress.

20. Josh Parry and Hugh Pym, "Hilary Cass: Weak evidence letting down children over gender care," BBC, April 10, 2024, https://www.bbc.com/news/health-68770641.

21. Reid J. Epstein and Laurel Rosenhall, "Newsom Splits with Democrats on Transgender Athletes: 'It's Deeply Unfair,'" *New York Times*, March 7, 2025, https://www.nytimes.com/2025/03/06/us/politics/gavin-newsom-transgender-sports-democrats.html.

22. Michelle L. Price and Patrick Whittle, "Trump spars with Maine's governor at the White House over transgender athletes," Associated Press, February 21, 2025, https://apnews.com/article/trump-janet-mills-governors-transgender-athletes-7cc3a7a6f29748d4b95eaf743b023926.

Chapter Nine: DEI Dies

1. Collin Rugg, March 26, 2025, https://x.com/collinrugg/status/1905007649466540478?s=42.

2. Ibram X. Kendi, "Ibram X. Kendi defines what it means to be an antiracist," June 9, 2020, https://www.penguin.co.uk/discover/articles/ibram-x-kendi-definition-of-antiracist.

3. 2020 Democratic Party Platform, August 17, 2020, https://www.presidency.ucsb.edu/documents/2020-democratic-party-platform.

4. Ilya Shapiro and Renu Mukherjee, "The End of the Beginning," *City Journal*, June 30 2023, https://www.city-journal.org/article/affirmative-action-ruling-is-the-end-of-the-beginning.

5. "More Americans Disapprove Than Approve of Colleges Considering Race, Ethnicity in Admissions Decisions," Pew Research Center, June 8, 2023, https://www.pewresearch.org/politics/2023/06/08/more-americans-disapprove-than-approve-of-colleges-considering-race-ethnicity-in-admissions-decisions/.

6. "Ending Illegal Discrimination and Restoring Merit-Based Opportunity," White House, January 21, 2025, https://www.whitehouse.gov/presidential-actions/2025/01/ending-illegal-discrimination-and-restoring-merit-based-opportunity/.

7. Christopher Caldwell, "The Biggest Policy Change of the Century," *Free Press*, January 27, 2025, https://www.thefp.com/p/christopher-caldwell-dei-trump-executive-order.

8. Dana Kennedy, "Inside the CEI system pushing brands to endorse celebs like Dylan Mulvaney," *New York Times*, April 7, 2023, https://nypost.com/2023/04/07/inside-the-woke-scoring-system-guiding-american-companies/.

9. Ibid.

10. T.J. Moe, January 11, 2025, https://www.facebook.com/TJMoe28/videos/dei-firefighters/573410925666248/.

11. Martin Luther King Jr., "I Have a Dream," August 28, 1963, https://www.americanrhetoric.com/speeches/mlkihaveadream.htm.

12. Boeing, *Global Equity, Diversity & Inclusion Report 2023*, January 2024, https://static.poder360.com.br/2024/01/boeing-relatorio-equidade-global-diversidade-inclusao-2023.pdf.

13. "FAA's Diversity Hiring Practices Were Under Scrutiny Long Before the Crash," *Washington Times*, January 30, 2025, https://www.washingtontimes.com/news/2025/jan/30/faa-diversity-hiring-practices-scrutiny-long-air-d/.

14. Mississippi Center for Justice. "Brigida v. FAA." Accessed July 9, 2025. https://mslegal.org/cases/brigida-v-faa/.

15. "Records Show Critical Race Theory Propaganda at West Point," Judicial Watch, June 20, 2022, https://www.judicialwatch.org/crt-propaganda-at-west-point/.

16. Tamar Lapin, "Air Force Cadets Undergo Gender-Inclusive Training," *New York Post*, September 22, 2022, https://nypost.com/2022/09/22/air-force-cadets-undergo-gender-inclusive-training/.

17. Jeff Schogol, "Army hits its annual recruiting goal in eight months," Task & Purpose, June 4, 2025, https://taskandpurpose.com/news/army-beats-2025-recruiting-goal.

18. Interview with the author, June 24, 2025.

Chapter Ten: Trade War II

1. Bryan Mena, "Key takeaways from Trump's 'Liberation Day' tariffs," CNN, April 2, 2025, https://www.cnn.com/2025/04/02/economy/key-takeaways-from-trumps-liberation-day-tariffs/index.html.

2. Alexandra Hutzler, "Trump announces 'historic' tariffs as he says America's been 'looted, pillaged,'" ABC News, April 2, 2025, https://abc7.com/post/donald-trumps-liberation-day-arrives-he-gambles-big-risky-tariff-policy/16118351/.

3. Josh Boak, "Trump announces sweeping new tariffs to promote US manufacturing, risking inflation and trade wars," Associated Press, April 3, 2025, https://www.ap.org/news-highlights/spotlights/2025/trump-announces-sweeping-new-tariffs-to-promote-us-manufacturing-risking-inflation-and-trade-wars/.

4. John McCormick, "Trump Calls Tariffs the 'Most Beautiful Word,'" *Wall Street Journal*, October 17, 2024, https://www.wsj.com/livecoverage/harris-trump-election-10-16-2024/card/trump-calls-tariffs-the-most-beautiful-word--YMVPAupw4EjBRp6yobOy.

5. Asma Khalid, "Why Trump loves former President McKinley so much," NPR, February 3, 2025, https://www.npr.org/2025/02/03/nx-s1-5272753/why-trump-loves-former-president-mckinley-so-much.

6. Tom Giovanetti, "President Reagan on Trade & Tariffs," IPI Roundtable, June 5, 2019, https://www.ipi.org/policy_blog/detail/president-reagan-on-trade-tariffs.

7. Michael Wayland, "Trump finds unexpected ally in auto union leader over tariffs," CNBC, March 10, 2025, https://www.cnbc.com/2025/03/10/trump-uaw-auto-union-shawn-fain-tariffs.html.

8. Grant LaFleche, Laurence Mathieu-Léger, Ioanna Roumeliotis, and Matthew Pierce, "From old grievances to new allies: Trump's history with tariffs," CBC News, February 28, 2025, https://www.cbc.ca/news/canada/trump-tariff-history-1.7469877.

9. Greg Grunberg, January 4, 2019, https://x.com/greggrunberg/status/1081589973898354689?lang=en.

10. https://www.cbsnews.com/news/ge-reshore-800-jobs-to-the-us-why/.

11. https://www.cbsnews.com/news/ge-reshore-800-jobs-to-the-us-why/.

12. https://www.youtube.com/watch?v=rGg8bWbWklo.

13. https://www.youtube.com/watch?v=-TBI6G8qpdM.

14. Erick Erickson, May 20, 2025, https://x.com/EWErickson/status/1924840730217861207.

15. https://www.washingtonpost.com/business/2025/03/01/paper-straws-plastic-trump-business/.

16. https://x.com/EricLDaugh/status/1942919163418173716.

17. John Carney, "The Forgotten Economic Theory Behind Trump's Tariffs," *Breitbart Business Digest*, April 10, 2025, https://www.breitbart.com/economy/2025/04/10/breitbart-business-digest-the-forgotten-economic-theory-behind-trumps-tariffs/.

18. Transcript of US Treasury Secretary Scott Bessent Interview with Tucker Carlson on President Donald Trump's Tariff Plan and Its Impact on the Middle Class, April 7, 2025, https://home.treasury.gov/news/press-releases/sb0073.

19. John McCormick, "Sen. Elizabeth Warren Says Trump Tariff 'Chaos' Will Hurt U.S. Investment," *Wall Street Journal*, April 14, 2025, https://www.wsj.com/livecoverage/stock-market-trump-tariffs-trade-war-04-14-25/card/sen-elizabeth-warren-says-trump-tariff-chaos-will-hurt-u-s-investment-NyXloTiSQEstrixPXgKK.

20. Barack Obama's February 12 Speech, *New York Times*, February 12, 2008, https://www.nytimes.com/2008/02/12/us/politics/12text-obama.html.

21. Batya Ungar-Sargon, *Second Class: How the Elites Betrayed America's Working Men and Women* (New York: Encounter Books, 2024).

22. Interview with the author, May 5, 2025.

Chapter Eleven: Unleashing American Energy

1. Reuters, "Fossil Fuels Show Staying Power as EU Clean Energy Output Dips." Reuters, July 10, 2025. https://www.reuters.com/markets/commodities/fossil-fuels-show-staying-power-eu-clean-energy-output-dips-2025-07-10/.

2. https://www.cnbc.com/2025/07/03/trump-one-big-beautiful-bill-oil-gas-coal-solar-wind-ira-tax-incentive-repeal.html.